THE LAW OF
PERFECT
FREEDOM

THE LAW OF

PERFECT FREEDOM

by

MICHAEL S. HORTON

MOODY PRESS

CHICAGO

ISBN: 0-8024-6374-6

3 5 7 9 10 8 6 4 2

Printed in the United States of America

To my father, James Franklin Horton

CONTENTS

FOREWORD

The first thing to say about the Ten Commandments is that they exist and their status is that of divine command. They are not Moses' bright ideas, but God's categorical requirements. Scripture affirms that the two tables of the law were written directly by God (Exodus 31:18). Thus God told the world what sort of behavior pleases Him: He made this very clear by His ten prohibitions of any other sort of life. Though stated as part of God's covenant with Israel, the Decalogue shows God's will for all His human creatures and is thus the place where all mankind's moral and spiritual education needs to begin. That was true in Moses' day and is just as true in ours.

The second thing to say about the Commandments is that we have largely lost them, and that is our folly. Until quite recently they were basic to the religious training that Western nations gave their young. Before I was ten I was made to memorize them—at a public school!—and so were most children of my day. But all that has changed. Prejudice against memorizing as an educational discipline, against the Old Testament, against law in the church, and against religion in schools has led to a state of affairs in which few in the churches, and fewer outside, can repeat the Ten Commandments, let alone explain them. The Reformers and Puritans, who wrote literally dozens of catechisms for Christian education based on the three classic formularies, the Commandments, the Creed, and the Lord's Prayer, would weep over us if they knew how far we had fallen from the standards they set. In a godless and immoral age like ours, ignorance of the Commandments is as great a spiritual weakness as one can imagine. But it is, alas, widespread, and on moral issues we fumble accordingly.

The third thing to say about the Commandments is that they are in fact foundational to Christian morals, as has been implied already. The positive principles implicit in their negative form, when set in the context of the Christian reality of Christ's kingdom and life in the Spirit, stand as a family code for God's redeemed children everywhere. Appeals to the ethic of Christ and the apostles that fail to find their roots in the Commandments (roots that are made very plain in the New Testament, be it said) slip and slide into all sorts of misconceptions. The unity of biblical ethics, starting with the Decalogue, needs rediscovery today.

The fourth thing to say about the Commandments is that Michael Horton's exploration of what they mean for Christian people today is a fine entry point for anyone who wishes to reappropriate their message. There is much wisdom here. Make it yours. It is wisdom that we all need.

J. I. PACKER
Sangwoo Youtong Chee
   Professor of Theology
Regent College
Vancouver, B.C.

ACKNOWLEDGMENTS

Thanks to the staff at Christians United for Reformation (CURE) for giving me the flexibility to write this book. I am especially grateful to the assistance afforded by my associate, Alan Maben, and also to Kim Riddlebarger, Loretta Johnson, Rod Rosenbladt, and Shane Rosenthal for their help.

CHAPTER ONE

DOING THE RIGHT THING

Writing this book has been something like a Midwestern farmer drawing a map of downtown Manhattan—I feel not a little like the wrong person for the job. Nevertheless, this has been a burden of mine for some time, not because I think I'm particularly good at following the course we will discover in the following chapters, but because I hear two voices calling us to the task.

First, God's voice is clear and unmistakable in the pages of Scripture. Having redeemed us from both the guilt and bondage of our sins, God now calls us to glorify and enjoy Him forever, beginning now, beginning here. But there is a second voice that makes a recovery of the Ten Commandments vital for our time. It is the voice of our neighbors: secular, not particularly given to religious justifications for what they do, but nevertheless searching for something that gives weight to their actions. *Newsweek* referred to the question over values as "a deep, vexing national anxiety . . . about the nagging sense that unlimited personal freedom and rampaging materialism yield only

13

greater hungers and lonelier nights." Furthermore, "the acting out has been bipartisan. Self-actualizing liberals have
been obsessed with personal freedom to the point of self-
immolation; predatory conservatives have been obsessed
with commercial freedom to the point of pillage." One
thing is clear, according to *Newsweek*'s Joe Klein: "Both
these indulgences have run their course. The 30-year spree
has caused a monster hang-over. There is a yearning for
something more than the standard political analgesics."[1]
The real question is whether evangelical Christians are,
generally speaking, prepared for the larger spiritual issues
or whether they will simply continue to align themselves
with short-sighted, "standard political analgesics."

As we approach Christianity's third millennium, the
mood of secular culture is clearly shifting from a disregard
for religious, spiritual, and moral direction to a renewed
willingness to listen. Of course, this means that they will listen to almost anyone and everyone, as the popularity of
new-age mysticism, the mushrooming of Islam, and an expanding universalistic sentiment demonstrate. But, as
demonstrated by the leading pollsters, there is one thing
our secular neighbors will not put up with any longer, and
that is what one writer called "The Bible Belt Inquisition."
There must be answers, intelligently argued, defending
the basis of core *beliefs*, not just assertions, slogans, and the
rhetoric of power games. Although the central point of
Christianity is not morality or direction in life (contrary to
what most people expect religion to be about), the transcendent beliefs out of which the Christian life grows and
matures, however feebly, give purpose, direction, and
meaning to life that cannot be matched by mere sentiment
and secular whim. Nor can it be matched by platitudes
from the left-wing or from right-wing ideology, with occa-
sional proof-texting from Scripture. What we really need is
a massive reeducation in the basics. And the world is more
ready for this now than it was just five years ago.

A striking example of this openness is an essay by
Time magazine's former editor-in-chief and ambassador to
Austria, Henry Grunwald:

We are beset by a whole range of discontents and confu-
sions. For a great many, the dunghill has become a natural
habitat. Derain and other observers of depravity would, in
fact, be stunned by the chaos of manners and speech, by
the hellish ubiquity of crime and the easy—one might almost say the democratic—availability of drugs; by the new
varieties of decadence—rock songs about rape and suicide,
pornography at the corner newsstand, commercials for
S&M clubs on your friendly cable channel, not to mention
telephone sex. . . . We are witnessing the end, or at least
the decline, of an age of unbelief and beginning what may
be a new age of faith. . . . We will need a new sense of drive,
less emphasis on "rights" and more on responsibility—in
short, we must create a new psychological climate.

Of course, it was our own evangelical forebears—
especially Luther and Calvin—who emphasized responsibilities over rights, the latter being the modern obsession.
The Bible, particularly the Ten Commandments, calls us
to discover our obligations to God and to our neighbor and
society. It calls the people of God to their posts in society,
not as a special interest group demanding its rights alongside everyone else, but as called-out men and women who
have a heavy sense of moral duty—not to save their own
souls, for that is by grace apart from works, but to bring
glory and honor to that gracious King. What Grunwald
calls for in terms of "a new psychological climate," where
responsibilities are emphasized over rights, was championed
earlier in our history as evangelical Christians. How ironic
that, in order to be relevant and on the cutting edge, we
must retrieve beliefs from the past. Grunwald concludes:

> One of the most remarkable things about the 20th
> century, more than technological progress and physical vi-
> olence, has been the deconstruction of man (and woman).
> We are seeing a reaction to that phenomenon. Our view of
> man obviously depends on our view of God. The Age of
> Reason exalted humankind but still admitted God as a sort
> of supreme philosopher-king or chairman of the board
> who ultimately presided over the glories achieved by rea-

son and science. The humanist 19th century voted him out. It increasingly saw reason and science irreconcilabl; opposed to religion, which would fade away. Secular humanism (a respectable term even though it became a right-wing swearword) stubbornly insisted that morality need not be based on the supernatural. But it gradually became clear that ethics without the sanction of some higher authority simply were not compelling. The ultimate irony, or perhaps tragedy, is that secularism has not led to humanism. We have gradually dissolved—deconstructed—the human being into a bundle of reflexes, impulses, neuroses, nerve endings. The great religious heresy used to be making man the measure of all things; but we have come close to making man the measure of nothing. The mainstream churches have tried in various ways to adapt themselves to a secular age. . . . The major Protestant denominations also increasingly emphasized social activism and tried to dilute dogma to accommodate 20th-century rationality and diversity.

But none of these reforms [is] arresting the sharp decline of the mainstream churches. Why not? The answer seems to be that while orthodox religion can be stifling, liberal religion can be empty. Many people seem to want a faith that is rigorous and demanding.[2]

Respected social commentators, such as Thomas Molnar, are increasingly open to intelligent religious options. Molnar explains:

The Ten Commandments, and many other biblical texts, used to be for me pious, nondescript, and rather gratuitous statements. That was youth. With maturity and age, they began to reveal (the right word) an immeasurable depth of wisdom, whose exploration occupied the life of a Pascal and a Chesterton. Our contemporary "culture" (various paganisms, abortion/euthanasia, inclusive language, overall politization) has demoted those texts to the level of bored clichés or outright mystifications. Hence the need to focus on them again.[3]

But there is also a renewed interest in transcendent answers to real-life problems from the *popular* culture.

Commenting on the 1992 tour of the band *U2, Rolling Stone* magazine concluded: "Their message? Thou shalt not worship false idols, but who else is there?"[4]

So, Grunwald concludes, "Where will all this lead? Just possibly, to a real new age of faith. Not a new universal religion, or the return of a medieval sort of Christianity overarching all of society—nor, one hopes, the resurgence of what might be called the Bible Belt Inquisition. But we may be heading into an age when faith will again be taken seriously, and when it will again play a major part in our existence."[5]

Tom Wolfe suggested that ours is not an age that is likely to produce great heroes. But biblical faith has always created heroes: nurses who devoted their lives to caring for the sick, parents who sacrificed for their children's education, businesspeople who know how to create wealth *and* use it for the benefit of the community, children who took care of their parents in their old age, employers who took care of their workers, and employees who threw in that extra bit to help the company become successful, people who helped their neighbor fix his roof. For the sake of our searching neighbors, for our own sake and, above all, for God's sake, let's prove Grunwald right and Wolfe wrong.

GOD'S WILL FOR YOUR LIFE

Growing up in the church, I can remember the anxiety I used to have over God's will for my life. Whom shall I date? Where does God want me to go to college? With a horror at the possibility of missing out on God's best ("plan A") for my life, I sought God's will earnestly, not knowing exactly what it would sound or look like once I discovered "it." Since then, my basic understanding of what it means to discover God's will has been transformed. Let me explain briefly what I mean.

"The secret things belong to the LORD our God, but the things revealed belong to us and to our children forever, that we may follow all the words of this law" (Deuteronomy 29:29). This verse distinguishes two categories:

"secret things" and "revealed things." It is fairly easy to determine what are the "revealed things": the Ten Commandments are a good example. But what happens when we get to questions about marriage and education, whether we should pursue this calling or relocate to that city? Surely we would search our Bible concordance in vain to find a text informing us of God's will for our life in these areas. That does not mean, of course, that God has not determined our future down to its most trivial details; what it does mean is that He has not decided to let us in on them. If God really is in charge, there is no "perfect will" we step in or out of, depending on how good we are at reading tea leaves or discerning "signs" of God's leading. He even works sin, suffering, and evil out to our good (Romans 8:28), so that everything is a part of His plan to bring Himself glory.

What this does for those burdened with anxiety over knowing God's will is amazing. It places our search for God's will, not in the subjective hunches we often attribute to the Holy Spirit, but in the revealed will of God. We may not get an advance copy of God's game plan as to the people, places, occupations, and moves He has in our future, but we already have more than we seem to have digested in God's *revealed* Word concerning the direction of our lives as Christians. To those seeking God's will for their life, the prophet Micah replies, "He has shown you, O man, what is good. And what does the LORD require of you? To act justly and to love mercy and to walk humbly with your God" (Micah 6:8).

But this search for God's *revealed* will for our lives has not only been interrupted by the search for His *secret* will or plan, but by other factors as well, which we shall consider briefly.

Biblical Illiteracy

According to George Gallup, "Americans revere the Bible—but by and large, they don't read it. And because they don't read it, they have become a nation of biblical illiterates." In fact, although four out of five Americans believe the Bible is "the literal or inspired word of God," most of them cannot recall the Ten Commandments. "Three-quarters of Americans said they make at least some effort to follow Jesus' example," Gallup reports, but they evidently don't have the slightest idea of what that example consists. Six in ten cited a personal relationship with Jesus Christ of some sort, but this evidently is a relationship of convenience, since they do not see it in terms of obligation.[6]

The authors of *The Day America Told The Truth* have this to say:

> It's the wild, wild West all over again in America, but it's wilder and woollier this time. You are the law in this country. Who says so? You do, pardner. . . . There is absolutely no moral consensus at all in the 1990s. Everyone is making up their [sic] own personal moral codes—their own Ten Commandments. Here are ten extraordinary commandments for the 1990s. These are real commandments, the rules that many people actually live by.
>
> 1. I don't see the point in observing the Sabbath (77 percent).
> 2. I will steal from those who won't really miss it (74 percent).
> 3. I will lie when it suits me, so long as it doesn't cause any real damage (64 percent).
> 4. I will drink and drive if I feel that I can handle it. I know my limit (56 percent).
> 5. I will cheat on my spouse—after all, given the chance, he or she will do the same (53 percent).
> 6. I will procrastinate at work and do absolutely nothing about one full day in every five. It's standard operating procedure (50 pecent).
> 7. I will use recreational drugs (41 percent)
> 8. I will cheat on my taxes—to a point (30 percent)
> 9. I will put my lover at risk of disease. I sleep around a bit, but who doesn't (31 percent)?
> 10. Technically, I may have committed date rape, but I know that she wanted it (20 percent have been date-raped).[7]

In spite of the fact that nearly all Americans say they believe in God, "the overwhelming majority of people (93 percent) said that they—and nobody else—determine what is and what is not moral in their lives. They base their decisions on their own experience, even on their daily whims."[8]

Again and again, in survey after survey, Christians and non-Christians respond in almost identical ways when questions are raised concerning greed, hedonism, and racism.[9] Clearly, something is rotten in our own backyard. We do not even seem to know right from wrong anymore, even as Christians. This ought to make us wonder what we are getting in our churches and in our Christian homes. That is why, throughout this book, we will make a conscious effort to see these commandments not merely as stones to throw at secular society, but as a witness to our unfaithful record at the end of the twentieth century. We need to relearn some things that we may have taken for granted. Before we go off on moral crusades, aligning ourselves with the secular Left or the secular Right, we would be well-advised to settle again in our minds what it is that God requires of us—and that is the exciting rediscovery awaiting us in the Ten Commandments.

Ambiguity About the Old Testament

Many of us were raised not knowing what to do with that first half of our Bible. The idea was, Israel in the Old Testament was under the law and Christians in the New Testament are under grace. This means that the Old Testament equals works-righteousness and the New Testament equals the gospel of grace.

However, this is out of keeping with the biblical text on a number of points. First, God made one covenant with Abraham. It was an unconditional gift of eternal life to him and to all of his spiritual descendants. Justified by grace alone through faith alone, just like any believer today, Abraham became the spiritual father of all who trusted in Christ, including us (Galatians 3:7). In fact, "[Not] because they are his descendants are they all Abraham's children. On the contrary, 'It is through Isaac that your offspring will be reckoned.' In other words, it is not the natural children who are God's children, but it is the children of the promise who are regarded as Abraham's offspring" (Romans 9:7–8). Jesus made clear to the Jews of His day that they were not simply children of Abraham by racial descent. In fact, the gospels make plain that because they rejected the promise (i.e., the gospel), the Jews ceased to be children of Abraham (Matthew 3:9). The writer to the Hebrews cautions early Christians against repeating the folly of the Israelites in the wilderness, who also "had *the gospel* preached to [them,] . . . but the message they heard was of no value to them, because those who heard it did not combine it with faith" (Hebrews 4:2, italics added).

Therefore, "law" does not equal "Old Testament," while "grace" or "gospel" equals the New Testament. "Law" refers to any command, from Genesis to Revelation. "Gospel" refers to any place in either testament where the promise of salvation by grace alone through faith alone is found. The law tells us what we *ought* to do, and this leads us to despair of meeting God's standard. Then the gospel tells us what God *has* done for us already in Christ, meeting the standard as our substitute and taking our punishment on Himself so that we could be regarded as righteous.

Seen in this light, the believer today ought to be as interested in the Old Testament as in the New. Although the gospel is more clearly articulated in the New Testament, surely there is no loss of gospel imagery in God's clothing of Adam and Eve Himself with skins from an animal He Himself sacrificed, or in Abraham's offering of Isaac, or in the Exodus from Egypt, and in the myriad of other examples of God's rescuing grace, in spite of the depravity of His people. Therefore, the Old testament still speaks to us today. When God confirms His promise (the gospel) to Jacob, that is for us today. When God commands Israel from Mt. Sinai, these commandments are for us as well.

But what about the sacrifices and all of those other laws that governed Israel's civic life? Surely we are not called to execute adulterers, are we? To answer this question, we must make a crucial distinction between what biblical scholars have called the *moral, ceremonial,* and *civil* laws. In the first category—the moral—we have the Ten Commandments, with all of their repeated charges and extrapolations in the New Testament. Individuals are to love God with all of their heart, soul, mind, and strength, and their neighbor as themselves.

But there is another cluster of laws in the Old Testament governing religious ceremonies. There are the special feasts and fasts, together with the elaborate sacrificial system and temple worship. Every *ceremonial* law was to be precisely obeyed. As we go back and read some of these laws, we wonder at the detail. Why did God get caught up in the question of whether a priest cut the animal's throat, or whether the one offering the sacrifice did the deed? We can only see the importance of these rituals in retrospect, as we see, for instance, the importance of the sinner's identifying directly with the victim substituting for his sins. That is why each person had to take the life of the sacrificial victim himself. It was not merely the Jews or the Romans who crucified Jesus Christ: we were all there, driving the sword into His side, transferring our sins to Him just as the presenter in the Old Testament put his hands on the scapegoat, signifying a transfer of guilt from the sinner to the victim.

As we can see, especially from the book of Hebrews, all of these types and shadows are fulfilled in Christ. They all pointed to Him. He was the temple, so why go on with temple worship? He was the sacrifice, so how could we offend God by thinking there was still a need for a better or fuller sacrifice for sins? Therefore, the ceremonial laws vanish with the coming of the one they were designed to foreshadow.

Then there is the third category: the *civil* laws of Israel. Just as Israel's ceremonial laws prefigured Christ as the great prophet and priest, so her civil laws prefigured Christ as the great king. And just as He does not cease to be our prophet or priest with the fulfillment of the ceremonial laws, so too he does not cease to be our king with the fulfillment of the civil laws. Furthermore, just as we must not go back to the shadows of the promise in the ceremonial law when we have the fulfillment of that promise in Christ, so too we ought not to seek to return to the Jewish theocracy when we have the fulfillment of Christ's kingdom in His spiritual reign through the proclamation of the gospel. Through Israel, God gives us object lessons about the kingdom that will come with Christ's ministry. As the kings of Israel were to drive out the idolatrous nations (unlike Adam, who entertained God's enemy instead of driving him out of the land), so Christ will separate the sheep from the goats, the wheat from the weeds, at the end of the age (cf. Matthew 25:31–46; and also 13:25–29). But the reality of the kingdom is not seen in its political, military, or social might, but in its advance through the gospel of Christ crucified for our sins and raised for our justification.

This is especially important to reiterate at a time when America is being confused with Israel as a chosen nation destined by God to bring salvation to the ends of the earth. When the Puritans and Pilgrim separatists settled New England, the aim was evangelistic ministry: "to advance ye kingdom of Christ" through the proclamation of the Word, administration of the sacraments, and the exercise of godly discipline and order. But as America secularized (as soon as the War for Independence), the vision of "Christian America" destined to spread its political gospel of life, liberty, and the pursuit of happiness continued, and evangelicals, instead of protesting the confusion of Christ and culture, have, especially in recent decades, helped to foster it. The Reformers argued that there are two swords: one ruling the temporal sphere (the state) and one ruling the eternal sphere (the church). The first sword is made of metal; the second of ink and paper. According to Calvin, nations are to be governed by laws created on the basis of "general equity," of which he believed even pagans were capable because of the image of God stamped on every person and the general revelation of justice, right, and wrong anchored in nature and in the human conscience.

That is why J. Gresham Machen, leader of the intellectual crusade against liberalism in the twenties and thirties, insisted that the church has a purely spiritual function—to speak for God, where God has spoken for Himself in His Word. Although Christians may involve themselves in moral and political crusades, Machen insisted that whenever the church as a divine institution did so it violated its sacred mission and confused the gospel with civil righteousness.

In the New Testament, we not only do not find explicit calls to obey various ceremonial or civil laws of the Old Testament, we find it expressly forbidden, as a return to shadows after the reality has come. However, the New Testament does reiterate the *moral* laws of the Old Testament, giving them fuller explanation and a particular New Testament application (i.e., in terms of the believer's responsibility to God and neighbor). In Jeremiah 31:31–33, we read:

> " . . . I will make a new covenant
> with the house of Israel
>   and with the house of Judah.
> It will not be like the covenant
>   I made with their forefathers
> when I took them by the hand
>   to lead them out of Egypt,
> because they broke my covenant,
>   though I was a husband to them,"
>   declares the LORD.
> "This is the covenant I will make with
>   the house of Israel
>   after that time," declares the Lord.
> "I will put my law in their minds
>   and write it on their hearts.
> I will be their God,
>   and they will be my people."

Joel also prophesied that in the last days the Holy Spirit would be poured out on every believer, not merely on those who were called out as prophets, priests, or kings.

Finally, the people of God would became what God intended the community to be: a whole *nation* of prophets and priests, declaring by the power of the Holy Spirit the good news of the gospel and the blessings of the covenant. At Pentecost, this prophecy was fulfilled, and since then every believer has been filled with the Spirit and given, in the new birth, a heart that has God's law, His revealed will, embroidered into it. This is why Paul calls Christian obedience the "fruit of the Spirit," because it is not the product of our own virtue or character, but the direct effect of having the law written on our heart and the Spirit working within us to produce a new obedience.

Every person—even the most perverted or confused person—has the law written on his or her conscience, Paul tells us in the first two chapters of Romans. But only believers have the law written on their heart; in other words, only through the new birth can one truly delight in God's law. Before, it only condemned and cursed, but now, because we are regarded as having fulfilled that law perfectly because Christ fulfilled it in our place, it can only direct us in our Christian life. It can never make such threats as "If you don't do your part, God won't do His." After all, God *did* "our part" through the perfect life and death of His own Son. Now, not only does this unconditional promise bring life to us who cannot gain a single part of the promise through our own obedience or effort; it brings a new heart that loves God's law for the first time. Notice that, instead of removing the law from the life of the believer, Paul declares, "You show that you are a letter from Christ, the result of our ministry, written not with ink, but with the Spirit of the living God, not on tablets of stone but on tablets of human hearts. . . . He has made us competent as ministers of a new covenant—not of the letter but of the Spirit; for the letter kills, but the Spirit gives life" (2 Corinthians 3:3–4, 6).

This is not, as many have thought, to set the Spirit against the Word or law of God. Rather, it is to say that apart form the life-giving Spirit, God's commands (as well as His gospel promise) are dead. Or, better still, it is to say that *we* are dead. The law cannot give us life. We cannot gain life (or keep it or become more "filled with the Spirit," or whatever you want to call it) by trying to achieve it. It all belongs to every believer. Only the Spirit can take those "dead in trespasses and sins" (Ephesians 2:1) and make them alive. And once one is made alive, he or she is able to respond positively and affectionately to the law of God for the first time.

So the believer today is just as much an heir to the promise as Abraham was, and as much obligated to the moral law of God as he was. The designation of Israel as "a kingdom of priests and a holy nation" (Exodus 19:6) is now applied to the New Testament church, composed of all of Abraham's children, Jew and Gentile (1 Peter 2:9).

Popular Preaching on the Old Testament

Very often, the preaching we get from the Old Testament these days is little more than *Aesop's Fables:* a clever story, with a moral at the end. A sermon on David is sure to focus on his willingness to stand up to Goliath, with the easy (one might say, insipid) application to whatever "Goliaths" we happen to be facing in our lives. But, of course, this is not the author's intention at all. We might be reading the text, but what is coming from the pulpit or the Sunday school room is not an exposition of the passage, making the point we are really supposed to draw from it.

It is ironic that in churches that so stress the literal nature of passages that are self-consciously apocalyptic, parabolic, or poetic, so much allegorizing of *historical narrative* passages of the Old Testament goes on. Whenever we turn Joshua or Gideon into characters whose main purpose in the Bible is to teach us a moral lesson, we are following the medieval method of interpretation, which sought to spiritualize, moralize, and allegorize historical narrative, rather than the Protestant method, which is aimed at explaining the passage according to its own context. An Australian evangelical, Graeme Goldsworthy, demonstrates the seriousness of this business:

The Old Testament is dead—dead at the conspiratorial hands of rationalists, Jews, medieval allegorists, theological liberals, existentialists, evangelicals and others. The Jews denied the Old Testament its appointed goal in the gospel and thus transformed it into a dead legalism. Medieval church scholars followed Origen by capitulating to Gnostics who said the Old Testament was materialistic and unspiritual. Rationalists, liberals and existentialists bowed to the philosophical fads of their day and found the Old Testament incompatible. But are evangelicals, the "people of the Book," involved in the conspiracy? We evangelicals are more guilty than all. We have prided ourselves on honoring the whole Bible as God's Word and have cast pharisaic stones at the adulterous higher critics and liberals. . . . Where are the sermons on the Old Testament that preach Christ without bumbling allegorizing or untheological character studies? Where are the evangelical Sunday school courses which teach the Old Testament without legalistic moralizing? . . . And the new-birth oriented "Jesus-in-my-heart" gospel of evangelicals has destroyed the Old Testament just as effectively as nineteenth-century liberalism.[10]

Christianity is a historical religion. Whereas existentialists point out the meaninglessness of life (a realistic and appropriate reaction apart from Christ), the biblical revelation assures us that life and history have meaning because God elected, redeemed, called, and justified a people throughout human history and within human history, from Eden to the present and on into eternity, and all of this has centered on the entrance of the Son of God Himself into time and space history to redeem. Christianity is not a message about inner peace or being born again or having Jesus in my heart. Whereas there is an unmistakable personal aspect, the message of Christianity is *Christ.*

From Genesis to Revelation, every figure, every story, every image, every lesson is the wrapping in which we find God's gift, Jesus Christ. Even in the Ten Commandments, Christ is not only prefigured in Moses, but is present as the one who has won His right to rule His people by the redemption He has accomplished for His people in the Exodus, a down payment on the great redemption to be accomplished, this time not through the signs and wonders of Moses in Pharaoh's court, demanding "Let my people go!" or in the parting of the sea, nor by feeding His people with bread in the wilderness, but by raising the dead, bearing the wrath of the divine justice for His brothers and sisters, and by *being* the Bread of Life from heaven (John 6). The Old Testament is not merely the part of our Bibles that predicted a coming Messiah and was rendered irrelevant when that Messiah arrived; it is part of one full, complete, running drama of redemption, and beginning with Matthew's Gospel is like walking into a movie halfway into the story. It is like thinking you are telling a good joke when all you can remember is the punch line.

David really lived in history. And the usefulness of that life, measured by the fact that the Bible records great segments of it, is not determined by how many instructive lessons we can learn from character studies, for there were greater men and women of character, no doubt, who never made it into the Bible. David's inclusion into the canon of Holy Scripture is defined by the place he had in redemptive history—not only as a precursor of Christ, the Son of David, but as someone to whom the gospel promise came, in spite of all his failures and unfaithfulness. "Blessed is he whose transgressions are forgiven, . . . whose sin the LORD does not count against him" (Psalm 32:1–2) wicked David cried, after confessing his utter depravity. In other words, we ought to be asking, "How is God's redemptive program advancing in this place and time, during the reign of David?" "Where is the gospel in this passage?" "How is Christ revealed, even in a shadowy way?" We read of Abraham, not to learn what Abraham, a liar, cheater, and schemer, did for God, but what God did for this sinner and, through him, for the rest of us who are wicked. These figures are not there primarily for our imitation, but for our instruction in the gospel.

The Pharisees of Jesus' day took the view that we often hear in our own churches. Our Lord castigated them for missing the forest for the trees: "You diligently study the Scriptures, thinking by them you possess eternal life. These are the Scriptures that testify about me, yet you refuse to come to me to have life" (John 5:39). They saw the Scriptures (our Old Testament) essentially as a moral code, a handbook for living. Although the Old Testament does contain moral commands (as does the New Testament), they are commands given to people who have already been redeemed and promised unconditionally that through faith in the promise they shall inherit the heavenly Promised Land on the other side of death. The moralistic and pictistic approach many of us have taken toward the Old Testament may be the reason many Christians have been bored by it and turned off to it, but a view that attempts to see the redemptive theme advancing throughout the history of God's people will revive our generation's sense of belonging to this people of God, this family of Abraham. With Isaac, Jacob, David, Rahab, and the prophets, we too inherit the family treasures: the law and the promise.

LAYING DOWN THE LAW

Most biblical scholars are agreed that the Old Testament is a legal document, a covenant between God and His people. The Ten Commandments are merely a summary —perhaps the best—of the covenantal arrangement for God's people. Before the commands are given, there is a preamble. We are used to preambles in covenants, treaties, and contracts. In our own Constitution, the Preamble reads, "We the people, in order to form a more perfect union, to provide for the common defense and to ensure to ourselves and to our posterity domestic tranquillity, do ordain and establish this Constitution of the United States of America."

Similarly, the Ten Commandments begin with the source of their authority: "I am the LORD your God, who brought you out of Egypt, out of the land of slavery" (Exodus 20:2). God is represented here as the Great King who has just rescued a tiny, helpless state from the clutches of an oppressive regime. But this rescue does not leave them to themselves, to be invaded and tyrannized again sometime in the future. Instead, God Himself assumes the reign of Israel as its Redeemer-King. We often speak of "letting God" do this or that, or of "making Him Lord," but the biblical idea could not be more different. God *is* Lord by right. "It is he who has made us, and not we ourselves"—so He is our Lord by right in creation—for "we are His people and the sheep of His pasture" (Psalm 100:3 NKJV), making Him our Lord by right in redemption. The Lord creates the covenant and does not bargain with us concerning its content. Instead of "we the people" or "I the believer," it is "God the Redeemer" who gives this covenant its binding nature. Instead of our making Him our Lord, in the covenant, God makes us His people.

Unlike the Preamble of the American Constitution, this divine preamble governing the people of God, the church, derives its authority not as an arrangement of the people covenanting together to obey God or to set up a kingdom, but as an arrangement of God Himself. It is not a contract where the two parties are equal, but a covenant in which God the Redeemer declares "I will take you as my own people, and I will be your God" (Exodus 6:7).

Whereas the promises concerning the physical land were conditional (Exodus 19:5; Ezekiel 33:21–29), the promise of everlasting life through faith in God's redeeming arm was unconditional (Deuteronomy 31:6; Romans 11:29; 2 Timothy 2:13). This is the promise we inherit, along with Jews who turn to Christ. Of course, the church is not an heir to any plot of land in Palestine, but it is the heir to the unconditional promise made to Abraham. For this, and not the earthly territory, was the ultimate hope of Israel (Hebrews 11:9, 14–16). Because God has already redeemed us by grace alone, we can serve in perfect freedom, not fearing the terrors of the law, but delighting in its precepts. We gain freedom through the gospel, not through the law; but the freedom we gain through the gospel is a freedom to obey for the first time, from our hearts, not to be left to ourselves. God redeems and God rules His people. The New Testament reiteration of this Old Testament preamble can be found, among other places, in 1 Peter 1:18–19, where we are told, "For you know that it was not with perishable things such as silver or gold that you were redeemed from the empty way of life handed down to you from your forefathers, but with the precious blood of Christ, a lamb without blemish or defect." We must never start with the first commandment, as though we entered into new life, or were somehow made acceptable to God by our performance and conformity to the commands, but must always begin right here, with the preamble, where God Himself does, in making His claim to His people on the basis that He has already done everything—including fulfilling the conditions of obedience to the law. He does this for us, in our place, through the person and work of our Lord Jesus Christ, God incarnate.

THE NATURE OF THE LAW

At Mount Sinai, God delivered to His people, through Moses, the famous Ten Commandments. But this was merely a republication of the eternal will of God already stamped on human nature. Paul argues, "For since the creation of the world God's invisible qualities—his eternal power and divine nature—have been clearly seen, being understood from what has been made, so that men are without excuse" (Romans 1:20). The problem people have is not, first and foremost, a lack of data. In spite of this law written on the conscience, humans "have become filled with every kind of wickedness, evil, greed and depravity. They are full of envy, murder, strife, deceit and malice. They are gossips, slanderers, God-haters, insolent, arrogant and boastful; they invent ways of doing evil; they disobey their parents; they are senseless, faithless, heartless, ruthless" (vv. 29–32).

Therefore, God published His eternal will again. Christians have found at least three purposes for this written law: a civil use, a theological use, and a moral use.

Civil Use

The list Paul gives us in the passage quoted above does not leave much room for trusting human nature. That is why the civil authority must respect both liberty (because of the divine image in humanity) as well as justice (because of the fallenness of humanity). Unfortunately, when we want to break the bounds of the law, the only thing that stops some of us is the threat that law imposes. Therefore, this first use of the law is that of a deterrent in the civil sphere, with the police and prisons to back up the threat.

Theological Use

Also called the pedagogical use, taken from Paul's reference to the law as God's tutor, leading us to faith in Christ (Galatians 3:24), the law shows us how hopelessly we fall short of the righteousness God requires. Just when we think we are not quite as bad as the guy down the street living with so-and-so, the law puts us on trial and compares us—not to other fallen men and women, but to God. This is meant to drive us to despair so that we seek our shelter from God's wrath in Christ's righteousness alone.

Moral Use

Since the law is the expression of God's eternal character, it does not change. We must remember that God first gave the law, written on the human conscience, not to drive people to Christ (for they were not lost), nor to threaten them with civil penalties (for they were not criminals). The law was first given as a realistic expectation for human behavior because God had created Adam and Eve with moral excellence. After the Fall, of course, human beings are incapable of conforming to this law. Even if they have not physically abused another person, they have murdered through gossip or slander. Even if they have not stolen from their neighbor by slipping into his home at night, they have not done everything they could to protect their neighbor's possessions. Even Christians cannot conform perfectly to this law, and they ought never to approach the law as though they could even come close to its moral excellence. Rather, believers ought to approach the law as the perfect standard God requires as the expression of His moral character and live, not in order to *meet* God's requirements (for that is achieved only in Christ), but in order simply to *obey* God's requirements. In the former approach, one sets out to *earn* God's favor by *attaining* His own righteousness; in the latter, one sets out to obey a gracious heavenly Father simply because He has *already accepted* him or her as righteous and holy.

For those, like the Pharisees, who sought to be justified by their own righteousness, the law comes to condemn and to judge. But for those, like David, who have known the liberating good news of God's free justification of the wicked, the law comes to lead and guide in the paths of righteousness: "I run in the path of your commands, *for* you have set my heart free" (Psalm 119:32, italics added). "He has revealed his word to Jacob, his laws and decrees to Israel. He has done this for no other nation; they do not know his laws. Praise the LORD!" (Psalm 147:19–20). Only those who know the privilege of adoption can say with the psalmist, "Open my eyes that I may see wonderful things in your law!" (Psalm 119:18).

NOTES

1. Joe Klein, "Whose Values?" *Newsweek*, 8 June 1992, 19.
2. Henry Grunwald, "The Year 2000: Is It the End—Or Just the Beginning?" *Time*, 30 March 1992, 74.
3. Thomas Molnar, *Chronicles: A Magazine of American Culture*, December 1992, 14.
4. *Rolling Stone*, 10–24 December 1992, 39.
5. Grunwald, "The Year 2000," 76.
6. George Gallup and James Castelli, *The People's Religion* (New York: Macmillan, 1989), 60.
7. James Patterson and Peter Kim, *The Day America Told the Truth* (New York: Plume, 1992), 201.
8. Ibid., 25–26.
9. George Barna and James Mackay, *Vital Signs* (Westchester, Ill.: Crossway, 1984), 140–41.
10. Graeme Goldsworthy, *Verdict* 2, no. 1 (February 1979), 5–10.

CHAPTER TWO

NO OTHER GODS

*You shall have
no other gods before me.*

"I believe in God. I'm not a religious fanatic. I can't remember the last time I went to church. My faith has carried me a long way. It's Sheilaism. Just my own little voice."

Such was the response of Sheila Larson, a typical American interviewed by Robert Bellah and his colleagues.[1] Bellah and his team contrast the communal, confessional faith of the New England Puritans with the individualistic and subjective diversity of contemporary religious attitudes. "This suggests the logical possibility of over 220 million American religions, one for each of us."

Ninety-six percent of the American population say they believe in God. In fact, 40 percent say they have had a born-again experience or "a turning point in [their lives when they] committed [themselves] to Jesus Christ," according to George Gallup. A third of the population claims to be evangelical.[2] In spite of the fact that there does not seem to be the slightest effect, 84 percent of adult Americans said in 1988 that they believed Jesus was God or the Son of God, up 6 percent from the previous decade.[3] The

United States is second only to the Republic of Ireland in church attendance. So is Sheila Larson really all that typical of the average modern American?

Gallup cites a statement made by Lincoln Barrett in an article in the *Ladies Home Journal:* "Although 95 percent of the Americans say they believe in God, it is by no means clear that they acknowledge the God of biblical revelation, who speaks to man from beyond himself and awakens in him a sense of dependency, moral unworthiness and obligation to obey his will. . . . Here indeed is a revelation of man's final sin, which Luther defined as the unwillingness to admit that he is a sinner."[4] The authors of the best-selling survey of American attitudes, *The Day America Told the Truth,* add, "This is not the 'jealous God' of the Old Testament—six in seven people think that it is okay not to believe in God. Rather, Americans seem to use God to refer to a general principle of good in life. . . . For most Americans, God is not to be feared or, for that matter, loved."[5] Thus the American paradox: while knowledge of God and the Bible plummets, along with any commitment to a common set of core beliefs, "Americans are even more 'religious' today than they have been in the past."[6] President George Bush praised America as "the most religious nation on earth," to the applause of his audience of Christian Broadcasters in January 1992.

That last comment brings us to a hill in first-century Athens, where the indefatigable apostle Paul addressed his pagan audience, congratulating them in a backhanded way for their religiosity. Earlier, Paul had been whisked out of Thessalonica for his own safety and escorted by friends to Athens. They left him there while they went looking for Silas and Timothy. In their absence Paul was not about to stay put and do nothing. He toured the world-famous cultural center and used his observations as the point of contact in presentations of the gospel he made in the marketplace and in the synagogue:

> While Paul was waiting for them in Athens, he was greatly distressed to see that the city was full of idols. So he

reasoned in the synagogue with the Jews and the God-fearing Greeks, as well as in the marketplace day by day with those who happened to be there. A group of Epicurean and Stoic philosophers began to dispute with him. Some of them asked, "What is this babbler trying to say?" Others remarked, "He seems to be advocating foreign gods." They said this because Paul was preaching the good news about Jesus and the resurrection. Then they took him and brought him to a meeting of the Areopagus, where they said to him, "May we know what this new teaching is that you are presenting? You are bringing some strange ideas to our ears, and we want to know what they mean." (All the Athenians and the foreigners who lived there spent their time doing nothing but talking about and listening to the latest ideas.) (Acts 17:16-21)

In other words, Paul's defense of the faith before the Jews and God-fearing Greeks got him a spot on the ancient world's equivalent to "The Oprah Winfrey Show": the Areopagus, where the Athenians and foreigners "spent their time doing nothing but talking about and listening to the latest ideas."

Upon arriving in the arena, Paul "stood up in the meeting of the Areopagus" and brought up some of the observations from his tour. "Men of Athens! I see that in every way you are very religious. For as I walked around and looked carefully at your objects of worship, I even found an altar with this inscription: TO AN UNKNOWN GOD. Now what you worship as something unknown I am going to proclaim to you" (Acts 17:22–23). As Gallup noted, the ironic upsurge in American religiosity at a time when the population knows less and cares less than ever about the one they supposedly worship, so Paul observed a similar irony in the Athenians. They were "in every way very religious"—so religious, in fact, that they had all of their bases covered. Not only did they have a god for everything, they even had an altar to an unknown god, in case they had left someone out. But instead of appealing to that vague religious commitment and praising the Athenians for their interest in spiritual things, Paul told them that this unknown God was, in fact, the only true God (vv. 24–36):

> "The God who made the world and everything in it is the Lord of heaven and earth and does not live in temples built by hands. And he is not served by human hands, as if he needed anything, because he himself gives all men life and breath and everything else. From one man he made every nation of men, that they should inhabit the whole earth; and he determined the times set for them and the exact places where they should live. God did this so that men would seek him and perhaps reach out for him and find him, though he is not far from each one of us. 'For in him we live and move and have our being.' As some of your own poets have said, 'We are his offspring.'
>
> "Therefore, since we are God's offspring we should not think that the divine being is like gold or silver or stone—an image made by man's design and skill. In the past God overlooked such ignorance, but now he commands all people everywhere to repent. For he has set a day when he will judge the world with justice by the man he has appointed. He has given proof of this to all men by raising him from the dead."
>
> When they heard about the resurrection of the dead, some of them sneered, but others said, "We want to hear you again on this subject." At that, Paul left the Council. A few men became followers of Paul and believed. Among them was Dionysius, a member of the Areopagus, also a woman named Damaris, and a number of others.

Let's take this speech apart in an effort to discover what Paul might say to modern-day "Sheilaism." First, the apostle describes the one true God as "the God who made the world and everything in it," by which he meant that He is "the Lord of heaven and earth." God is sovereign because He created, upholds, governs, and will judge the world. People cannot elect Him to His post. He is not a candidate who requires acceptance by a constituency. Nor is He a deity who indulgently tolerates other gods (work, pleasure, relationships, things, or other religions), so long as He is honored from time to time. This one true God is the world dictator, the Sovereign of the universe. As the potter controls his wheel and the clay, so God governs His creation (Isaiah 29:16). This government even includes the most minute details of every person's life: "He determined the times set for them and the exact places where they should live" (Acts 17:26). Nebuchadnezzar, the Persian king in the Old Testament, learned this the hard way. While he was walking on the roof of his palace, soaking in the magnificence of "the great Babylon I have built as the royal residence, by my mighty power and for the glory of my majesty" (Daniel 4:30), God struck the king with some sort of insanity that made him a recluse, with fingernails like eagles' claws. The story is reminiscent of Howard Hughes's last years. But Nebuchadnezzar finally comes around:

> At the end of that time, I, Nebuchadnezzar, raised my eyes toward heaven, and my sanity was restored. Then I praised the Most High; I honored and glorified him who lives forever.
>
> His dominion is an eternal dominion;
>> his kingdom endures from generation to generation.
> All the peoples of the earth
>> are regarded as nothing.
> He does as he pleases
>> with the powers of heaven
>> and the peoples of the earth.
> No one can hold back his hand
>> or say to him: "What have you done?"
>
> . . . . Now I, Nebuchadnezzar, praise and exalt and glorify the King of heaven, because everything he does is right and all his ways are just. And those who walk in pride he is able to humble. (vv. 34–35, 37)

"Those who walk in pride he is able to humble"—including Sheila. The root misunderstanding for pagans in all ages (including "Christian" ones) concerns the sovereignty of God. In paganism, gods exist to make people happy and provide moral examples of the good life. This is the concept referred to by Roger Patterson and James Kim in *The Day America Told the Truth:* "Americans seem to use God to refer to a general principle of good in life."[7] In paganism, God exists for humans, not humans for God. It is as though God depends on creatures for His happiness and power and the success of His plans. Man provides something (a sacrifice, a mantra, sacrificial incarnation, or magical rite) which then obligates the god or gods to respond in the way they have determined. But the true God, Paul declares, is not served by human hands, "as if he needed anything, because he himself gives all men life and breath and everything else" (Acts 17:25). Paul asks in Romans 11:35–36, "Who has ever given to God that God should repay him? For from him and through him and to him are all things. To him be the glory forever!"

We slip into paganism by thinking that somehow what we do for God will create an obligation on His part: "Look how much I've sacrificed for You!" we tell God. Or we say, "If You do this for me, I promise to do that for You." Paganism fails to understand that our relationship with God is on the level of ruler-and-ruled rather than a mutual partnership. We do not bargain with God. He makes no deals.

Let us, therefore, take a closer look at each of these areas in an effort to discern where precisely we have allowed other gods to take their place in our pantheon.

WHAT IS IDOLATRY?

We often take for granted that we know what idolatry is. What *is* this sin that lies at the heart of all human rebellion and deceit?

The famous *Shema* of the people of God, "Hear, O Israel: The LORD our God, the LORD is one. Love the LORD our God with all your heart and with all your soul and with all your strength" (Deuteronomy 6:4), is perhaps the oldest creed in church history. In it Israel anchored all of its beliefs and activity. The surrounding nations were marked by the abundance of deities. There were gods of agriculture, entertainment, government, love, and war, and the lives of the pagans were ruled by these impersonal forces. Religion was simply a separate compartment of life, as were man's other activities. No better is Israel's belief in one Sovereign God contrasted with paganism than during the Egyptian exile.

John Timmer has conducted an excellent survey of the meaning of the great sign-demonstrations done before Pharaoh.[8] God transformed Aaron's rod into a serpent because of the geography:

> With the exception of a long, narrow strip of arable land on either side of the River Nile, Egypt consisted of nothing but desert region. In this region, so the Egyptians believed, no gods resided. Only snakes, dangerous snakes. By having Aaron's rod swallow up the rods of the Egyptian magicians, God demonstrates that he has power where Egypt's gods do not: over the desert.

Next, God turns the Nile River into blood. Since the farming communities depended on the overflooding of the Nile for the productivity of their otherwise dry and unusable land, and the god Hapi was credited with this annual rite, this powerful sign clearly demonstrated that it was Israel's God, not Hapi, who had power over the Nile. Then God sends the plague of the frogs. Again, this had a particular significance for Egypt, according to Timmer:

> Each year, Egypt experienced a frog season when, all along the banks of the Nile, people were forced, night after night, to listen to a cacophony of croaking frogs. The god in charge of regulating this annual affliction was Hekht. This female deity "protected the crocodiles in the river; these were the enemies of the frogs. On the other hand a plague of frogs means a promising rise in the level of the Nile. So Hekht was also regarded as the symbol of fertility" (Knight, *Narration,* 62). With unheard-of numbers of frogs overrunning the country, things clearly have gotten out of Hekht's hand. Once more, Yahweh has proven himself mightier than Egypt's gods.

In addition, God sent a plague on the domestic animals in order to demonstrate the ridiculousness of the sovereignty claimed for the various local deities who looked after these animals. Similarly, the plague of darkness demonstrated God's sovereignty over Amen-Ra, the Sun-god, who was thought by the Egyptians to be "'the source of all life, whom even Pharaoh worshiped as his divine father' (Knight, *Narration*, 79)." As Timmer writes, "The eclipse of the sun means the eclipse of Amen-Ra."

The modern reader may find this confrontation rather primitive, since our generation is particularly given to self-congratulation for being wiser than those who have gone before. The presence of microwave ovens, NASA, television, medical and genetic advances, and other rapidly unfolding products of modern life masks a deeper foolishness and immaturity in our intellectual, emotional, spiritual, and moral development. At a lecture I attended in Strasbourg, France, the gentleman in charge of drafting political legislation on genetic engineering for the European Parliament said that the ambiguity of his job is exacerbated by the fact that people often assume that technological sophistication implies a corresponding ethical and intellectual sophistication. But, he complained, we are wise in figuring out how things work and foolish in our capacity for knowing the meaning of it all. We must not think, based on material prosperity and scientific achievement, that we are anything but backward, unsophisticated neopagans who have drifted again into superstition and foolishness. This is not only evident in the New Age movement but in similar revivals of blatant paganism, such as the revival of feminine and earth cults at major universities.

We can even see in our own Christian circles traces of this shift from the idea of a Sovereign God, who has revealed Himself in real time and space history, to the notion of local deities managing the separate compartments of our life, guaranteeing success and happiness in their respective spheres. It is rarely declared but often practiced: God is in charge of the area called "religion," but life itself is ruled by a pantheon of deities: career, possessions, greed,

self-esteem, family, friends, entertainment, fashion. Whenever we make a decision to violate God's revealed will in favor of one of these "deities," we are putting other gods
before the one true and living God. A decision to doctor
the figures just a little bit in order to get that raise or to exaggerate one's success slightly in order to secure a contract
or to charge that dress to the credit card when it is beyond
one's means—these are all particular acts of idolatry, every
bit as primitive, crass, and formal patterns of worship as Israel experienced, and occasionally engaged in, while in
Egypt.

Whenever we compartmentalize our life, gifts become
burdens and tokens of God's blessing become demons.
Take, for instance, work. God instituted work in the Garden before the Fall. It is a divine ordinance, and it only
takes on an aspect of drudgery because of the Fall itself. In
the film *Chariots of Fire,* Eric Liddell, a Scots Presbyterian, is
contrasted with Abrahams, a secular Jew. Both are runners
at Cambridge University, and both end up qualifying for
and participating in the Olympics. Yet, Abrahams runs for
his own glory and fears losing so much that he cannot even
take pleasure in winning. Liddell, on the other hand, sees
beyond running. While recognizing that God had called
him to China as a missionary, Liddell also recognized that
God had given him athletic gifts. "God also made me fast,"
he explained to his sister. "And when I run, I feel his pleasure!" Many of us have become so successful at dividing
our lives into spiritual and secular realms that on Sundays
we read the Bible, pray, give, and speak of the things of the
Lord like Liddell and then go about our business on Monday morning like Abrahams. Do we feel God's pleasure at
work? Or has it become an obsession, an idol, that has lost
its joy? Whatever we do not take captive as a good gift of
God and bring into the service of His glory will end up becoming a demon. Alcohol, a good gift of God, ends up in
alcoholism if it becomes an idol instead of a gift of the one
true God. All of the "isms" of contemporary psychological
taxonomy are nothing more than what people used to call

idols. Our basic problem is not psychological disease. Addiction is simply a newer euphemism for idolatry.

This happens on a grander scale, too. Modern science, at least in the West, was born out of the zeal of Christians to understand the order of a universe they knew had been ordered by the same God they praised on Sunday morning. Their work, therefore, was an extension of that worship—bringing knowledge of God's visible world to the people. But today, as Nobel laureate Sir John Eccles observes, modern science "has become a superstition" by trying to take the place of religion and explain things that transcend its competence.[9] For instance, the famous Cambridge scientist, Stephen Hawking, argues, "The eventual goal of science is to provide a single theory that describes the whole universe."[10] Hawking is working for this because "it would be the ultimate triumph of human reason—for then we would know the mind of God."[11] When modern science declares the universe to be eternal, it is simply re-echoing the paganism of Plato, "worshiping the creature [matter] rather than the Creator." When it speaks of matter creating itself or of chance creating matter, it creates idols just as rude and primitive as the Canaanite gods, regardless of how well the idea is wrapped in sophisticated jargon.

Deism, the prevailing religion of science since the Enlightenment, maintains that the universe is governed by laws. Whereas God set them into motion (and is, therefore, generously dubbed "Creator"), He only occasionally intervenes. Most of the time, He simply watches the laws do their thing, as any good delegator would. But, of course, deism is nothing new; it is not merely a product of eighteenth-century empiricism. Paganism in cultures around the globe has always worshiped separate "forces," with perhaps a chief "force" at the top of the totem pole. Mortimer Adler writes of our century, "A cultural delusion is widespread in the twentieth century. The extraordinary progress in science and technology that we have achieved in this century has deluded many of our contemporaries into thinking that similar progress obtains in other fields of mental activity. They unquestioningly think that the twentieth century is superior to its predecessors in all the efforts of the human mind."[12] Like other paganisms, deism, the religion of most modern scientists, parcels out God's providence and sovereignty over creation to lesser "gods" or "laws." Nevertheless, Israel's God, the one true God, comes to the altar of technology to mock the gods of today's secular high priests, much as Elijah mocked the priests of Baal.

But in postmodernism, some scientists—some very well-known ones—are turning from their rigid materialistic orthodoxy to the other extreme: mysticism. "Still, a few big name physicists have stepped cheerfully beyond the bounds of the strictly scientific," Robert Wright observes in a *Time* magazine article. "In the 1950s, the pioneering quantum physicist Erwin Schrodinger, author of *What Is Life?* wrote about the hidden oneness of all human minds. More recently, the American physicist John Wheeler has drawn diagrams that depict a symbiosis of mind and matter and look like they came from the scrolls of some occult society."[13] Oxford's William D. Hamilton, the most important evolutionary biologist today, suggests the possibility that Earth is "a zoo for extraterrestrial beings," noting that this is "a kind of hypothesis that's very, very hard to dismiss."[14] That the hypothesis that our planet is a zoo for extraterrestrial beings, whose existence in the first place has not a shred of evidence, is a better explanation than the theory of God's existence appears to many, such as myself, to be a bit of stretching on the part of those who are too dogmatically and rigidly committed to their religious beliefs to entertain theism (belief in God).

Happily, there are many scientists, such as Harvard's leading astrophysicist Owen Gingerich, an evangelical, who argue that the more we learn about the purpose and design of the cosmos, the more irresistible is the conclusion that there is a Being responsible for it all. Nevertheless, this is where natural theology (i.e., the truth about God that we can obtain from nature alone) ends. Science cannot explain why we are here or where history is going ultimately. It is essential, therefore, that we do not settle for *a* god, but for the only true God who has revealed Himself in the Scriptures and in His only eternally born, incarnate Son.

My fear is that we evangelicals have been willing to settle for *a* god, like the "unknown god" of Athens or the Baals of Israel's neighbors. Evangelical leaders who want to see prayer in the public schools and invoke Him at civic functions assume that *a* god is enough, but Paul reminds us that the antidote for secularism is not religion of any kind, but religion of a particular kind revealed in the pages of Holy Scripture and in the doings and dying of a Jewish rabbi who rose from the dead for the salvation of men and women.

And now, while we continue to value technology, the popular culture is growing increasingly cynical about traditional science. Even respected Nobel prize-winning scientists advocate a blending of science and magic. The grandeur and rationality of science becomes first banal, then superstitious and irrational, when it tries to be something it is clearly not—God. Only when we see our hobbies, interests, sports, entertainment, vocation, relationships, food and drink, clothes, and cars as particular expressions of this particular God's goodness meant to remind us of His liberality toward us, and therefore to be used with respect and moderation, can we truly enjoy these gifts. What we moderns call "addictions" God calls "idols," and all of God's good gifts are meant to raise our eyes in thanksgiving to our benevolent heavenly Father, not to fix our eyes on the gifts themselves.

Who was better acquainted with the process of turning blessings into curses and gifts into gods than King Solomon? And yet when he turned gifts into gods, that very treasure—whether it was wisdom, riches, honor, or success—became "vanity," as the King James Version puts it. Only when Solomon recovered his God-centered focus was he able to regain the balance between abusing God's gifts by making them ultimate entities (i.e., gods) and rejecting them as though they were bad gifts. Only when Solomon restored gifts to their rightful role of glorifying the God who is ultimate could he say:

> Then I realized that it is good and proper for a man to eat and drink, and to find satisfaction in his toilsome labor under the sun during the few days of life God has given him—for this is his lot. Moreover, when God gives any man wealth and possessions, and enables him to enjoy them, to accept his lot and be happy in his work—this is a gift of God. He seldom reflects on the days of his life, because God keeps him occupied with gladness of heart. (Ecclesiastes 5:18–20)

Gifts are a source of pleasure and delight; idols end up destroying instead of saving.

WHAT IS EXPECTED OF US IN THIS COMMANDMENT?

The first commandment is not only a command, but a promise. In other words, one can even find the gospel in the commandment. Essentially, God is telling His people, "Look, I am the sovereign God of history who spoke this world into existence and led you out of slavery. I am the only one in this mess who *can* save you because I am all-powerful. But not only am I the only one who *can* save you, I *want* to save you, because I am gracious and merciful, in spite of the fact that you do not deserve it. Because I am sovereign, I am the only one who *can* save you; because I alone can unconditionally love, I am the only one who *wants* to save you and will continue to save you in spite of your sin and resistance."

Thomas Molnar, in *Chronicle,* adds: "It is first because it also contradicts the principal human tendency of locating the divine in ourselves and of bringing our exalted ego into the focus of adoration. . . . The decisive metanoia is to make the first commandment your own: resist the temptation of worshiping yourself, of regarding yourself as the center of creation."[15] The "spark of divinity" in every person, the goodness in everyone, self-esteem, whatever you call it—we attempt to anchor our faith, our confidence, and our hope somewhere inside of ourselves. It is too risky, not to mention, too humbling, to anchor it in someone outside of us. Luther believed that the commonest, and most dangerous, form of idolatry was works-righteousness. Refusing to trust the righteousness of someone else (viz., Christ), we seek to establish our own, like Paul's countrymen (Romans 10:2). In this way, we worship our own righteousness, our own virtue, our own moral strength.

The Protestant Reformers explained the obligation implied by the first commandment in terms of adoration, trust, invocation, and thanksgiving. To adore God means to submit one's conscience to Him in worship, agreeing with Him that He has the right to rule us and that His rule is just and good. We trust God when we place all of our weight on Him for our salvation and the liberation of our conscience from the painful realization that we have a shameful record in the history of His reign over us. By invoking His pardon and forgiveness, we are calling on the name of the Sovereign God, who is not only the judge to whom we must answer but the redeemer who meets the obligations of justice on our behalf. Thanksgiving is the only appropriate response. As in Luther's day, Christians today are often encouraged to obey God so that they can get something out of it. "If I do this, God will do that," many reason. But Luther insisted that the gospel—including the part about human helplessness and God's omnipotent grace—needs to be so clearly preached that those who hear it will not need to be coaxed, harassed, or frightened into obedience. The gospel, not bare commands, is the motivation for thanksgiving. If we are unclear about this point, we cannot have thankful hearts. "If I do not know these things, I cannot worship, praise, thank, or serve God," Luther declared. "For I shall never know how much I owe to God and how much to myself."

We violate the first commandment when we worship, trust, invoke, or thank others in God's place. Which deity has our allegiance on a Sunday morning—our career or an entertainment? Or how about Monday morning? Do we trust God completely, or do we still rely on our own willpower or effort to gain acceptance with God? Do we think that God sees something in us worthy of His love or grace?

Do our decisions, our "free will," even our commitment to Christ give us more confidence in ourselves than in God? Do we invoke God to the exclusion of all other deities? When we are in trouble, upon whom or what do we call? When we are in trouble, do we say to ourselves, *I can take care of this myself,* or perhaps run to other gods for help— materialism, alcoholism, mindless absorption in entertainment? Do we thank God not only for our salvation but also for the gifts He gives us at work, at play, and with our family and friends? Do we see Him as the provider of all of our needs, not just of our eternal redemption? How we answer these questions determines much in terms of the commandments that follow.

WHAT ARE OUR IDOLS?

We are familiar with the obvious idols of money, sex, power, and success. Not much has changed since Sir Francis Bacon wrote, "There are four classes of idols which beset men's minds. To these for distinction's sake I have assigned names,—calling the first class *Idols of the Tribe;* the second, *Idols of the Cave;* the third, *Idols of the Market-Place;* the fourth, *Idols of the Theatre.*"[16] It is easy for us to see idolatry in the obsessions many have with nationalism (the tribe), superstition (the cave), business (the marketplace), and entertainment (the theatre). In fact, these gods seem to have set up shop in some of our churches, with nationalistic campaigns, superstitious demon-chasing, marketing approaches, and entertainment models replacing worship of the one true God in Spirit and truth.

In our own day, we see a rebirth of raw paganism, in the worship of the Earth and female deities. It is often in mainline churches where such ideas find their freest expression these days, with breast-bearing crucifixes and neutered liturgies. Never mind the Trinity, God is now Father, Mother, Child, and Spirit. And we can live without the humanity of Christ (requiring a specific gender), or so radical feminists tell us. But most readers of this volume will not find themselves enmeshed in confusion over issues of divine gender and the veneration of mushrooms.

But what are the idols we harbor, even we conservative Christians? Thomas Molnar adds to the definition of contemporary idolatory.

> The more dangerous idols we currently worship are more subtle in their idolatry: science, history, a way of life, this or that regime, satisfaction with one's own goodness, a cause like progress, utopia, an "ism." All these are absolutized with the greatest of ease—not because we believe they are perfect, but because it is *we* who adore them. In other words, self-idoltry is so immensely tenacious that whatever it chooses to embrace becomes *ipso facto* an absolute.[17]

Could it be that the feeling that the advance of God's kingdom rides on who occupies the White House at any given time makes an idol out of the American presidency? Paul said something about God raising up Pharaoh and Nero, two notorious persecutors of God's people, but we have forgotten God's sovereignty over history. Do we make an idol out of our political ideology or moral agenda by thinking, if subconsciously, that everything will be all right and America will be saved if we just achieve these particular secular goals, even if we consider them religious ones? Molnar is right: by worshiping *our* agenda, *our* goals, *our* nation, *our* group, *our* movement, *our* whatever, we are able to, in short measure, worship ourselves.

The pagans of the ancient near east carved their wood into the shapes of animals, not because the animals themselves were gods, but because they represented some transcendent deity. One might surmise from the mission of the last three and a half decades that Christians themselves have sacrificed more than once to the image of the elephant and the donkey. But what about other idols Christians may harbor and even nurture and encourage as supposedly faithful to God's revealed will?

Faith in Faith

"You've got to believe in something; I believe I'll have another beer," reads a southern California bumper sticker. Os Guinness has said that "faith in faith is a characteristically American heresy," evidenced in an evangelistic tract bearing the title "How to Have Faith in Faith."

Americans believe there is a power in faith, a magic in believing, and this is every bit as "primitive" as the Egyptian, Roman, and medieval superstitions we have described. The *act* of faith is what really counts; the *object* of faith is peripheral. The prosperity evangelists talk about "decreeing" things into existence by the "force of faith," just as God created the world by His faith-filled words. But according to scripture, faith is not a power. Faith itself can do absolutely nothing. If faith could save, heal, or bring prosperity, faith would be God. The New Age mystics and prosperity preachers, in attributing to faith the attributes of deity, are propagating idolatry. Faith is like a telephone wire—it cannot create a conversation between two people, but can only be the instrument through which two people communicate. Faith in anyone or anything other than the true God as He has revealed Himself in Christ and the written Word is idolatry, even if it is faith in good, worthwhile, and noble things.

It is always easy to spot idolatry when someone makes a god out of cheap bourbon, but how about when the false god is a theological system that so misrepresents God's own self-disclosure in Scripture that it creates an idol of speculation and imagination? To bring this even closer to home, is it possible to violate this commandment by attributing to human beings a power that belongs exclusively and properly to God alone? The famous Baptist evangelist, Charles Spurgeon, was not afraid to distance himself from this idol:

> If you believe that everything turns upon the free-will of man, you will naturally have man as its principal figure in your landscape. . . . I do not serve [that] god . . . at all; I

have nothing to do with him, and I do not bow down before the Baal they have set up; he is not my God, nor shall he ever be; I fear him not, nor tremble at his presence. . . . He may be a relation of Ashtaroth or Baal, but Jehovah never was or can be his name.[18]

Faith in any human activity or decision is not only counterproductive to the gospel, it is, in fact, another gospel. Consequently, to the extent that the creature is "the principal figure in your landscape," as Spurgeon put it, the creature will be worshiped rather than the Creator (Romans 1:25).

Faith in Experience

"You'll never convince me it's not true: I *experienced* it!" This is the sort of response we often hear even from deeply committed Christians. Instead of going to the Scriptures to be told what we ought to experience, we view experience as normative and go to the Scriptures to justify what we have already concluded.

"I just feel right about that," is another giveaway of the attitude. We ought to be wary of believing something that "feels right," "sounds right," or "looks right." Remember, the forbidden fruit was "a delight to the eyes," and the religion of the natural man or woman is extremely attractive. Belief in some inherent human goodness and worth attaches itself to the bone of human nature. Teachings that exploit this natural religion are always going to find a ready audience. Telling people to believe in themselves resonates with human experience. Calling pagans to follow their heart is not a challenge to faith and repentance, but an invitation to add the "Jesus trip" to their resume of quasi-religious experiences.

We must even, as believers, beware of making our "personal relationship with Christ" an idol. It is possible to be in love with the idea of marriage instead of one's spouse, and it is also possible to be so obsessed with one's relationship with Christ that there is not enough knowledge of and concern for Christ Himself to constitute a meaningful relationship. Sometimes, especially when one's conversion experience was radical, that person will say, "I know I'm saved because of that night in Wichita, in 1968," and again, this risks placing one's faith in the idol of experience rather than in the God who saves.

"Sheilaism" is further characterized by the oft-heard phrase, "My idea of God is . . ." Even professing Christians often depend on their own intuition rather than on God's self-revelation. This has never been more widespread than now, when relativism threatens to shape our minds and hearts, illustrated (albeit, in a more pious way) in such phrases as "I don't care about theology or doctrine—just so long as you love Jesus." It is ironic that the devil has diverted our attention from worldliness in these extremely sensitive areas to focusing our gaze on the supposed worldliness of card games, movies, dances, and secular literature. Whenever a brother or sister bases a religious claim on his or her own personal experience, that person has usurped God's throne. Our faith depends on divine revelation, not on human speculation, and if we are truly to put that conviction into practice, there can be no more dalliance with the sort of subjective relativism that allows, in essence, "Whatever helps you in your personal relationship with Jesus." Personal faith without a clear understanding of the object of that faith is idolatry.

Faith in Love

An all too typical Christian idol is "love," better characterized as "sentiment." Notice the warning of the English writer, Harry Blamires:

> A curse of contemporary Christendom has been the replacement of traditional theology by a new system which we may call *Twentieth-century Sentimental Theology*. Sentimental theology has invented a God: it insists that he is a God of love, and implies that it is therefore his eternal concern that a thumping good time should be had by all. Are we in the dumps? Pray to this God and, at a word, he restores us to self-confident buoyancy. . . . Five minutes of

prayer to this many-sided God, and we shall be able to re-joice indiscriminately with sinner and saint; we shall be able to spread the family spirit of Christian charity like a blanket over every disloyalty and infidelity conceived in Hell and planted in men's hearts.

So runs the Sentimental Creed. Because this God loves all men equally, therefore, we must live in agreement with all men, smiling indulgently upon every vanity and be-trayal. Because this God is a God of Love, we must never differentiate between good and evil, for judgment partakes of uncharity and presumption. Because this God is a God of mercy, we must pretend that sins have not been commit-ted, that evils under our own noses do not exist.

But Blamires doesn't think that this idol stands up to life's trials, much less to biblical revelation:

If we try to change the face of eternal God, we indulge in the supreme idolatry, beside which perhaps, in the scale of sin, adultery weighs like a feather and murder like a far-thing. Yet the sin is committed among us, within Christen-dom, within the Church—maybe within ourselves; for are we sure, after all, that we prayed to the true God this morn-ing? The God whose face is the face of the living and dying Christ? Or was it this God who, in grand avuncular benevo-lence, slyly slips us half-a-crown and tells us to have a good time?[19]

According to one survey, nearly half of the evangeli-cal students polled at Bible colleges and seminaries agreed that facing unbelievers with the reality of judgment and hell was "in poor taste."[20] God's love has lost its meaning in the Christian imagination because it has lost its corollary: wrath. If we begin with "God loves you and has a wonder-ful plan for your life," what is the problem? From what does the unbeliever need to be saved? We have forgotten that people are condemned eternally, not primarily be-cause they did not accept Christ, but because *God* did not—could not, if He remained just and holy—accept *them*. Un-less we are clothed with Christ's righteousness, God cannot enter into a relationship of covenant love and faithfulness with us. It is God's problem with us, not just our problem with God, that must be faced if we are to avoid setting up an idol of love in the place of the true God. This was poignantly illustrated in the assurance I heard not long ago from a televangelist. "You can say it either way: God is love; love is God." We have read the verse "God is love" to argue as if God had only one attribute, or at least one attribute to which all His other character traits had to bow. If God is love, He cannot *really* hate, show His wrath, execute His justice, or display His glory in a manner judged by sentimental moderns to be "unloving." This is to make an idol of one of God's attributes in the place of God Himself.

This idol of love not only confuses our evangelistic message and goals, it also inhibits discipline in the body of Christ. Whenever a Christian leader goes into print with a novel interpretation of a particular passage that may have negative consequences in Christian faith and practice, anyone who criticizes the leader's views is immediately treated with disdain. In fact, it might be said that in our society of mindless sentimentalism, the only way to really be run out on a rail in some Christian circles these days is to criticize "the Lord's anointed." Love is more important than doctrine or holiness, we are told, so we must overlook the differences. But in actuality, whenever love and unity become more important than truth and loyalty to God Himself, they become idols.

We are commanded not to love the idol of love, but to love God with our whole being, and our neighbors as ourselves. This love must be informed, intelligently directed, and thoughtfully nurtured. We must be focused clearly on the object if we are to avoid creating a rival deity.

There are many other examples one might offer to demonstrate the lure of idol-making even when those idols are dressed in pious, spiritual clothes. The religious imagination, like the secular imagination, is busy creating fabrications of the real thing. We must be especially keen in preserving ourselves from the adoration, trust, invocation, and gratitude toward false gods.

Faith in Self

"To love oneself is the beginning of a life-long romance." These words from the controversial British hedonist Oscar Wilde. "To love yourself is to be truly religious." These words from televangelist Robert Schuller.[21] By sharp contrast, Jesus said that if anyone wishes to become His disciple, he must deny himself. Luther said that "man can seek only his own interests and love above all things. This is the essence of all his faults." But Robert Schuller has written, "Self-love is, or should be, the basic will in human life."[22] What Christians have, in the past, called vice, many today are calling virtue. But that is just one more sign of a confused church, when people call evil good and good evil.

Our media culture is locked in, it seems, to Oscar Wilde's definition of life's chief end. Each of us thinks himself a little god, at the center of his own universe, with other people—even God, Himself—existing to make his own personal life more meaningful. *Newsweek* writer Gary Wills writes, "The imperative 'to feel good about oneself' has become a national and personal priority. It has become a patriotic, even religious, duty."[23] And in his best-selling book, *The Culture of Narcissism,* Christopher Lasch observes, "Self-absorption insulates Americans against the horrors around them—poverty, racism, injustice—and 'eases their troubled conscience.'"[24] Secular writers are becoming increasingly impatient with the narcissism of popular culture, but it is still taking Christians a while to catch on that, once more, just as we got to the dock, the ship embarked for yet another port.

The restless American soul is still looking for the meaning of it all, a quest that took it to various ports of call in this century. In the '50s, it was the mental health craze; in the '60s, revolution and sexual liberation; in the '70s, the "me generation"; in the '80s, money fever; and in the '90s, power. Meanwhile, the one group that claims to be the most "separated" has become the most worldly branch of Christendom. Yale professor George Linbeck writes, "Playing fast and loose with the Bible needed a liberal audience in the days of Norman Vincent Peale, but now, as the case of Robert Schuller indicates, professed conservatives eat it up."[25] In this not only are we *unfaithful* once more (as in Jeremiah's day, when God's people committed spiritual prostitution "wherever the shade is pleasant," as God put it), we are *late* once more, following rather than leading popular taste. *Newsweek* devoted a cover story in February 1992 to the American plague, with "The Curse of Self-Esteem" splashed across the cover. With other social institutions, "churches have discovered that 'low self-esteem' is less off-putting to congregants than 'sin.'"[26] Unless people love themselves and think they are worthy of God's love, self-esteem advocates like Robert Schuller insist, they will never come to Christ. After all, the basic nature of the fallen human condition is not wickedness, but fear that comes from a low self-worth.

Schuller observes that "once a person believes he is an 'unworthy sinner,' it is doubtful if he can really honestly accept the saving grace God offers in Jesus Christ,"[27] whereas Jesus said it was the immoral person who cried out, "Lord, be merciful to me, a sinner," rather than the Pharisee with self-worth, who "went home justified that day" (Luke 18:19–14). Gone is the idea of total depravity—the belief that the glorious creature made in God's own image plunged himself into bondage to corruption, replaced by the idea that the reason Jesus died for us was that He thought we were worthy of it all. But, as Lutheran writer Don Matzat argues, that is somewhat akin to telling a serial murderer that he should derive a sense of self-worth from the enormous bail the court placed on him. To see the cross is not to see the measure of how worthy I am, but of how *un*worthy, shameful, and guilty I am apart from the imputed righteousness of Christ alone.[28]

It has always been difficult to get people to take it all seriously—you know, the bad as well as the good. We are looking for something that will give us what we need—or at least what we want—without taking anything away. We want to be in charge, so give us something we can use, employ, put into practice—treating religion like some diet plan—to improve our own lives. We want to be gods ourselves. But don't tell us that we're helpless to save ourselves, that we're "dead in trespasses and sins," enslaved to our own selfishness. Instead, tell us sweet and pleasant things. Tell us that heaven is a state of self-indulgence, and that hell is the state of unrealized self-fulfillment. Tell us that our root problem is not that a holy and just God must somehow satisfy His own moral character in the face of our sinfulness; in fact, tell us that it doesn't have anything to do with God at all. Our real problem is that we just don't love ourselves enough, and that God fits into the plan by providing that missing link to personal fulfillment.

What we really need are preachers like George Burns, who, in his unlikely role as God, tells John Denver, "If you find it hard to believe in me, it might help you to know that I believe in you." Not far off from the title of a best-selling Christian book, *Believe in the God Who Believes in You.* Nice sentiment, but on the whole unhelpful for people who need answers somewhere beyond the fortune cookie. Theologian Mary Hatch nicely observes that the main problem with churches these days is that "they give out the worst schlock in the culture. . . . The preaching and teaching people actually get in the churches simply reify what people get from the newspaper and television."[29]

The apostle Paul warned Timothy, "There will be terrible times in the last days: Men will be lovers of themselves" (2 Timothy 3:1). Evangelicals, it seems, have forgotten that this was a warning, not an invitation. The people of God are not most unfaithful when they are sleeping with their neighbor's wife, as serious as that is, but when they are prostituting the biblical message for the passing fads that will always be part and parcel of fallen humanity's self-love. And, like the prophets in Jeremiah's day, there will always be plenty of "lying prophets" to peddle it. Of all the idols of our time, perhaps this is the one that has given birth to the many demigods of materialism, sexual fulfillment, vanity, and hedonism.

Faith in Happiness

Americans are, or have been, the most optimistic people in the industrialized world, it seems. But happiness has become an idol. Richard Niebuhr pointed out the dangers of the optimism of Protestant liberalism earlier this century: "It tends to define religion in terms of adjustment to divine reality for the sake of gaining power rather than in terms of revelation which subjects the recipient to the criticism of that which is revealed." Thus, "man remains the center of religion and God is his aid rather than his judge and redeemer."[30]

Pop-psychology assists in giving modern men and women the sense that everything, God included, exists for its own personal happiness and fulfillment. We divorce when our spouse does not fulfill every craving of our heart (which we dub "needs"), and we move from self-help programs to religion and back again with the ease of a shopper sampling for the best product. It is not truth, but happiness, we seek most. But, alas, when we worship happiness, the things and people with whom we entrusted this commission eventually let us down and the worship of happiness turns into a nightmare of disillusionment, fatigue, and depression. This is what philosophers call "the hedonistic paradox." John Stuart Mill said it best, after preaching the gospel of happiness for some years himself: "But I now thought that this end [happiness] was only to be attained by not making it the direct end. For those are only happy . . . who have their minds fixed on some object other than their own happiness."[31]

God will never let us down; the truth will never fail us, because truth is true, if you will pardon the tautology. This explains the joy the Reformers experienced when they abandoned their own happiness and gave themselves entirely to the pursuit of God and truth. Columbia University historian Eugene F. Rice observes just this point. The God-centeredness of the Reformation, he said, "spans the gulf between the secular imagination of the twentieth century and sixteenth-century Protestantism's intoxication with the majesty of God. We can only exercise historical sympathy to try to understand how it was that the most sensitive intelligences of an entire epoch found a supreme, a total, liberty in the abandonment of human weakness to the omnipotence of God."[32]

What is your chief end? "To glorify God and enjoy him forever"? Or to glorify yourself, and enjoy yourself forever? How one answers that question will determine what decisions he or she makes in the course of any given day.

There are many other examples one might offer to demonstrate the lure of idol-making even when those idols are dressed in pious, spiritual clothes. The religious imagination, like the secular imagination, is busy creating fabrications of the real thing, and we must be especially keen in preserving ourselves from the adoration, trust, invocation, and gratitude toward false gods.

HOW MANY GODS?

We return to Israel's *Shema:* "Hear, O Israel: The LORD our God is one." The most basic affirmation of the Christian faith, according to both testaments, is monotheism. In paganism many deities reign over their own spheres, but our "Atlas"—the God of Israel—bears the whole world on His shoulders. He alone is sovereign over land and sea, church and state, the holy and the common, providence and miracle, salvation and culture, Sunday and Monday. There is no corner of our lives that escapes His scrutiny, concern, and authority. All besides God are in the category of creature and are dependent on the one who alone is self-existent, autonomous, and self-sufficient.

The essence of the pagan (whether ancient or modern) reaction to this commandment is threefold. First, it is restrictive; it does not make room for the variety of gods, powers, idols, and saviors. Especially as our society becomes increasingly pluralistic, Christianity is going to be required to make certain dogmatic sacrifices. It can no longer declare, with God's people through all ages, "Hear, O Israel! the LORD your God is one"—that is, if it wants to be accepted. But biblical faith violates this precious tenet of modern culture by accepting the self-testimony of one who said, "I am the way and the truth and the life. No one comes to the Father except through me" (John 14:6). A second objection from a pagan culture, both ancient and modern, is that biblical religion, framed by this first commandment, is theocentric (God-centered), not anthropocentric (man-centered). Religion, according to paganism, is for the well-being, happiness, and prosperity of human beings. But according to biblical faith, revealed in part here in this commandment, God makes all of life a matter of glorifying and enjoying Him, not glorifying and enjoying ourselves.

Finally, paganism new and old objects because it is dogmatic and objective rather than psychological and subjective. This commandment calls us to focus our attention on a person outside of ourselves. Instead of finding the "god within us" or the "spark of divinity" concealed in our heart, this faith calls us away from our own subjective, inner life as a source of hope, salvation, or life. Paganism appreciates mysticism—the feeling of ecstasy. Even rationalistic scientists may dabble in this sort of harmless religion, so long as it does not make rational claims itself. Once Christianity makes truth claims about events such as resurrections happening in time and space history, thus requiring the same assent from everybody as the facts of Napoleon's life, it is regarded as narrow-minded and bigoted. As long as religion stays within the bounds of the oft-heard reply, "As long as it helps you," pagans will even help celebrate its annual rites.

This affirmation may seem so basic as to be almost trite, but it is nonetheless denied implicitly in a number of ways in our day, even increasingly in Christian circles. Chief among these threats to monotheism is universalism.

Universalism

No one likes the idea that people go to hell. Those who do find the notion attractive ought to seek profession-al help. It is perhaps the most disturbing part of the confession of faith that is required of us as Christians. We have no sentimental difficulty with Hitler spending eternity in hell, but when Gandhi is said to have the same fate, something inside the human heart recoils. Regardless of how good we think our theology is, there is still something in all of us that tells us there is a class of people called "good" who do not actually deserve God's wrath.

In James Davison Hunter's surveys of evangelical students, this belief was pointed up again and again. "When asked about Gandhi's fate, some were absolutely certain he was saved, a few were certain he was not, but most were unsure of either."[33] In fact, one Christian college student responded, "The human part of me wants to say that Gandhi would be good enough to get him eternal life, but I think Scripture would indicate that he is not." A Bible major went even further. "I would say that the Lord would know his heart and somehow would judge him fairly. I hope the Lord would judge his heart and if he was a good man and he knew to live an honest life and he was generous and loving, maybe the Lord would take him." Another response came from a Christian student. "At Judgment we are judged by our deeds and by the light we have to live by. . . . I don't believe in eternal torment—it may be but it seems to be inconsistent with God's nature."[34] And what is "inconsistent with God's nature" is whatever we deem such in our wisdom, apart from divine revelation. We make idols of ourselves in this way, too: by placing more confidence in our reason than in God's revelation.

Hunter concludes, "The introduction of these qualifications tempers the purity of the theological exclusivism traditionally held. Ultimate truth is not at issue here, only what people perceive to be ultimate truth."[35]

Maintaining convictions of a religious nature since the Enlightenment has been a precarious business. How do we justify our claims? In the age of the microscope and telescope, how can we *show* people conclusively that God exists and that He sent His Son to die for our sins and rise for our justification? The route we have commonly chosen to overcome this difficulty is the one called "fideism" (from the Latin *fides*, "faith"). The idea—and unfortunately it is a line of thinking many Christians have followed—is that we ought not set out to justify our faith in terms of the historical accuracy of the biblical record or the external evidences for the resurrection, since religion is outside the parameters of investigation. The decision of faith was a leap with no apparent rationale. One believes in atoms because their existence can be empirically verified; one believes that Napoleon lived because his existence can be historically verified; but one believes in God simply because one has decided to believe in God.

Keeping that definition of fideism in mind, let us consider another concept prominent in contemporary culture —pluralism. Cultural pluralism is the product of immigration and what the Canadian educator Marshall McLuhan has called the "global village," our world. Now in one sense no culture is intrinsically superior to another. In the United States, for example, the "melting pot" has been a source of national strength. Los Angeles, where I live, is the second largest Mexican city, El Salvadoran city, Korean city, and Vietnamese city, in addition to other records. Each community brings with it a rich diversity that contributes to the overall breadth and variety that makes this country so distinctive and strong. There is not, and ought never to be, a test of racial, socioeconomic, or cultural superiority in a democratic society.

But cultural pluralism is quite a different thing from religious pluralism. Only regenerate Christians go to heaven when they die. Yet we often mix cultural pluralism with religious pluralism. If a Christian spokesperson were to go on the "Phil Donahue Show" and say of Jesus what He said of Himself, he or she would be the immediate object of the most vituperative verbal abuse imaginable. After all, only a self-righteous, egotistical bigot whose teachings inspired division and confrontation between people of different faiths would dare to assert that there is only *one* way to God. Surely Christ was more inclusive than that. After all, everyone likes Jesus. He's the Gandhi of the ancient world.

But that is precisely what Jesus is not. He is indeed an exclusionist. He declared that He is the only way to God. "I am the way and the truth and the life," He said. "No one comes to the Father except through me. If you really knew me, you would know my Father as well" (John 14:6–7). "Whoever believes in [me] is not condemned," He said, "but whoever does not believe stands condemned already because he has not believed in the name of God's one and only Son" (John 3:18). "Do not suppose that I have come to bring peace to the earth. I did not come to bring peace, but a sword" (Matthew 10:34). Fathers and sons, daughters and mothers, would turn against each other. Families would be divided over the claim "Jesus Christ is Lord."

Like Judaism, Christianity is founded on monotheism: the declaration of the *Shema* that there is but one God. That means that God will never share the stage. He refuses to be simply a part of our life; He must have a full and complete right to our whole life and existence. He does not want to help us get things we have always wanted; He insists on telling us what we need. Consequently, though cultural pluralism may indeed be right, religious pluralism is entirely wrong. A faith founded on historical facts, one that demands exclusive loyalty and trust, will not enter into partnerships with competing allegiances. Christians need to quit confusing exclusivity in religious truth claims with exclusivity in racial, cultural, and socioeconomic backgrounds. After all, it is that conviction—Christ alone as Lord and Savior—that has bound together people of nearly every nationality who were otherwise divided by prejudice. Not only is Christianity not a roadblock to cultural pluralism, the former writes the latter into its very constitution: "'For You were slain and have redeemed us to God by Your blood out of every tribe and tongue and people and nation" (Revelation 5:9 NKJV).

What happens when fideism marries religious pluralism? When everyone is nominally Christian, the leap of faith is at least made in a group, which gives individuals a little bit of confidence that they are doing the right thing. But in a culture where Christianity is seen as only one faith among many, the marriage of fideism and pluralism creates the notion that "everyone ought to have his or her own belief system—whatever works for each person." To be sure, no one should be *forced* to embrace someone else's belief system, but Christianity insists that those who do not embrace Jesus Christ's person and work will suffer eternal misery. Any version of Christianity that does not insist on exclusivity, by definition ceases to be Christian: "No one can come to the Father except through me," our founder declared.

Not only did Jesus Christ say that He was the only *way* to the Father, He added that He was the only *truth*. "He who has seen Me has seen the Father," Jesus declared (John 14:9 NKJV). As God in the flesh (John 1), Jesus Christ not only tells the truth, He is the truth. "For in Christ all the fullness of the Deity lives in bodily form" (Colossians 2:9). Paul insisted that there was "one Lord, one faith, one baptism," and this is founded on the fact that there is only "one God" (Ephesians 4:5–6). If Jesus Christ is the only way and truth, then the exclusivity of Christianity extends not only to the person and work of Christ Himself, but to the teachings that testify to Him—both the Old and New Testaments.

Finally, Jesus Christ is the only *life*. No one obtains eternal life from any other source. A day is coming, Jesus warned, when He will separate the sheep from the goats (Matthew 25) and the wheat from the tares (Matthew 3:12). As His resurrection was a real time-and-space event in history, so this separation of the human race into the condemned and the justified will be a distinct event in history. The sad reality is that not only will many cruel and terrible people be among those suffering eternal loss, but so will many kind, generous, noble, and nice people. The exclusivity of the Christian claim does not turn on religious bigotry. It is not a matter of "our party" being God's favorites. After all, many professing Christians will be among the estranged number on that day. "Many will say to me on that day, 'Lord, Lord, did we not prophesy in your name, and in your name drive out demons and perform many miracles?' Then I will tell them plainly, 'I never knew you. Away from me, you evildoers!'" (Matthew 7:22–23).

School Prayer and the Jews

The issue of prayer in public schools is not just a public policy issue, but a theological concern as well. A test of our commitment to monotheism (the first commandment of the Decalogue) is whether we can say that unbelievers ought to pray. I know of no proponent of public school prayer who believes for one moment that the teachers, much less the students, will all be Christians. What, therefore, is the prayer of an unbeliever? Does one really require a mediator? Is Jesus Christ really the only mediator between God and humans? Or can unbelievers go directly to God without an intercessor? If Jesus is the only mediator and, therefore, the prayers of genuine Christians the only prayers God entertains, what is the purpose of a prayer that God never hears? Is it for the general moral welfare of the students, so that they will receive another inoculation to numb their symptoms of secularism and alienation from God? If so, we are engaging in antievangelism, the undermining of society's sense of lostness apart from Christ.

This is why I find it so shocking that it is the evangelicals who so often protest the loudest when schools cancel public prayer or when city officials do not allow civil prayers to be offered in mixed, public gatherings, without any reference to Christ. Or, when city officials refuse to place the nativity scene on the courtyard grounds along with Jewish and other religious symbols of the season. It is, after all, in the best interest of the gospel that Christ's birth is not celebrated alongside other religious festivals, that prayers are not offered in such a way as to give the impression that Christ is unnecessary as the only mediator. One is reminded of the Roman emperor who placed a crucifix in his private temple, alongside his pagan idols. Earlier, Christians were executed not because they believed in Christ (Rome allowed anything and everything that was judged good for morality and politics) but because they believed in

Christ *alone*. To be sure, Christians are to gather to pray for their rulers, but what are we to say of public gatherings and even prayer breakfasts where one's political or civic credentials outweigh one's faith, as secular leaders invoke God's blessing? All who are not in Christ Jesus are under a curse, and this fact is only blunted when we are more concerned about publicity and public support than in looking out for God's honor and our neighbor's salvation.

Another issue that points up a problem in our commitment to the first commandment is our assumption that Jews have a special relationship with God apart from Christ. Although he was a Jewish rabbi, the apostle Paul had no problem opposing this misunderstanding in the early church. He specifically stated, referring to believers, "There is neither Jew nor Greek, slave nor free, male nor female, for all are one in Christ Jesus" (Galatians 3:28). Moreover, "If you belong to Christ, then you are Abraham's seed, and heirs according to the promise" (v. 29). I have attended evangelical prayer breakfasts in which conservative Christians and Jews join together in prayer, and I have also heard evangelical brethren tell Jewish friends, "We worship the same God," a declaration these people would never make to a Muslim or a Hindu, and with good reason.

According to New Testament teaching, Jesus Christ is God in the flesh, and we cannot know the Father apart from the Son. To worship "God" apart from worshiping the Triune being who exists in three persons is to worship an idol, even if the Jews are relying on earlier biblical revelation. As redemption progressed through history, God revealed more concerning Himself than the Old Testament saints understood. By the time of Christ, people had to start making a choice: either to deny this fuller revelation or to embrace it to their soul's salvation. They still must make this choice. Evangelicals cannot do the Jewish people a greater disservice, even a more eternally consequential disservice, than to presume that they can enjoy a relationship with God apart from Christ. Apart from Christ, we are all—yes, including the Jews—God's enemies. He plays no favorites.

CONCLUSION

We have seen in this chapter how important it is that the one we are worshiping is the one described in the pages of Holy Scripture and visible in the person of Jesus Christ. In this commandment we find the law, forbidding us to place our faith in ourselves or in anyone or anything beside the one true God, who has reconciled us to Himself through the person and work of Jesus Christ. But it is also a gospel invitation: "For God so loved the world that He gave His only begotten Son, that whoever believes in Him should not perish but have everlasting life" (John 3:16 NKJV). Apart from this one true God—one in essence, three in person—there is no salvation. May God give us His grace to accept this and bring our thoughts and feelings into closer conformity to this commandment.

NOTES

1. Robert Bellah et al., *Habits of the Heart* (New York: Harper & Row, 1985), 221.
2. George Gallup and James Castelli, *The People's Religion* (New York: Macmillan, 1989), 93.
3. Ibid., 16.
4. Ibid., 7.
5. James Patterson and Peter Kim, *The Day America Told the Truth* (New York: Plume, 1982), 201.
6. Gallup and Castelli, *The People's Religion*, 251.
7. Patterson and Kim, *The Day America Told the Truth*, 201.
8. John Timmer, *They Shall Be My People* (Grand Rapids: CRC Publications, 1983), 28–29.
9. *U.S. News and World Report*, "Science Can't Explain," February 1985.
10. Stephen Hawking, *A Brief History of Time* (New York: Bantam, 1988), 10.
11. Ibid., 175.
12. Mortimer Adler, *The Great Ideas* (New York: Knopff, 1922), ix.
13. *Time*, 28 December 1992, 43.
14. Ibid., 44

15. Thomas Molnar, *Chronicles: A Magazine of American Culture,* December 1992, 15.
16. Francis Bacon, *Novum Organum,* Aphorism 1.
17. Molnar, *Chronicles,* December 1992, 14.
18. C. H. Spurgeon, *The Sermons of C. H. Spurgeon* (Grand Rapids: Baker), 1:240.
19. Henry Blamires, *The God Who Acts* (Ann Arbor: Servant, 1985), 50–51.
20. James Davison Hunter, *Evangelicals: The Coming Generation* (Chicago: Univ. of Chicago Press), 70.
21. Robert Schuller, *Self-Love* (Old Tappan, N.J.: Revell, 1981), 24.
22. Ibid.
23. Gary Wills, *Reagan's America* (New York: Penguin, 1988), 235.
24. Christopher Lasch, *The Culture of Narcissism* (New York: Warner, 1979), 62.
25. Frederic Burnham, ed., *Postmodern Theology* (San Francisco: Harper & Row, 1989), 45.
26. *Newsweek,* 15 February 1992, 46.
27. Robert Schuller, *Self-Esteem: The New Reformation* (Waco, Tex.: Word, 1982), 8.
28. Don Matzat, "A Better Way: Christ Is My Worth," in *Power Religion,* ed. Michael Horton (Chicago: Moody, 1992).
29. Quoted in Bellah et. al., *The Good Society* (New York: Knopf, 1991), 206.
30. Quoted in Schneider and Dornbuch, *Popular Religion: Inspirational Books in America* (Chicago: Univ. of Chicago Press, 1958), 47.
31. Ibid., 75
32. Eugene F. Rice, *The Foundations of Early Modern Empire* (New Hork: W. W. Norton, 1970), 136.
33. James Davison Hunter, *Evangelicals,* 38.
34. Ibid.
35. ibid.

CHAPTER THREE

WORSHIPING THE CORRECT GOD CORRECTLY

*You shall not make for yourself an idol
in the form of anything in heaven above
or on the earth beneath or in the waters below.*

Not only docs God command us to make sure we have the correct deity in mind when we worship, He also requires us to worship the correct God correctly.

One of the best lessons in all of scripture in this regard comes from the story of Jehu, the king of Israel in 841 B.C. The wicked duo, King Ahab and Queen Jezebel of Israel, had incorporated Baal worship, and only seven thousand Israelites were left worshiping the God of Israel (1 Kings 19:18). After the violent deaths of the royal couple, Jehu is anointed king and the prophet informs him that he must destroy the whole royal line of Ahab. Jehu tricked all of the prophets of Baal into showing up by sending word that he was going to offer a tribute to the false deity for his success. "Ahab served Baal a little; Jehu will serve him much," the new king deceptively declared (2 Kings 10:18). Placing guards at the exits of the temple, Jehu left strict orders that not one prophet of Baal was to escape. In addition to killing all of the priests and prophets

71

of Baal, Jehu and his army destroyed every implement used in the worship of this false god and turned the old Baal temple into public rest rooms. "So Jehu destroyed Baal worship in Israel" (v. 28).

Unfortunately that is not the end of the story. Having destroyed the worship of the wrong god, Jehu nevertheless "did not turn away from the sins of Jeroboam son of Nebat, which he had caused Israel to commit—the worship of the golden calves at Bethel and Dan" (v. 29). The worship of the golden calves was an attempt to worship the true God of Israel through images. It was not a violation of the first commandment ("You shall have no other gods before me") but of the second commandment ("You shall not make an idol in the form of anything in heaven above or in the earth beneath or in the waters below"). As much as Jehu had done, he still "was not careful to keep the law of the LORD, the God of Israel, with all his heart" (v. 31). After twenty-eight years of reigning over Israel, Jehu died, replaced by Joash. Even though Joash "did what was right in the eyes of the LORD," he too failed to remove the high altars, and the people continued to offer sacrifices and burn incense there, accommodating the worship of God to the pagan culture. It was the right God, but the wrong worship.

The human heart not only wants to worship false gods, it consistently seeks to invent new ways of worship even when worshiping the triune God of biblical revelation. People are convinced that God will be pleased with the patterns, forms, rules, and guidelines they have set up for His service. Or, worse, they invent new patterns of worship to accommodate themselves, with little thought to pleasing God.

WHAT IS FALSE WORSHIP?

Human-Centered Worship

You can tell who is being worshiped on Sunday morning in a given church by whom the service is attempting to please. Our evangelism is often human-centered, so we tell the unbeliever what we think he or she wants to hear: how God can do this for him or fill that need for her. Our public worship is therefore often geared toward the consumer —getting new people in—instead of raising the eyes of the people to heaven in praise and thanksgiving. If this is our focus, our worship will inevitably require innovations at every turn, and theological objections will almost always be undervalued. In contrast, biblical, God-centered, Christ-focused worship looks to the Word and the sacraments, not to entertainment, to inspire worship. This does not exclude contemporary worship styles. In fact, when worship was reformed in Geneva at the time of the Reformation, the return to biblical patterns (joyful congregational singing, instead of leaving it to the professionals; centrality of Word and sacrament, with no unscriptural ceremonies; sermons, prayers, and liturgy in the common language of the people) was at once considered radically contemporary. So lively were the psalms set to music that they earned the scornful nickname "Geneva jigs." Bach's congregational music for the German evangelicals borrowed much of its style from the popular secular operas of the day, a fact that won the famous composer a good deal of scorn from many of his contemporaries. Nevertheless, the Reformation composers did not blindly adopt the contemporary any more than they blindly adopted the ancient. The key question remained, How can we enable God's people to worship their Creator and Redeemer correctly in their day? not How can we pack 'em in this Sunday? The glory of God, not the lowest common denominator of popular fancy, drove every new adventure.

Robert Schuller says that "the Reformation erred in that it was God-centered rather than man-centered," since "man's greatest need is for self-esteem."[1] If we believe that religion ought to be man-centered and that man most needs self-esteem, we will view the congregation as consumers rather than worshipers. We will not be there to equip them, as members of a royal priesthood, to learn about God and His saving work in Christ, to share that faith with others, to treat their neighbors with concern, and to engage in their callings with integrity. The glory of God will be eclipsed by the glory of those who "let" Jesus have His way and "allow" Him to add something to their lives.

Almost overnight, the evangelical churches have been swept into the church growth movement, a diverse collection of strategies and methodologies vying for success. Among the most popular methods is the door-to-door or telephone survey, in which the unchurched are asked to describe the kind of church they would attend. Of course, there is nothing wrong with listening. In fact, we need to have our ears opened ever wider to the culture and to our unbelieving friends and neighbors. And yet, many of these pastors, anxious to develop a successful ministry, take their results and build a church that is "user friendly" —a congregation that accommodates to the preferences of those who do not attend church.

Why don't these people attend? Growth experts might want to convince us that it is simply because we have not made the option attractive, but Scripture compels us to conclude that the principal reason that people do not want to worship God is that they worship themselves instead. If they show up on Sunday morning and hear and see very little that challenges their secular outlook—a "happy," country-club type of atmosphere that strips the church bare of Word and sacrament, law and gospel—it is likely that what they have experienced is merely a transition service for Christians on their way to the unchurched category rather than the opposite. Why even show up on Sunday morning if one can get the same stuff from talk-shows and self-help books? Those who are more comfortable in a church with a chatty, talk-show atmosphere that makes no demands on the mind, heart, body, and soul than they are in a church with solid exposition, sound teaching, and reverent worship will soon find it just that much more comfortable to stay home and watch Sunday morning TV instead.

This does not mean, of course, that worship cannot be contemporary or relevant in terms of style. There is nothing more sacred about an eighteenth-century style of worship than a twentieth-century one. However, the principles of worship never change, regardless of changing applications. God is always the audience and we—all of us, not just the professionals in the bulletin and in the choir—are always the actors in this drama of worship. That does not mean that we all must use a prayer book or follow an ancient liturgy, but it does mean that somehow everyone must be involved in confession, prayer, thanksgiving, intercession, and praise. The sermon must always be central; the service must be reverent; and Holy Communion must have a prominent and well-defined place in confirming the proclamation of the Word. These principles may be applied in a variety of worship styles, but they must have the last word in every case.

Self-Centered Worship

It is but a small step from a human-centered religion to self-centered living. If God is there for me; if I, as a pastor, believe that I must conduct worship in a way that treats each person as though he or she were the main attraction on Sunday morning; and if the theology I teach gives them the impression that God exists for their happiness and pleasure, it is inevitable that the people present in the auditorium on Sunday will worship themselves, not God, on Monday. When we come to church in order to get something rather than to give something (namely, praise, thanksgiving, fellowship, and service), and when we come as members of an audience expecting to passively experience the events of the service rather than to actively participate in them as members of a congregation, what is going to challenge us to get beyond that sort of worldly thinking on Monday morning? Worship has the power to change us as no other activity. It trains not only our minds, but our hearts and bodies. Purely cerebral services in which lectures rather than sermons are offered cannot bring about the transformation of the total person that worship provides. It calls for a response that goes beyond taking notes and nodding our heads.

Many insightful challenges have been made to believers to get beyond Sunday religion and view God as a daily reality. The problem, I hear it often said, is that we have the right doctrine, but we just aren't living up to it. We're orthodox, but we don't live it, or so the common perception goes. I would like to suggest, rather, that we *are* living up to our theology—or, rather, *down* to it. We cannot be expected to put God at the center of our existence if He is not at the center of our theological system. If God and humans must share the stage in salvation, and if God must provide the fish and the loaves to hold the attention of His demanding consumers, it is inevitable that those who accept such an orientation will think of themselves first—at home, on the job, and in the neighborhood.

Jeremiah prophesied to a nation that thought everything was going well. The sanctuary was looked after, the people were religious and active in spiritual services. Tithes and offerings were pouring in. Then along came Jeremiah, telling them that their prophets were false shepherds filling them "with false hopes" and speaking "visions from their own minds, not from the mouth of the LORD" (Jeremiah 23:16). Far from rebuking those who despised God, they gave them a false assurance, saying "The LORD says: You will have peace" (v. 17), which sounds hauntingly similar to those today who keep telling unbelievers positive things in order to attract them. Is it acceptable to offend God in order to please men? Further, God declares, "I have heard what the prophets say who prophesy lies in my name. They say, 'I had a dream! I had a dream!' How long will this continue in the hearts of these lying prophets, who prophesy the delusions of their own minds?" (vv. 25–26). The people are commanded to cease their reckless claims to have heard words from the Lord, "because every man's own word becomes his oracle and so you distort the words of the living God, the LORD Almighty, our God" (v. 36).

Not only are the false gods worthless, but false religion and false worship of the true God are vain too:

> Do not trust in deceptive words and say, "This is the temple of the LORD, the temple of the LORD, the temple of the LORD!" If you really change your ways and your actions and deal with each other justly, if you do not oppress the alien, the fatherless or the widow and do not shed innocent blood in this place, and if you do not follow other gods to your own harm, then I will let you live in this place, in the land I gave your forefathers for ever and ever. But look, you are trusting in deceptive words that are worthless.
>
> Will you steal and murder, commit adultery and perjury, burn incense to Baal and follow other gods you have not known, and then come and stand before me in this house, which bears my Name, and say, "We are safe"—safe to do all these detestable things? (Jeremiah 7:4–10)

The people of Israel felt safe because they took God for granted. They thought that they could live however they chose and still assume that God would take care of them because of the temple and the mercy-seat. Gathering around them teachers who told them whatever they wanted to hear (one is reminded of the "itching ears" in 2 Timothy 4:3), the people in Jeremiah's day used religion for their own purposes. The temple existed for their safety and carnal security, not for the worship of God. Much could be said along the same lines today. People can so easily attend church and feel comfortable. Instead of being called to repentance, they are soothed with flattery and assurances that they are children of God simply because they belong to the church or simply because they walked an aisle or prayed a prayer. False worship begins on Sunday, when we worship ourselves through entertainment instead of praise, flattery instead of confrontation, the wisdom of a preacher rather than the wisdom of God, and continues throughout the week as we "look out for number one."

Amos also confronted false worship and reported what God had to say about it:

> I hate, I despise your religious feasts;
> I cannot stand your assemblies.

Even though you bring me burnt offerings and
grain offerings,
I will not accept them.
Though you bring choice fellowship offerings,
I will have no regard for them.
Away with the noise of your songs!
I will not listen to the music of your harps.
But let justice roll on like a river,
righteousness like a never-failing stream!
(Amos 5:21–24)

False worship, therefore, can exist even in the presence of apparent success. We often associate unfaithfulness with secularism, outright idolatry, and naked immorality, but the prophets and our Lord Himself argue again and again that false worship is often part and parcel of a church that thinks it is healthy when in reality it is ill. The Israelites, after all, were bringing their offerings and sacrifices just as they were commanded. Their songs were loud and joyful. But there was no connection of theology and life, no realization that honoring and worshiping God included what one did at work every bit as much as what one did in public worship. Hosea, combatting the spiritual adultery of Israel, speaks on behalf of God, "For I desire mercy, not sacrifice, and acknowledgment of God rather than burnt offerings" (Hosea 6:6). In other words, theology and ethics, grace and gratitude, are the marks of true worship—not mere ritual.

Growing up in churches that made regular sport out of crying down "rituals" and "traditions of men," I am amazed at just how cluttered my faith was with just those sorts of human innovations. We may not have had a grand ceremony such as the Mass, but our altar call served a similar purpose: infusing the faithful with fresh grace after backsliding. How difficult it is for us so often to think of worship as something more than quiet times, Bible studies, prayer meetings, and Sunday morning services. Our routines become rituals, and even though they are devised by human wisdom, to omit them is just as eyebrow-raising in our evangelical circles as any of the Reformation's criticisms of ritualism and formalism in the medieval church.

Imaginative Worship

Here we have to be careful, since the use of the imagination in worship is not only inevitable, but appropriate and God-given. And yet, this powerful faculty is also the most vulnerable to temptation in this matter of idolatry.

The most obvious violation of the second commandment since its institution is the practice of establishing physical representations of the eternal God. When God commanded the construction of the temple, He insisted that there be no physical representations of deity. There was much use of color and shapes and images from the natural world (fruit, trees, flowers, land, water), but there were no images of God Himself (1 Kings 6:16–18).

As we saw in the last chapter, the essence of paganism was (and is) a plurality of gods. The God of Israel is what we mean when we say we believe in "God." It is not enough to simply be a theist; one must believe in the one true God. But here we see that another aspect of paganism is the commitment to physical representations of deity as points of contact between the heavenly and earthly realm. Through this pole or that totem, this bronze statue or that gold figure, the gods carry on a relationship with the people. Whoever controls the point of contact controls the deity. The idol becomes a means of manipulating the gods into service. In paganism, the worshipers insist on having a direct relationship with their deities, experiencing them through powerful displays of blessing and cursing. The idol becomes the object through which this direct, sensual encounter can take place.

The religion of Israel was committed, however, to a *mediated* relationship with God. Individual Jews had a relationship with God only because they were part of a *community* of faith. This community was *represented* by mediators: prophets, priests, and kings. In the New Testament, the final prophet, priest, and king-mediator appears. Jesus

Christ is the point of contact between God and humanity. Because God is holy and worshipers sinful, the only way worshipers can stand in God's presence is through the intercession of a mediator. Idolatry, on the other hand, promises a direct encounter with deity. But ultimately more is desired. People insist on having power over the idol so that they can control their own destinies. In most ancient pagan religions, for example, the name of the god itself was said to have magical powers. To know the name of a particular spirit was to have control over that being and manipulate it for one's own ends.

With all of our technological sophistication, we have not advanced very far beyond this form of paganism in our own day. Even in some segments of the church today, one can "name and claim" prosperity, success, healing, or happiness—even salvation, simply by "using" God's name. Evangelist Kenneth Copeland tells his followers, "You need to realize that you are not a spiritual schizophrenic—half-God and half-Satan—you are all-God."[2] Once the line between Creator and creature is erased, Copeland can add, "Man had total authority to rule as a god over every living creature on earth, and he was to rule by speaking words."[3] Earl Paulk asserts that God "has given us the name of Jesus Christ like a blank check."[4]

This is nothing more than paganism, the human craving to be God, or at least to have control over one's god at the point where it has authority over one's life. Even when people insist that they are worshiping the correct God, they can be engaged in idolatrous worship. Like the children of Israel who used the golden calf as a means of worshiping the one true God, many professing Christians today use means other than those God commanded. We must smash the idols of false worship, for we do not have a "user-friendly" God who gives us power over Him through rituals (spoken words, a particular prayer, an altar call in which we promise to do X if God will do Y). Our God is sovereign and free from any "laws" or obligations we presume to place over Him. If He chooses, He may withhold our breath; if He likes, we may become poor. Death may come to us unexpectedly, or sudden wealth may become part of our lot in life. But all of this is determined by God.

You will recall that when Paul confronted the Greek pagans in Athens, God's sovereignty was a large aspect of his sermon. "From one man he made every nation of men, that they should inhabit the whole earth; and he determined the times set for them and the exact places where they should live" (Acts 17:26). Right worship begins with the recognition that the worshipers have absolutely no control over God, no claim on Him, and no magical power over their own destinies by knowing certain formulas, rituals or "laws."

But the imagination can also become a nemesis to true worship when it substitutes for clear declarations of God's Word. Not long ago, I attended a service in which the pastor called the people to close their eyes and imagine God smiling, bending down, and embracing them. I have heard other variations on the theme. Sometimes the people are asked to imagine God covering them with a warm blanket. At other times people are asked to imagine Him whispering something to them that ought to change them forever. All of this has to do with "the healing of memories." Whatever the purpose, the practice itself ought to be regarded as a violation of the second commandment.

Richard Foster encourages readers, "In your imagination allow your spiritual body, shining with light, to rise out of your physical body . . . up through the clouds and into the stratosphere . . . deeper and deeper into outer space until there is nothing except the warm presence of the eternal Creator."[5] Giving such priority to the imagination will always lend itself to doctrinal distortions, such as the idea that God's presence is somewhere deep in "outer space." Churches that would never represent God the Father in stained glass leave it to us, a TV generation, to decide which idol to create in our imagination. So the pastor of the world's largest church declares, "The only way for us to incubate [our future] is through our imaginations."[6] Never would a good evangelical bow to a statue of Jesus in a Roman Catholic church, but to do the same thing in a more privatized, individual way seems to take the sting out of idolatry.

ART IN WORSHIP

The use of art in worship has, of course, a long history of debate. Although symbols of Christ and Christian truth (a lamb, a peacock—symbolizing resurrection, and so on) abounded in the early church, there was a great deal of restraint concerning actual depictions of Christ Himself and no depictions of the Father and the Holy Spirit apart from symbols. A fourth-century bishop, Epiphanius, was shocked when he visited a church in Palestine and discovered a curtain with a depiction of Christ. After tearing the curtain down, the bishop launched a campaign to stop the spread of such images. Yet according to Owen Chadwick, "By 404, when [Epiphanius] died, portrayals of Christ and the saints were widespread."[7]

Again in the seventh century the controversy erupted, this time threatening to actually divide the Greek Church through a century of heated debate between the iconoclasts (those who opposed images) and iconodules (those favoring them). Kenneth Scott Latourette observes, "The iconoclasts pled the prohibition of the second commandment to make 'the likeness of anything' and held that to do so 'draws down the spirit of man from the lofty worship of God to the low and material worship of the creature.' They declared that 'the only admissible figure of the humanity of Christ . . . is the bread and wine in the Holy Supper.'"[8] The eighth-century Greek Father John of Damascus, however, argued that since God had become flesh, it was not improper to represent or depict "what is visible in God," that is, the incarnate Son of God.

The next significant debate over images took place at the time of the Protestant Reformation in the sixteenth century. Although practical piety has differed widely, official Roman Catholic teaching has never held that it is proper or, for that matter, allowable, to worship images. In fact, the only reason the people are to venerate the images is because of the honor due to those represented, not to the representations themselves. The magical, superstitious quality attached to the images was an aspect of popular medieval piety, not of official church teaching. Thomas Aquinas declared, "Not even to a statue of Christ is any reverence owed, since it is only a piece of carved wood." And yet, he continued, "men are more easily moved by what they see than by what they hear or read." Before we are too hard on the "Angelic Doctor," as he was called, we ought to remember that such bizarre, unscriptural rituals as "shaking, extreme terror, [and] being 'drunk with the Spirit,'" are being justified today on the basis that the written Word is not enough.[9] People are moved more by what they see and experience than by what they read or hear. But in opposition to spectacle, Calvin responded, "Because God does not speak to us every day from the heavens, there are only the Scriptures, in which he has willed that his truth should be published and made known unto even the end, they can be fully certified to the faithful by no other warrant than this: that we hold it to be decreed and concluded that they came down from heaven, as though we heard God speaking from his own mouth."[10]

The Reformers were eager to challenge images altogether, with Luther, Zwingli, and Calvin taking slightly different positions even among themselves. The chief defense of images was that they were the layperson's books. They provided instruction for those who could not read. Much like our own day, there was a wide gulf between the clergy and laity in terms of what was known. Even many of the clergy were self-taught itinerant evangelists themselves, ill-equipped to teach the people. Sometimes an image can teach more than a whole day's worth of reading scripture, the church argued. Luther disagreed.

> This is, in reality, establishing idolatry: undertaking to worship God without God's bidding, on the basis of one's own devout inclination. For he will not have us direct him how he is to be served. He intends to teach and direct us in this matter. His Word is to be there. This is to give us light and guidance. Without his Word all is idolatry and lies, however devout it may seem and however beautiful it may appear. ... For here you learn that it is not enough to say and

think: I am doing this for the glory of God; I intend it for the true God; I want to serve the only God. All idolaters say and intend just that.[11]

Idolatry always has good intentions. We want to help the people of God worship more effectively. We are certain that our clever means and methods will achieve success. But all worship that God has not expressly commanded is vain and is, in fact, counterproductive. The Heidelberg Catechism (1563) put it this way:

96. Q. What is God's will for us in the second commandment?
     A. That we in no way make any image of God (Dt. 4:15–19; Is. 40:18–25; Ac. 17:29; Rom. 1:23) nor worship him in any other way than he has commanded in his Word (Lev. 10:1–7; 1 Sam. 15:22–23; Jn. 4:23–24).

97. Q. May we then not make any image at all?
     A. God can not and may not be visibly portrayed in any way. Although creatures may be portrayed, yet God forbids making or having such images if one's intention is to worship them or to serve God through them (Ex. 34:13–14; 2 Kings 18:4–5).

98. Q. But may not images be permitted in the churches as teaching aids for the unlearned?
     A. No, we shouldn't try to be wiser than God. He wants his people instructed by the living preaching of his Word (Rom. 10:14–15, 17; 2 Tim. 3:16–17; 2 Pet. 1:19)—not by idols that cannot even talk (Jer. 10:8; Hab. 2:18–20).

Even today, well-meaning Christians establish new patterns of worship without finding it necessary to conform such practices to the theology of worship found in Scripture. Many Protestants are fond of criticizing Roman Catholics for their rituals, but at least those rituals have some root in Scripture, even though they have been embellished and, we would argue, corrupted, through the centuries.

However, such practices as the altar call, unknown to the church until the last century, are innovations in worship that are not only not commanded in Scripture but are actually prohibited by the God-centered character of worship and the Christ-centered character of mediation in worship. In altar calls, the minister steps in to mediate between God and the sinner, acknowledging hands and presenting himself and the altar up front as something of a point of contact with God. Regardless of what is intended by the preacher, the laity can easily gain the impression that the minister is the go-between and that the ritual, though not as long-standing as Roman Catholic rituals, has some efficacy.

Further, it is difficult to overestimate the role that images play in the television age. Ours is a religion of a book. No other religion, although Islam comes close, is so dependent on written words as Protestant Christianity. "It is written," was our Lord's defense against the image of the kingdoms of the world that Satan offered Him in exchange for homage. But how does a religion of a book survive in the age of the videocassette? How can churches hold the attention on Sunday morning of people who have been fed with thousands of spliced images throughout the week? Sermons must compare to sit-coms. They must be witty and light and contain a moral. How different is this from the image-centered medieval church? See if Calvin's characterization hits home:

> Nay, what one sermon was there from which old wives might not carry off more whimsies than they could devise at their own fireside in a month? For as sermons were then usually divided, the first half was devoted to those misty questions of the schools which might astonish the rude populace, while the second contained sweet stories, or not unamusing speculations, by which the hearers might be kept on the alert. Only a few expressions were thrown in from the Word of God, that by their majesty they might procure credit for these frivolities. . . . And here a very wide field for exposing your ignorance opens upon me, since, in matters of religious controversy, all that you leave to the faithful is to shut their own eyes, and to submit impli-

citly to their teachers. . . . Hence, I observe, [Cardinal] Sadoleto, that you have too indolent a theology, as is almost
always the case with those who have never had experience
in serious struggles of conscience.[13]

One is reminded by Calvin's description of medieval
sermons of the frivolous nature of much of popular preaching today. In *Amusing Ourselves to Death*, Neil Postman
wrote,

> Today, we must look to the city of Las Vegas, Nevada, as a
> metaphor of our national character and aspiration, its sym-
> bol a thirty-foot-high cardboard picture of a slot machine
> and a chorus girl. For Las Vegas is a city entirely devoted to
> the idea of entertainment, and as such proclaims the spirit
> of a culture in which all public discourse increasingly takes
> the form of entertainment. Our politics, religion, news,
> athletics, education and commerce have been transformed
> into congenial adjuncts of show business, largely without
> protest or even much popular notice. The result is that we
> are a people on the verge of amusing ourselves to death.[13]

And then Postman even has the nerve to use our own
Second Commandment on us:

> In studying the Bible as a young man, I found intimations
> of the idea that forms of media favor particular kinds of
> content and therefore are capable of taking command of a
> culture. I refer specifically to the Decalogue, the Second
> Commandment of which prohibits the Israelites from mak-
> ing concrete images of anything. . . . The God of the Jews
> was to exist in the Word and through the Word, an unpre-
> cedented conception requiring the highest order of ab-
> stract thinking. Iconography thus became blasphemy so
> that a new kind of God could enter a culture. People like
> ourselves who are in the process of converting their culture
> from a word-centered to image-centered might profit by
> reflecting on this Mosaic injunction.[14]

Postman, who is not an evangelical, goes on to contrast
the God-centered, literate culture of New England Calvinism

with the human-centered, anti-intellectual revivalism that eventually created televangelism. So powerful is the medium that God and the preacher are often confused. "Most of the religion available to us on television," Postman writes, "explicitly disdains ritual and theology in favor of direct communication with the Bible itself, that is, with God." Further, what Postman says about God's role on TV could be applied to His place in many churches today:

> Without ensnaring myself in a theological argument for which I am unprepared, I think it both fair and obvious to say that on television, God is a vague and subordinate character. Though His name is invoked repeatedly, the concreteness and persistence of the image of the preacher carries the clear message that it is he, not He, who must be worshipped. I do not mean to imply that the preacher wishes it to be so; only that the power of a close-up televised face, in color, makes idolatry a continual hazard. Television is, after all, a form of graven imagery far more alluring than a golden calf. . . . Jimmy Swaggart plays better than God. For God exists only in our minds, whereas Swaggart is there, to be seen, admired, adored. Which is why he is the star of the show. And why Billy Graham is a celebrity, and why Oral Roberts has his own university, and why Robert Schuller has a crystal cathedral all to himself. If I am not mistaken, the word for this is blasphemy.[15]

Of course, Postman is wrong when he says that God exists in our mind rather than on the screen. For He exists in reality, no more a product of our imagination than that of a television executive's. It is not too far-fetched to compare the superstitious attraction of a medieval peasant to a relic or image of a saint as a "point of contact" for a miracle to the attraction of the modern viewer to the image of a televangelist telling the folks to place their hand on the screen.

OPINION IN WORSHIP

Finally, the imagination not only creates material images and innovations in public worship that do not conform to Scripture, but false images can also be false ideas of God. Even though one may worship the true God in all essential matters (understanding His attributes), it is easy to base one's view of God and His way of operating on intuition or personal experience. We think it would be unfair for God to let a twelve-year-old child die from a tragic illness, but He ends up doing just that—and so we become angry because He has violated our image of Him. We assume somehow that it is in God's character to give us only joy and happiness. Then when things begin to fall apart, we lose our faith in the image.

As with the argument that material images and creative ceremonies serve a useful and pragmatic end, so too we often create images not to worship a false god but in order to worship the true God in a manner that appeals to us. Contextualizing—that is, bringing the changeless gospel into changing historical and cultural situations—can easily become a traffic in false images, as we create a theology and form of worship based on our own intuition, pleasure, entertainment, and practical wisdom.

As the Reformers refused to accommodate their practices and beliefs to the illiteracy of the Middle Ages and engage in superstition, so too we must return to the conviction that the Word (read, preached, taught, and understood) and the sacraments of baptism and the Lord's Supper are the *only* means of God's communication with us. We communicate with Him in prayer, and He communicates with us through these ordained means. Earlier we read God's warning in Jeremiah to the people and priests of Israel concerning their flippant reference to God's speaking apart from the inspired prophets:

This is what the LORD Almighty says:

"Do not listen to what the prophets are
prophesying to you;
they fill you with false hopes.
They speak visions from their own minds
not from the mouth of the LORD. . . .

"... This is what each of you keeps on saying to his friend or relative: 'What is the LORD's answer?' or 'What has the LORD spoken?' But you must not mention 'the oracle of the LORD' again, because every man's own word becomes his oracle and so you distort the words of the living God, the LORD Almighty, our God. This is what you keep saying to a prophet: 'What is the LORD's answer to you?' or 'What has the LORD spoken?'" (Jeremiah 23:16, 35–37)

I fear that this use of God's name to procure support for the product of our imagination is no less widespread in our day than it was in Jeremiah's or Luther's, from public worship to church growth strategies to inner healing to personal piety. In our imagination, we devise our own ideas of what pleases God, or worse, what pleases us. Like the Pharisees, we are even willing to set aside God's commands in order to obey our own counsel. In how many services do innovations (the altar call, special music, dramas, and the like) take preeminence over the proclamation of the Word and administration of Holy Communion? Whenever humanly devised customs and practices are more frequent in worship than the divinely ordained means of grace, something is clearly wrong. How often do we set up rules regulating behavior that make sense and have ingenious arguments in their favor but have absolutely no foundation in Scripture? And yet we think we are serving God by following our own fancy.

We cannot pretend that we are not idolaters simply because we refrain from setting up a statue of the Virgin Mary at the front of the church. We can just as much be idolaters if we place the pastor on a highly raised platform and treat him as the center of worship. Nor can we presume that we are keeping the second commandment if we lean on our own intuition and experience to guide us in our understanding of God and His way of dealing with us.

Imagination must once again become captive to the Word of God. We must learn all over again the character of God and the service He requires.

WHY NO IMAGES?

There is a rationale for God's prohibition of images. God does not forbid images because He is opposed to art. In fact, Solomon's temple was richly decorated with representations of the natural world. Rembrandt, shaped by the Reformation, celebrated everyday life and gave the natural world its own place, without requiring spiritual justification for his subjects. Nor were all depictions of Christ and the apostles forbidden. They simply were not to be used in worship or devotion. Why, then, is God so serious about keeping us from actually representing Him in worship?

God Is Spirit

Jesus told the Samaritan woman, "God is spirit, and his worshipers must worship him in spirit and in truth" (John 4:24). To depict God the Father in physical images or in our own imagination as an old man with a white beard is to worship a false image. God is ageless, an eternal spirit.

In the Old Testament, God revealed Himself in what are called *theophanies* (divine appearances) and often used *anthropomorphisms* (language that made it sound as though He really had hands, eyes, ears). Some speakers and writers erroneously maintain that these anthropomorphic statements are to be taken literally. They argue that when God says the He holds out His hands (viz., Isaiah 65:2), that means that He really does possess physical hands. Based on this literalism, God must also possess eagle's feathers (Exodus 19:4). The orthodox interpretation, to the contrary, has always maintained that the Bible contains not only one genre—literal narrative—but also a variety of modes of communicating: poetry, history, drama, parable, and apocalayptic literature. References in the Bible to human characteristics (anthropomorphisms) are simply God's way of accommodating to our weaknesses, much like a parent's use of baby-talk.

It is clear in Scripture that God is an eternal spirit and that He does not possess a material or physical aspect (2 Corinthians 3:17). This makes it difficult, admittedly, for Christians to worship their God as directly and to understand or experience Him as thoroughly as pagans can their idols, but that is where the incarnation comes in.

The Incarnation

If the Jews had been allowed to worship God through images they would not have had their hopes set on the coming Messiah. At least one purpose in forbidding the use of images is the fact that any representation of God other than Christ is not only false but an insult to His exclusive claim that "he who has seen Me has seen the Father"; "I and My Father are one" (John 14:9 NJKV; 10:30 NKJV).

Jesus Christ is called "the image of the invisible God" (Colossians 1:15). The Greek word used for image in the passage is *eikon,* from which we get the word *icon.* Jesus Christ is the only exact icon or physical representation of the invisible and unrepresentable deity. "For in Christ all the fullness of the Deity lives in bodily form" (Colossians 2:9). This is what paganism attempts with its idols—having a point of contact with God. By being close to the idol, the worshiper hopes to be close to God, for to his mind the idol possesses some degree of deity in itself. But just as God ridiculed the pagan idols as being blind, deaf, and dumb, so surely did Jesus Christ not only possess sight, hearing, and speech but give sight to the blind, hearing to the deaf, and speech to the dumb. He was God in the flesh, walking among us, talking to us, eating with us, weeping with us.

For us to set up our own images after Christ has come is even more of an affront to God than it was for the ancient pagans. How could we possibly find a means of worshiping God that would be more tangible, more precise, and more direct than we find in Jesus Christ? And yet, He is at God's right hand, and we demand direct encounters and experiences. So we turn to idols of our own making and imagination. We return to worshiping God in our own way, in a manner that makes sense to us and suits our tastes.

The second commandment is not abrogated, however. It still calls us to train our minds, hearts, and senses to look only to the Word and the sacraments. Eve found the fruit "pleasing to the eye, and also desirable for gaining wisdom" (Genesis 3:6). She and Adam trusted their senses and wisdom above God's Word. To look beyond God's Word for communication from God is, in effect, to forge our own worship, violating the second commandment. May we think about God? Absolutely, but only as He has revealed Himself. May we meditate on God's character and activity? Yes, but only as He has explained Himself and His actions in history. May we experience God? Without doubt, but only as we encounter Him in His own action of communication. The second commandment does not prohibit the senses any more than it discourages the use of reason, but it does command both to submit to the Word and the sacraments as God's means of feeding the reason and the senses. Through the means He has appointed He fills the mind with grand thoughts, intoxicates our senses with the realization that we are forgiven, and inspires us for creative and enthusiastic service in the world.

CONCLUSION

Every recent survey demonstrates that there is widespread biblical illiteracy, not only in an increasingly secularized American culture, but even within an apparently successful evangelicalism. According to Gallup, "Eight in ten Americans say they are Christians, but only four in ten know that Jesus, according to the Bible, delivered the Sermon on the Mount. Fewer than half of all adults can name Matthew, Mark, Luke and John as the four Gospels of the New Testament."[16]

Much like the medieval church, modern Christianity appears more attracted to images than to words, more given to subjective ideas and opinions than clear convictions drawn from serious biblical study and reflection. God declares of all such idols, "You shall not bow down to them or worship them; for I, the LORD your God, am a jealous God" (Exodus 20:5). God is jealous for our affection, reverance, trust, and praise. The English poet and preacher John Donne reasoned, "If thou carest not who I love, then thou lovest not me." What spouse who really loves his or her partner does not care whether the other person is promiscuous? The second commandment assures us that God has chosen us for Himself, set us apart for His own pleasure, and has given us the necessary means through which we can have an intimate, personal relationship, mediated through the living and written Word. It is not enough to worship the correct God; we must worship the correct God *correctly.*

NOTES

1. Schuller, *Self-Esteem: The New Reformation* (Waco, Tex.: Word, 1985), 63–64.
2. Kenneth Copeland, *Believer's Voice of Victory,* February 1987, 9.
3. Kenneth Copeland, *The Power of the Tongue* (Ft. Worth, Tex.: Kenneth Copeland), 6.
4. Earl Paulk, *Satan Unmasked* (Atlanta: Dimension K, 1984), 59.
5. Richard Foster, *Celebration of Discipline: The Path to Spiritual Growth* (San Francisco: Harper & Row, 1988), 27.
6. Paul Yonghi Cho, *The Fourth Dimension* (Plainfield, N.J.: Logos, 1980), 40.
7. Henry Chadwick, *The Early Church* (New York: Penguin, 1989), 281.
8. Kenneth Scott Latourette, *A History of Christianity* (New York: Harper & Row, 1975), 1:294.
9. John Wimber and Kevin Springer, *Power Evangelism* (San Francisco: Harper & Row, 1975), 105.
10. John Calvin, *Institutes of the Christian Religion,* 1.7.1
11. Ewald Plass, *What Luther Says: A Practical-in-Home Anthology for the Active Christian* (St. Louis: Concordia, 1987), 680.
12. John Calvin, in *A Reformation Debate*, ed. John Calvin and Jacopo Sadoleto (Grand Rapids: Baker, 1976), 65–70.

13. Neil Postman, *Amusing Ourselves to Death: Public Discourse in the Age of Show Business* (New York: Viking Penguin, 1986), 9.

14. Ibid.

15. Ibid., 122–23.

16. George Gallup and James Castelli, *The People's Religion* (New York: Macmillan, 1989), 60.

CHAPTER FOUR

GUARDING GOD'S REPUTATION

*You shall not misuse
the name of the LORD your God.*

A shocking story is recorded in Leviticus 10:1–3. Aaron's own sons were ministering in the sanctuary, but they added their own form of worship—an unauthorized offering. They thought that would please God, but instead it enraged Him. The connection between worshiping the correct God correctly and protecting God's holy name is illustrated in this tragic event:

> Aaron's sons Nadab and Abihu took their censers, put fire in them and added incense; and they offered unauthorized fire before the LORD, contrary to his command. So fire came out from the presence of the LORD and consumed them, and they died before the LORD. Moses then said to Aaron, "This is what the LORD spoke of when he said:
>
> > 'Among those who approach me
> > I will show myself holy;
> > In the sight of all the people
> > I will be honored.'"
>
> Aaron remained silent.

Though he had understood Moses' argument, Aaron's problem was not intellectual, but emotional. His own sons had distinguished themselves in God's sanctuary, committing their whole lives to His service, and now there they were, lying in the front of the sanctuary where they had simply sought to perform their own service in their own way. That is how seriously God takes His name. As the writer to the Hebrews put it, "It is a dreadful thing to fall into the hands of the living God" (Hebrews 10:31).

During my seminary years I had an apartment on the corner of a busy intersection. Students from a nearby elementary school walked past my window in the morning and afternoon. Although I realize that every generation cries out against the greater sins of the next, I was shocked at the language these schoolchildren—not yet teenagers—used, much of it consisting of the misuse of God's name in some form. The easy explanation of this profane use of God's name is the secularization of our culture.

But the problem, as I see it, is not that we have "taken God out of the public schools" or that we have "removed public acknowledgment of God at the courthouse." It is that we have taken God out of the *churches* and have removed public acknowledgment of God and His attributes from our personal and public lives as Christians. Why should Christians lament the day when the Ten Commandments were taken down from the wall in the classroom when few of them can name these decrees themselves? When the world forgets God, the church is called upon to proclaim Him more widely. But what happens when the church forgets God? Who speaks for Him then? Frankly, I am more offended by the hucksters, heretics, and healers who misuse God's name than those kids who passed by my window each day, whose profanity did far less damage to the coinage of the divine name.

This was the dilemma the prophets faced in the Old Testament. They spoke for God when God's people and priests secularized and corrupted divine worship. You will recall that God's covenant with His people was in the form of a Near Eastern treaty: God bound Himself to Israel as an emperor to a vassal king, to protect His people from enemies; in turn, the nation, as a vassal king, was to remain loyal to God, the Great King. Whenever Israel defaulted on its covenantal obligations, God sued the nation as a landlord might sue his tenants. It is just this sort of legal trial Hosea records:

> Hear the word of the LORD, you Israelites,
> because the LORD has a charge to bring
> against you who live in the land:
> "There is no faithfulness, no love,
>   no acknowledgment of God in the land.
> There is only cursing, lying and murder,
>   stealing and adultery;
> they break all bounds,
>   and bloodshed follows bloodshed.
> Because of this the land mourns,
>   and all who live in it waste away;
> the beasts of the field and the birds of the air
>   and the fish of the sea are dying.
>
> "But let no man bring a charge,
>   let no man accuse another,
> for your people are like those
>   who bring charges against a priest.
> You stumble day and night,
>   and the prophets stumble with you.
> So I will destroy your mother—
>   my people are destroyed from lack of knowledge.
>
> "Because you have rejected knowledge,
>   I also reject you as my priests;
> because you have ignored the law of your God,
>   I will also ignore your children. . . .
>
> " . . . a people without understanding will come
>   to ruin!"
>
> (Hosea 4:1–6, 14)

First, God assembles the court and reads His charges: "There is no *hesed* [covenant loyalty], no love, no acknowledgment of God in the land." Notice that even though Israel was a chosen nation (the only nation in history to have enjoyed this privilege), God did not place the blame on the politicians and government officials. Loyalty to the covenant, genuine love of God and neighbor, and acknowledgment of God were all dependent on the health of the sanctuary. If God's name were blasphemed here, it would surely eventually be blasphemed among the Gentiles (Romans 2:24).

Second, in place of covenant loyalty, love, and acknowledgment of God there is a casual violation of all human relationships. Here we notice the link between God and neighbor. Whenever the bond between God and His people dissolves, any human relationships founded on that religious commitment unravel. When truth concerning God (i.e., theology) no longer matters, truth in human dealings (i.e, ethics) becomes increasingly tenuous. The connection between theology and ethics is inextricable. We must not see morality or ethics as self-contained, self-evident facts that do not require theological justification, but merely legal enforcement. We cannot expect in the world an integrity that is missing in the church.

Third, God announces the ruin of Israel unless things change: "A people without understanding will come to ruin." It is the priests who are chiefly to blame, and the prophets also, who, with the priests, told the people whatever they wanted to hear. Ignorance was bliss. "My people are destroyed from lack of knowledge" (Hosea 4:6).

The trial in Hosea could well be undertaken in our day, when, as Nathan Stone writes, "There is little real knowledge in these days of the one, true God."[1] How can we honor God's name when we do not even know enough about God to respect Him or to command our interest? The well-know Bible translator J. B. Phillips wrote the following in his 1961 best-seller, *Your God Is Too Small:*

> No one is ever really at ease in facing what we call "life" and "death" without a religious faith. The trouble with many people today is that they have not found a God big enough for modern needs. While their experience of life has grown

in a score of directions, and their mental horizons have been expanded to the point of bewilderment by world events and by scientific discoveries, their ideas of God have remained largely static. It is obviously impossible for an adult to worship the conception of God that exists in the mind of a child of Sunday-school age, unless he is prepared to deny his own experience of life. If, by a great effort of will, he does do this he will always be secretly afraid lest some new truth may expose the juvenility of his faith. And it will always be by such an effort that he either worships or serves a God who is really too small to command his adult loyalty and cooperation.[2]

With much of popular preaching and evangelism conforming to the mentality of the bumper sticker that sports "God is my copilot," there ought to be little wonder why God's name is not hallowed in our society. For it is not hallowed in our churches. Our prophets and priests have falsely handled the Word, attributing more to human beings than to God. In Scripture, God is the potter and we are the clay. Salvation "does not . . . depend on man's decision or effort, but on God's mercy. . . . Therefore, God has mercy on whom he wants to have mercy, and he hardens whom he wants to harden" (Romans 9:16–21). But in popular religion, God is there for me. I am the potter and He is the clay. After all, He can't do anything if I don't "let Him have His way." Only if I decide to let Him do this or that can He fulfill his will. After all, "Jesus is a gentleman who will not violate our free will," or so I was told growing up.

The biblical God is clearly something other than this finite god of American religion. Taking God's name seriously depends on taking God Himself seriously, and that requires a God-centered theological perspective.

We cannot, therefore, blame the courts, public schools, media, or government for our own theological unfaithfulness. We are the ones—the prophets and priests —who have contributed to this "Ichabod," this departure of God's glory in our time. Only by returning to sound, effective God-centered preaching and teaching can we restore the confidence not only of Christians themselves in God's greatness, but of an unbelieving world that is more apathetic toward our benign, helpless, happy deity than hostile.

How, then, do we violate the third commandment?

By Using God

In the last chapter, we noticed how the "lying prophets" were claiming revelatory status for "visions from their own minds" (Jeremiah 23). Many today similarly use God for their own ends. The practice is not always intentional; in fact, many of those who so use God think they are serving His best interests. Nevertheless, it is easy to corrupt the truth and refuse any possibility of being challenged by claiming divine authority for one's own speculations.

One of the best recent examples of using God for one's own ends is apartheid in South Africa. Afrikaner theology argued that the European settlers were the chosen people of God, conquering their Promised Land by driving out the Canaanites, a vision not altogether different from our own treatment of the native Americans during the same time. The leading Christian opponents of apartheid in more recent years insisted that it was not Christian theology, but a twisting of Scripture in order to suit purely secular political and ideological aims.[3]

In Germany, the evangelical church became the "Reich's Church," the state church of Naziism, and all but a group of Lutheran and Reformed clergymen who insisted that Nazi ideology was heretical signed the oath of allegiance to Hitler. So far was Christianity used to prop up Christendom that the enormous atrocities of the Crusades in the middle ages were actually conceived of as divinely inspired. It is easy to *use* God's name instead of *fearing* it.

When I was about ten years old, my father was the manager of a Christian campgrounds in the Sierra mountains. One week, when the director of the camp came up for an inspection, my parents had grounded me for a week by denying me the use of a friend's snowmobile. Now I saw my opportunity. I took the snowmobile for a two-hour ride, and when I found my angry parents waiting for me, I simply told them that Pat, the director, *told* me to go pick something up for him on the snowmobile. How could I refuse the director? I never thought my parents would actually ask Pat what happened. When they did, I suffered the ultimate embarrassment. My parents didn't confront me— Pat did, and I felt like a fool. I had claimed his authority for my own disobedience. We do this with God whenever we claim God's authority and direction for our own decisions—even when those decisions are not necessarily right or wrong.

In the story of Nadab and Abihu, Aaron's sons, the heart was in the right place—they wanted to render service to God. The problem was that it was their own service, not the service authorized by God. One of the ways in which we profane God's name, then, is to use God—His name, authority, or direction—as a blank check for our own decisions and activities. In the cases mentioned above—the Crusades, the Holocaust, slavery, the slaughter of Native Americans, and apartheid in South Africa—the exploitation of God's name brings enormous discredit and scandal to the name of God and the cause of Christ in history. The evils in which professing Christians have participated (and even created) in the name of God (and continue to participate in) set the progress of the gospel back decades.

Those today who hear in a word such as *fundamentalist* a ring of ideological fanaticism that uses religion to achieve temporal power over people are numerous. We can either cry out about the media's unfairness in painting Christ's church into a corner with the Ayatollah, or we can bend over backwards to "act justly and to love mercy and to walk humbly with [our] God" (Micah 6:8), instead of using religion to support our own political agenda. In the past twenty years, God has been used to justify American nationalism, militarism, opposition to child care for working mothers, and even such debatable issues as the retention of the Panama Canal. He has been used as a mascot for the conservative, white, middle-class establishment, the guarantor of such evangelical rights and family values as that of owning submachine guns. This smacks of "using God" and exploiting religion when evangelicals do it every bit as much as it does when mainline liberals paint God red.

When Amos chastized Israel for its ignorance, unfaithfulness, and social injustice, he encountered more hostility from the religious leaders than from the civil servants. Amaziah, the priest of Bethel, saw his chief end in life to be yes-man to the king. Amaziah sent a message to King Jeroboam: "Amos is raising a conspiracy against you in the very heart of Israel. The land cannot bear all his words" (Amos 7:10). Any criticism of Israel's confusion of God's purposes with Jeroboam's agenda was regarded by Amaziah as a conspiracy. "Then Amaziah said to Amos, 'Get out, you seer! Go back to the land of Judah. Earn your bread there and do your prophesying there. Don't prophesy anymore at Bethel, because this is the king's sanctuary and the temple of the kingdom'" (vv. 12–13). In other words, it is God who serves Israel, not Israel that serves God. Religion serves the purpose of social glue, providing national identity through civil religion. It is not God's sanctuary and God's temple, but "the king's sanctuary and the temple of the kingdom" of Jeroboam. When we confuse the kingdoms and aims of this world with God's, we are bringing shame and dishonor to God's name. That is why, in the Lord's prayer, the petition "Hallowed be your name" is followed by the petition "*Your* kingdom come, *your* will be done on earth as it is in heaven" (Matthew 6:9–10, italics added).

Hypocrisy

"It is," wrote the Puritan Stephen Charnock, "a sad thing to be Christians at a supper, heathens in our shops, and devils in our closets." We bring disgrace to the name of God when we profess much and possess little. Self-righteousness is the greatest sin of all, but it is rendered even more grotesque when it combines with hypocrisy. No self-righteous person has ever attained the righteousness of which he boasts, so when he falls his fall is great. Everyone notices, and not a few take pleasure in it.

Jesus warned about those who would be surprised at the last day to learn that their use of His name was vain. "Not everyone who says to me, 'Lord, Lord,' will enter the kingdom of heaven, but only he who does the will of my Father who is in heaven. Many will say to me on that day, 'Lord, Lord, did we not prophesy in your name, and in your name drive out demons and perform many miracles?' Then I will tell them plainly, 'I never knew you. Away from me, you evildoers!'" (Matthew 7:21–23). Notice that these people are professing Christians ("Lord, Lord," they call Him) and they even insist that they prophesied, drove out demons, and performed miracles in the name of Christ. They were using His name in vain.

In our lives, therefore, we must always be aware of the fact that we are representatives of our heavenly Father. If we are engaged in scandal, we necessarily include God in the charges the world makes. When we mark up a product in our store beyond that which is reasonable, simply because the demand is there, and our customers see a fish symbol on our calling card, it reflects on God's own character. Whenever we perform poorly at work, we are giving an opportunity for cynicism. Our motivation for excellence —in education, at work, in relationships, in the home— must be the sanctity of God's reputation. We are "out there" in the world as chosen representatives of His government. Whatever we do reflects on our head of state.

Of those who had been corrupted both in their doctrine and life, Paul warns Titus, "They claim to know God, but by their actions they deny him" (Titus 1:16). False doctrine can itself be a form of blaspheming the name of God, and Paul could just as easily have said, "They claim to know God, but by their doctrine they deny him." That brings us to the next means of violating the third commandment.

Heresy and Error

Just as using God as a mascot for our own causes brings dishonor to His name, so too using the Bible to support heresy is a serious and soul-imperiling exercise.

Peter warned about the heretic's use of scripture. "They will secretly introduce destructive heresies, [and] many will follow their shameful ways and will bring the way of truth into disrepute. In their greed these teachers will exploit you with stories they have made up. Their condemnation has long been hanging over them, and their destruction has not been sleeping" (2 Peter 2:1–3). Heretics have little respect for the Word and do not allow it to speak for itself. Where it is clear, they make the meaning confusing until at last they can substitute the plain meaning for their distortion. Even Paul's letters "contain some things that are hard to understand, which ignorant and unstable people distort, as they do the other Scriptures, to their own destruction" (2 Peter 3:16).

But heresy is not the only way in which God's name is corrupted. When in sermons we learn more about the history of the preacher through personal anecdotes than the history of redemption through biblical revelation, the name of God is not given its due. When the minister uses the twenty to thirty minutes he is given to offer his own opinions, speculations, or insights, he is taking liberties with the name of God. When illustrations can be recalled better than the morning's text, God's name is not hallowed in the church halls.

Nor is God's name protected when we use it in a profane, crass, irreverent manner: "God is rad; He's my dad" springs to mind. When "Praise the Lord!" or similar catchphrases roll off of our tongues as a Christian equivalent of "That's great!" we are using God's name in vain; that is, unnecessarily. Casual use of God's name is prohibited precisely because it wears away our sensitivity to the enormous reverence we owe it. Once we are able to think lightly of God's name even in our discussions with other Christians—even when our intentions are pious—it is not so difficult to lower our perception of the market price of God's name in more pernicious respects.

Blasphemy

The case is recorded in Leviticus 24 of a boy who "blasphemed the Name" (v. 11). God commanded Moses to take the youth outside the camp and have the entire assembly stone him. "Say to the Israelites: 'If anyone curses his God, he will be held responsible; anyone who blasphemes the name of the LORD must be put to death'" (v. 15).

In very few evangelical circles would a dirty joke be considered appropriate, and yet such expressions as "Good Lord!" "Lord of Mercy!" as well as "God!" and "Oh my God!" do occur in our circles with disturbing frequency. This is a form of blasphemy, and it required execution in the Old Testament. So sensitive were the Jews about God's name that they never even pronounced it or spelled it. And yet, today I see T-shirts being sold at evangelical conventions bearing such slogans as "This blood's for you!" a take-off on the "This Bud's for you!" beer commercial. Whenever we cheapen God's name by vain repetition, irreverent sloganeering, or by actual cursing, we engage in a violation of the third commandment.

WHY IS THIS SO IMPORTANT?

We saw the rationale behind the first commandment: every major Christian doctrine is based on the affirmation that there is only one true God and only one being who is "the way and the truth and the life" (John 14:6). The rationale behind the second commandment is equally clear: to worship even the true God in our own way is to open the door to speculation, superstition, and apostasy. After all, "God is spirit, and his worshipers must worship in spirit and in truth" (John 4:24). But why does God take His name so seriously?

Although I would take exception to his view of the civil law, Gary North offers a helpful illustration of this commandment:

One way for a modern American to begin to understand this commandment is to treat God's name as trademarked property. In order to gain widespread distribution for His copyrighted repair manual—the Bible—and also to capture greater market share for His authorized franchise—the Church—God has graciously licensed the use of His name to anyone who will use it according to His written instructions. It needs to be understood, however, that God's name has not been released into the public domain. God retains legal control over His name and threatens serious penalties against the unauthorized misuse of this supremely valuable property. All trademark violations will be prosecuted to the full limits of the law. The prosecutor, judge, jury, and enforcer is God.[4]

Elohim, one of the divine names, refers to God's omnipotence. *Yahweh,* translated "LORD" in capital letters, to distinguish it from *Adonai,* the title "Lord," is God's personal name. From the verb "to be," it expresses the essence of God's character: that he is a self-existent, self-sufficient Sovereign who depends on no one and nothing, but is rather the one on whom and for whom all depends. "I am he: before me there was no *Elohim* formed, neither shall there be after me. I, even I, am *Yahweh;* and beside me there is no savior" (see Isaiah 43:10–11).

The meaning of *Yahweh* is directly related to the idea God communicated to Moses when the prophet asked whom he shall say sent him to the children of Israel. "Indeed, when I come to the children of Israel and say to them, 'The *Elohim* of your fathers has sent me to you,' and they say to me, 'What is His name?' what shall I say to them? And God said to Moses, 'I AM WHO I AM.'" (see Exodus 3:13–15 NKJV). *El Shaddai* is translated "God Almighty," or "the Sovereign Lord" (NIV). *Yahweh-Yireh* is first used in Genesis 22, when Abraham is called upon to offer Isaac as a sacrifice. It means "the Lord will provide" and referred to God's ultimate provision for Abraham and his spiritual heirs by the sacrifice of His Son. *Yahweh-Rophe* is "the Lord who heals"; *Yahweh-Nissi* is "the Lord my banner" (Exodus 17:15), referring to God's role in providing security for His people in the presence of their enemies; "the Lord of Holiness" is *Yahweh-M'Kaddesh; Yahweh-Shalom,* of course, is "the Lord of Peace"; *Yahweh-Tsidkenu* is translated "the Lord our Righteousness," referring to God's gift of justification through His own imputed righteousness.

Other names and titles could be listed, but it is enough for our purposes here to recognize that each of the divine names was packed with information—not with magical power or spiritual energy, but with doctrinal content. Each name teaches us something crucial about the way God relates to us as His people.

Therefore, whenever we undermine belief in God's sovereignty, we call into question His character as *El Shaddai.* Whenever we question His provision by setting out to acquire happiness, wealth, or even salvation by our own strength and for our own good, we deny God as our *Yahweh-Yireh.* If we set out, as Paul's Jewish brothers did, to establish our own righteousness (Romans 10:2–3), we deny God as *Yahweh-Tsidkenu.*

Thus protection of God's name is essential primarily for theological reasons. Each name is an affirmation of faith, and, taken together, they all form a confession of faith. To hold God's sovereignty, righteousness, peace, providence, and holiness in high esteem is to reverence God himself. Likewise, to discredit any of these names is to pour contempt on the very person of the one we worship. That is why I find it incongruous for Christian brothers and sisters to say, "I don't want to get caught up in all that theology. I just want to know the Lord." To know the Lord is necessarily to get "caught up in all that theology," for, as the names suggest, it is impossible to know the true God apart from His self-disclosure. Equally disastrous, of course, is the tendency to get caught up in theology without getting caught up with the personal God Himself.

Finally, just as the prohibition of images was ultimately due to the uniqueness of Christ as the one who was to be "the *image* of the invisible God" (Colossians 1:15, italics added), and the prohibition of other gods is due to the exclusivity of Christ as "the way and the truth and the life," so too the third commandment has a Christ-centered focus. We are not to misuse the name of God primarily because it is by this name that we are saved.

Earlier in this book we discussed the form of the Ten Commandments in relationship to treaty forms in the Near East. The Ten Commandments (indeed, the entire Old Testament) is cast in the form of an ancient Near Eastern treaty between an emperor (a "great king" or suzerain) and a lesser king (a vassal). Whenever the lesser king saw his realm in military danger, he called upon the name of the suzerain, his protector. By invoking the suzerain's name, the lesser king was officially invoking the clause in the treaty that promised protection in the case of danger. From that time, the invading army would know that its enemy was not the lesser king, whose territory they were plundering, but now the "great king" with whom they would have to do battle. In the same way, Israel could rely on God to defend her whenever she was invaded—except in the cases where God Himself sent Israel into captivity because of her disloyalty to the treaty.

Christ has fulfilled all of the terms of this treaty—not only His end of the bargain, but ours. When we are invited to "call upon the name of the Lord," what is involved is not merely our asking God for something He may or may not grant. The reference is to a clause in a treaty that we sign by faith: "Everyone who calls upon the name of the Lord will be saved" (Romans 10:13). We are called, therefore, to bind God to us in a covenantal obligation. This is not, of course, an obligation of merit. God is not obligated to us because we have done anything that would put Him under obligation (cf. Romans 11:30). Rather, He is obligated because He Himself has promised to bind Himself to all who call upon His name. No longer do we have to worry that our failure to meet the conditions will somehow shorten God's arm, or at least His willingness, to save. He has committed himself to rescuing all who have been invaded and held captive by oppression. We are merely to call upon His name. After all, Jesus Christ is Himself the LORD God, the second person of the Holy Trinity. The Father "has given him the *name* that is above every name" (Philippians 2:9, italics added). We are to "believe in the *name* of the Son of God" (1 John 5:13, italics added). To call upon Christ's name is to call upon the name of *Yahweh-Tsidkenu,* "The Lord our Righteousness."

We protect God's name because we are saved through calling upon it. We also bear God's name as children of God and brothers and sisters of Christ. In the Old Testament God's people are referred to as "my people, who are called by my name" (2 Chronicles 7:14), in contrast to those who sought to "make a name for [themselves]" at the Tower of Babel (Genesis 11:4). For, unlike any name we could make for ourselves, "the name of the LORD is a strong tower" (Proverbs 18:10), defending us from the invading forces of the world, the flesh, and the devil.

It is through the person and work of Christ that God gains for Himself the greatest glory due His name. When the Israelites returned to Jerusalem from Persian captivity to find the City of Peace buried in weeds, there was a renewal of the covenant, with weeping and repentance. But it did not take long for the children to long for the ways of Persia. Worship, service, and duty to God and neighbor fell by the wayside as secularism invaded the congregation. "'A son honors his father, and a servant his master. If I am a father, where is the honor due me? If I am a master, where is the respect due me?' says the LORD Almighty. 'It is you, O priests, who show contempt for my name.' But you ask, 'How have we shown contempt for your name?'" (Malachi 1:6). The Lord's table is defiled (v. 7), the people bring their least costly offerings instead of the best of their flocks and fields, and all the while everyone thinks that God is pleased. But God himself thunders:

> "Oh, that one of you would shut the temple doors, so that you would not light useless fires on my altar! I am not pleased with you," says the LORD Almighty, "and I will accept no offering from your hands. My name will be great among the nations, from the rising to the setting of the sun. In every place incense and pure offerings will be brought

to my name, because my name will be great among the nations," says the LORD Almighty. (Malachi 1:10–11)

In Christ, this resolution is fulfilled. His name is great, not only in Israel, but "among the nations," where the name of Christ is known and honored. Around the world incense, representing the prayers of the saints (Psalm 141:2; Revelation 5:8), is rising to God's throne, and God is making for Himself *living* sacrifices out of those who were "dead in trespasses and sins" (Ephesians 2:1; see also Romans 12:1). As the book of Hebrews makes clear, the advent of Christ fulfills the shadows of the Mosaic economy. What the temple service, theocracy, and Torah could not accomplish, Jesus Christ Himself accomplished as our Temple, God's kingdom presence, and the Word made flesh. "The Son is the radiance of God's glory and the exact representation of his being, sustaining all things by his powerful word. After he had provided purification for sins, he sat down at the right hand of the Majesty in heaven. So he became as much superior to the angels as the name he has inherited is superior to theirs" (Hebrews 1:3–4).

May His name be hallowed by us at work, at play, in school, and in the home. May politicians in our day speak for the weak, as did the Dutch theologian and prime minister at the turn of this century, Abraham Kuyper. May educators execute their calling with excellence and leave politics and public relations to the world of big business. May businesspeople carry out their honorable vocation with uncommon dignity, integrity, and respect for their clients, consumers, employees, and employers. Let Christians become widely known again as the best workers an employer could hire, and let homemakers and homebuilders set their compass toward creating dynasties of faith, their children taking their own places in society as salt and light. Just as moral scandal followed upon the heels of doctrinal ignorance in Hosea's day, so we today "are destroyed from lack of knowledge" (Hosea 4:6). Let us long for the day that God's name is no longer blasphemed among the Gentiles because of us, a day when "the earth will be full of the knowledge of the LORD as the waters cover the sea" (Isaiah 11:9).

NOTES

1. Nathan Stone, *The Names of God* (Chicago: Moody, 1944), 7.
2. J. B. Phillipps, *Your God Is Too Small* (New York: Macmillan, 1964), 7.
3. John W. de Gruchy, *Liberating Reformed Theology: A South African Contribution to an Ecumenical Debate* (Grand Rapids: Eerdmans, 1991; and Allan A. Boesak, *Black and Reformed: Apartheid, Liberation, and the Calvinist Tradition* (New York: Orbis, n.d.).
4. Gary North, *Chronicles: A Magazine of American Culture*, December 1992, 15.

CHAPTER FIVE

REST ASSURED

*Remember the Sabbath
day by keeping it holy.*

Are Christians allowed to go into work on Sunday afternoon to cover for another employee? Is it wrong to attend
sporting events on the Lord's Day? Just what is the purpose of the Sabbath, and does it have the same meaning
for Christians that it had for Jews in the Old Testament?
These are some of the practical—and thorny—questions
raised by the fourth commandment.

THE ORIGIN OF THE SABBATH INSTITUTION

Within the classical Christian tradition a number of
views concerning the Sabbath ordinance have been maintained. One of the most hotly debated points surrounds
the question of whether the Sabbath has its origin in creation or in the Mosaic institution. In other words, did God
institute the Sabbath as a creation ordinance or as a special
sign of His favor to Israel? As Geerhardus Vos states, "This is
important, because with it stands or falls the general validity
of the commandment for all mankind."[1] If God gave the

fourth commandment to humanity as an institution of creation, it is universally binding, but if it has a Mosaic origin, it is a unique privilege and possession of God's people. It must be said that the former view (rooting it in creation) has more support among Protestant exegetes, particularly through the influence of the Puritans. Geerhardus Vos himself argues this position, but many, like myself, remain unconvinced.

The second view, locating the origin of the Sabbath in the Ten Commandments, which formed God's special charter for His people, seems to make more sense in the light of the texts. The first time the Sabbath appears in Scripture is in Genesis 2:2: "By the seventh day God had finished the work he had been doing; so on the seventh day he rested from all his work. And God blessed the seventh day and made it holy, because on it he rested from all the work of creating that he had done." But notice that although "God blessed the seventh day and made it holy," nothing is said about bringing creatures into this enjoyment of God's rest until the fourth commandment, recorded in Exodus 20:8–11. Similarly, although we could say that "God blessed the seventh day and made it holy" in an objective way at creation, so that *He* could honor and enjoy His rest, it is not until the Mosaic institution of the Sabbath that we read, *"Observe* the Sabbath, because it is holy *to you"* (Exodus 31:14, italics added).

Only under Moses, therefore, does God invite—indeed, command—His people to share His rest with Him. That is part and parcel of fellowship with God—enjoying Him in rest.

Therefore, it is best to regard the Sabbath as an ordinance for the people of God, not as a universal principle that ought to be enforced on unbelievers who are not as yet in fellowship with God —for how can unbelievers share in his rest?

THE PURPOSE OF THE SABBATH

God created the Sabbath rest because He had finished His work. It was not simply because He was tired. This excludes the possibility that the primary purpose behind the Sabbath is its usefulness to us. The most commonly held purpose behind the Sabbath is its practical utility for those who follow it. After all, it only makes sense that people should take one day off from work. God is only looking out for our best interest. But once more, as so often is the case with the other commandments, this explanation is a human-centered rather than a God-centered and Christ-centered way of looking at it. There is much more to the Sabbath institution than the service it renders to us. The Protestant Reformers argued that the primary purpose of the Sabbath was to advance the kingdom of Christ.

Luther argued that the Sabbath meant that "we should fear and love God, and so we should not despise his Word and the preaching of the same, but deem it holy and gladly hear and learn it" (Small Catechism). Calvin spoke of the usefulness of the Sabbath day because of human weakness. We need one day out of the week for instruction and meditation; otherwise, we might find it even more difficult than it is to make time throughout the week.

Nevertheless, the Reformers *did* understand the eternal significance of the Sabbath. It was not merely for them a *useful* institution, but a *sign-bearing* one. Calvin, for one, viewed the primary use of the commandment in terms of spiritual rest, pointing to Christ, in whom believers "lay aside their own works. . . . We are taught in many passages that this foreshadowing of spiritual rest occupied the chief place in the Sabbath."[2]

So now we move beyond a merely practical, functional purpose, to a theological one. To do this, we need first to review the sweep of the biblical record on this point.

Ever since God finished His work of creation, He has been resting. We must not view this rest in the common, earthly, physical way, since God is spirit. God the Creator is still God the Preserver, Provider, Redeemer, and Judge. He is still very active in the affairs of this world, so His rest is not a cessation from activity. Scholars have pointed out that the Hebrew word for "rest" is very close to the word for "peace." Wherever God is, there is peace and rest: In His holy place ("Jerusalem" means "City of Peace/Rest") or in His holy time (the Sabbath). But, of course, God exists in eternity and is not a creature of time. He exists in an eternal state of rest and peace, even though He is very active.

In the Garden of Eden, God sought to bring heaven to earth in a small way, by making the garden a holy place of rest and giving a Sabbath time of rest. If Adam had held out until the end in obedience, he too would have entered the eternal Sabbath rest, for he would have been given the fruit of the Tree of Life. Instead, he chose the way of rebellion, and the Sabbath rest was no longer a *creation* ordinance, but a *redemption* ordinance. In other words, it was no longer given to man as man, but only to those with whom God entered into covenant. The Jews were those special people with whom God entered into covenant. This, and not creation, is the reason we find God inviting—in fact, commanding—His people to enter into His Sabbath rest. It is a call of salvation, a shadow of the gospel proclamation, that was to go out to the people of God and, through them, to the whole world. When the Jews celebrated the Sabbath, they looked forward to the end of their suffering and labor, sacrifices and ceremonies, to the final rest. God would come at the end of the age (week) and set things right.

In the New Testament, the light has come. With the dawn of Christ's coming we have the end of the Jewish "week" and the beginning of the new age and the new creation. The Jews looked for the Messiah at the end of the week, but we look backward to Christ at the beginning of the new week. When the Second Adam came, he fulfilled all obedience due to God and, unlike the first Adam, won for us access to the Tree of Life and entrance into the eternal Seventh Day that God Himself enjoys. The Sabbath is, therefore, eternal life in the presence of God.

It is one thing to state a purpose, quite another to defend it. Nevertheless, this is more of a major theme of Scripture than we often realize. In Scripture the idea of providing rest extends beyond a Sabbath day. Immediately following the commandment in Exodus 30 concerning the Sabbath day, God adds a Sabbath for the land every *seventh year*. Similarly, in the *seventh month of each year* the Day of Atonement is to be observed. Finally, *every fiftieth year* is to be a major Sabbath, the Year of Jubilee, in which prisoners, slaves, and debtors go free, their debts canceled. "Consecrate the fiftieth year and proclaim liberty throughout the land to all its inhabitants" (Leviticus 25:10).

But again, although these Sabbaths do indeed serve the best interests of the people by providing physical rest, socioeconomic liberation, and even a rest for the land (which modern agricultural science and environmentalists would aggressively endorse), the purpose is not utilitarian. It just so happens that the effect of doing things God's way produces effective results, since God's law reveals divine wisdom. But it reveals much more than God's wisdom. We must not base our defense of God's law on its rationality, although it is superbly rational. We must not locate its defense in its utility, although it is supremely useful. The main point of all of God's laws, including this Sabbath decree, is *theological*. It teaches us something about God, not something about ourselves. It points the way to enjoying God, not to enjoying ourselves. It is not concerned with making life easier for us, but with teaching us about the age to come that God has prepared.

This brings us to the heart of the biblical argument. In Psalm 62:1, 5, God invites His people to share in His rest—and the psalmist takes Him up on it: "My soul finds rest in God alone; my salvation comes from him. . . . Find rest, O my soul, in God alone; my hope comes from him." Notice the connection between the rest and the fact that salvation comes only from God. Now hold that thought, as we move to Psalm 95:7:

> Today, if you hear his voice,
> > do not harden your hearts as you did at Meribah,
> > as you did that day at Massah in the desert,

where your fathers tested and tried me,
    though they had seen what I did.
For forty years I was angry with that generation;
    I said, "They are a people whose hearts go astray,
    and they have not known my ways."
So I declared on oath in my anger,
    "They shall never enter my rest."

We often hear the baby boomer generation referred to as a "lost generation," especially after the destruction experienced by a loss of hope, addiction to drugs, casual relationships, and a fear of the future. The Bible knows of a similar generation. After the Exodus (prefiguring redemption in Christ) and the giving of the law on Mount Sinai, some of the Jews were discovered to be unbelievers. That should not come as any surprise, since, as Augustine said of the church, "There are many sheep outside and many wolves inside." Judging by what the people of Israel saw—the afflictions of freedom compared to the relative affluence of slavery in Egypt—many grew cynical about God's ever coming to fulfill His promise to Abraham. The psalmist describes that unbelieving generation as those who "spoke against God, saying, 'Can God spread a table in the desert?'" (Psalm 78:19). Contrasted with this unbelief, the psalmist declared, "You prepare a table before me in the presence of my enemies. You anoint my head with oil; my cup overflows. Surely goodness and love will follow me all the days of my life, and I will dwell in the house of the LORD forever" (23:5). It was because of the "lost generation" of Israel that the psalmist reminded Israel of God's great acts of redemption:

He decreed statutes for Jacob
    and established the law in Israel,
which he commanded our forefathers
    to teach their children,
so the next generation would know them,
    even the children yet to be born,
    and they in turn would tell their children.

> Then they would put their trust in God
> and would not forget his deeds
> but would keep his commands.
> They would not be like their forefathers—
> a stubborn and rebellious generation,
> whose hearts were not loyal to God,
> whose spirits were not faithful to him.
>   (78:5–8)

God declared of an entire generation, "They shall never enter my rest." So the children of Israel wandered for forty years. None of the cynical unbelievers ever entered the Promised Land, even though they were ancestral heirs of Abraham.

When we recall the psalmist's confession, "My soul finds rest in God alone; my salvation comes from him" (62:1), we can see how the real issue of the Israelite "lost generation" was one of faith. The reason they did not enter the rest of the Promised Land was not that they were not sufficiently obedient, nor that they did not offer enough sacrifices or perform enough ceremonies. They were barred eternally from God's rest because of unbelief. They refused to locate their rest in God alone. They refused to declare that their salvation was entirely in His hands and refused to believe that they were at God's mercy and that God would graciously provide. They took matters into their own hands and decided to save themselves. When they could not do this, they complained about God. That is the backdrop for the discussion of the Sabbath rest in Hebrews 4.

First, the writer to the Hebrews establishes the priority of Christ over Moses (Hebrews 3:5–6). In the New Testament believers not only *have the promise* of a Sabbath from the mouth of Moses, they actually *enter into* the Sabbath rest in Christ. To reject the command to enter God's rest as issued by Christ Himself, especially after He has accomplished everything that the Old Testament people had only in the form of a promise, is the height of unbelief.

Second, after the writer to the Hebrews recalls the warning recorded in Psalm 95, he says:

> See to it, brothers, that none of you has a sinful, unbelieving heart that turns away from the living God. . . . We have come to share in Christ if we hold firmly till the end the confidence we had at first. As has just been said:
>
>> "Today, if you hear his voice,
>>   do not harden your hearts as you did in the rebellion.". . .
>
> So we see that they were not able to enter, because of unbelief. (3:12–15, 19)

Again, it was unbelief that kept the Israelite "lost generation" from entering the Promised Land. But just because the Jews did not enter God's Sabbath rest in the Old Testament, that does not mean that God has canceled His promise: "Therefore, since the promise of entering his rest still stands, let us be careful that none of you be found to have fallen short of it" (4:1). But how can this promise still stand for New Testament believers, both Jew and Gentile, if it was merely a promise of a plot of earthly territory? That is why the same author writes that even those believers who did finally enter Palestine realized that that was only a shadow of the eternal Sabbath rest: "Instead, they were longing for a better country—a heavenly one" (11:16).

Therefore, the lost generation was not only barred from entering the earthly rest, but because the people did not trust God's promise, they were barred from the heavenly rest as well. It is that heavenly rest that remains open to us as believers:

> For we also have had the gospel preached to us, just as they did; but the message they heard was of no value to them, because those who heard did not combine it with faith. Now we who have believed enter that rest, just as God has said,

> "So I declared on oath in my anger,
>   'They shall never enter my rest.'"

And yet his work has been finished since the creation of the world. For somewhere he has spoken about the seventh day in these words: "And on the seventh day God rested from all his work." And again in the passage above he says, "They shall never enter my rest."

It still remains that some will enter that rest, and those who formerly had the gospel preached to them did not go in, because of their disobedience. (4:2–6)

Notice, both the believers in the wilderness and believers today have the same gospel preached to them (v. 2). We are faced with the same decision, the same crisis event. The unbelievers in the wilderness had known the promise and had participated in the rituals and ceremonies that constantly reminded them of that promise. Yet they did not combine the regular hearing with faith; they did not respond to the gospel, but simply took it for granted and then, when times grew tough, decided to make it on their own. This process is familiar to many of us who have seen family members and friends—maybe even ourselves—go from a Christian home to a disregard for the things of God and then, finally, to a complete rejection of Christ, in practice if not in theory.

But God invites us into His Sabbath day. The offer still stands, but we must not be like those who failed to trust God's promise of salvation, even though we have heard the good news again and again. The Promised Land and the promised rest cannot ultimately refer to the physical land of Palestine, "for if Joshua [who led the children of Israel into the land] had given them rest, God would not have spoken later about another day. There remains, then, a Sabbath-rest for the people of God; for anyone who enters God's rest also rests from his own work, just as God did from his" (2:8–10). This is the key to the entire passage, and in my view, to the entire purpose behind the Sabbath institution. This is what the Sabbath points toward: "Anyone who enters God's rest also rests from his own work, just as God did from his." As Paul wrote, "To the man who does not work but trusts God who justifies the wicked, his faith is credited as righteousness" (Romans 4:5). The lost generation failed to enter into the promise, not because they failed to do or achieve something, but because they would not stop trying to enter the land by their own efforts and scheming.

In the same way, we are barred from God's seventh day, His eternal rest, unless we cease our striving after God's favor and trust in Christ alone. For that eternal rest is none other than Christ Himself. By our union with Christ, we are already living in the seventh day, the eternal Sabbath of God. God commanded the Sabbath observance through Moses, but Christ Himself is the Sabbath for His people, as He says in the book of Matthew: "Come to me, all you who are weary and burdened, and I will give you rest. Take my yoke upon you and learn from me, for I am gentle and humble in heart, and you will find rest for your souls. For my yoke is easy and my burden is light" (Matthew 11:28–30). Joshua may have led Israel into the earthly Promised Land, but that was a mere foreshadowing of a greater triumph, a greater land, a greater rest.

In fact, the text in Matthew, where Jesus invites people to share in His rest, is immediately followed by Christ's proclamation of Himself as "Lord of the Sabbath." After telling the people that He was their rest, the Lord was confronted by the Pharisees, who were disturbed that Jesus' disciples were not observing the Sabbath properly. Jesus reminded the Pharisees that on the Sabbath the priests were busy working. "Haven't you read in the Law that on the Sabbath the priests in the temple desecrate the day and yet are innocent? I tell you that one greater than the temple is here. If you had known what these words mean, 'I desire mercy, not sacrifice,' you would not have condemned the innocent. For the Son of Man is Lord of the Sabbath" (12:5–8). The Pharisees were busy trying to enforce the outward keeping of the Sabbath but were utterly blind to the fact that the whole purpose behind the Sabbath institution was standing before them in the person of

Christ. Rather than embrace Christ as their Rest incarnate, the Pharisees chose instead to use this shadow as a source of works-righteousness.

After this discussion, Jesus walked to the synagogue and healed a man with a shriveled hand in the sight of the Pharisees, so enraging the religious leaders that they began plotting His death. Nevertheless, the Lord moved on to another place and healed the sick. All of this, we are told, "was to fulfill what was spoken through the prophet Isaiah":

> Here is my servant whom I have chosen,
>   the one I love, in whom I delight;
> I will put my Spirit on him,
>   and he will proclaim justice to the nations.
> He will not quarrel or cry out;
>   no one will hear his voice in the streets.
> A bruised reed he will not break,
>   and a smoldering wick he will not snuff out,
> till he leads justice to victory.
>   In his name the nations will put their hope.
>   (Matthew 12:17–21; cf. Isaiah 42:1–4)

Therefore, in this one chapter of Matthew, we have Jesus Christ proclaiming Himself as the Sabbath rest, demonstrating Himself as the Lord of the Sabbath, and attributing to Himself the fulfillment of the prophecy concerning the Chosen Servant who would care for the broken and weary, unlike the religious leaders who had given themselves to casually breaking off bruised reads and snuffing out smoldering wicks. To those with weak faith, He would give hope instead of fear; to those with doubts and spiritual insecurity, He would provide a place of rest.

ARE WE OBLIGATED
TO KEEP THE SABBATH TODAY?

This practical question is what many readers have been waiting to see answered since they began reading this chapter. Nevertheless, it cannot be adequately answered apart from the preceding "big picture." Sabbath-keeping is the fourth of the Ten Commandments; therefore, if we believe that Christians are obligated to obey the Ten Commandments, aren't we saying that they are to keep the Sabbath? And if the Sabbath is a literal day of the week on which "you shall not do any work, neither you, nor your son or daughter, nor your manservant or maidservant, nor your animals, nor the alien within your gates" (Exodus 20:10), does that not create a practical crisis of conscience for many Christians?

First, let me say that, based on Paul's advice to Christians in Romans 14, one ought never to transgress one's conscience. If I really believe that I am obligated to keep the fourth commandment according to its ceremonial use (i.e., a literal day of cessation from labor), then I am sinning against God in my conscience if I violate it. If I believe that I am sinning against God—even if I am not violating His commandment—I am in my heart rebelling against God. That is far more destructive of our character over the long term than transgressing a known law. Therefore, we ought never to treat lightly one's conscientious objection to working or engaging in various forms of recreation on Sunday.

Having said that, the believer who views Sunday as the Christian Sabbath must be careful not to violate the freedom his or her brother or sister enjoys in this matter. Just as other ceremonial issues were left up to the individual conscience by the apostles (cf. Galatians), so we ought to give each other freedom to hold differing views on this matter. As Paul wrote, "One man considers one day more sacred than another; another man considers every day alike. Each one should be fully convinced in his own mind. He who regards one day as special, does so to the Lord" (Romans 14:5–6). Nevertheless, I wish to make the case for my conviction that the fourth commandment belongs in what we call the "ceremonial" rather than the "moral" part of the law. Remember, the "moral" part of God's law is what is eternally binding on believers in both testaments, whereas the shadows of Christ in the civil and ceremonial laws disappear when the reality (Christ) appears. To suggest that the fourth commandment, then, is part of the *ceremonial*, rather than the *moral*, law is to say that it is no longer binding for Christians.

First, the apostle Paul argues in the first two chapters of Romans that the law written on the conscience and the law written on tablets of stone are one and the same. In other words, the moral law (Ten Commandments) is the written expression of the natural law engraved on the human conscience. So universal is that law that every tribe and culture is aware, according to Romans 1 and 2, that there is a God with particular attributes and demands. Paul makes it clear that not only the second table of the law (concerning our obligation to other people), but the first table as well (concerning our obligation to God), is stamped on every person by creation. Nevertheless, as I have already argued, the Sabbath is unique among the Ten Commandments. It is not, I would maintain, stamped on the human conscience because of creation; rather it is an ordinance, like circumcision, for the redeemed community of Israel pointing forward to Christ. Whereas pagans know that setting up idols in the place of God is wrong, but do it anyway, it is difficult to find a universal principle of Sabbath. It can be argued as useful and practically justified, particularly in cultures that have already had a religious tradition of observing the Lord's Day, but one would be hard-pressed to simply take a native in the South Pacific and ask him or her to come up with anything equivalent to the Jewish Sabbath. That is because it is the only commandment of the ten that is not given to all people by way of creation, but is a special gift for the people of God, pointing them in a unique way to their coming Messiah.

Second, the reason we give for accepting the moral law (i.e., the Ten Commandments) is that its precepts are repeated in the New Testament. The ceremonial and civil laws are not repeated, but every single one of the Ten Commandments is reissued in one way or another, many times over, in the New Testament—with one exception, the fourth commandment. We search in vain to find one single New Testament commandment concerning the Sabbath. We do find believers commanded to continue regularly meeting together (Hebrews 10:25), and this was done on the first day of the week (Sunday) rather than on the last (Saturday) in the early church (Acts 20:7; 1 Corinthians 16:2), but there was surely more to this austere Old Testament commandment than getting together on a regular basis. In fact, "Whoever does any work on the Sabbath day must be put to death" (Exodus 31:15).

The reason God took the Sabbath observance so seriously was that it was pointing to something utterly essential: the coming of Christ and salvation by resting rather than working. If God allowed any work on the Sabbath, how could it serve as a valuable foreshadowing of the eternal promise? Does God allow us to contribute even the slightest activity to our own redemption? Is there one place where we can say, "Look, that's what I did; that was my part!"? Surely not, and those who trust in their own effort, however slight, are put to death for all eternity. This is precisely what is foreshadowed in the Old Testament legislation. That is why God demands the severest punishment—physical death, foreshadowing a severer death, eternal death—for rejecting Christ as our rest.

Thus, it is quite impossible to truly obey the Sabbath commandment with the rigor required by the Old Testament law apart from reinstituting a theocracy (a prospect, by the way, that I find both frightening and appalling for biblical-theological as well as practical reasons). But not only is the ceremonial observance of the commandment not possible for us in all of its details; it is not called for in the New Testament. The apostle Paul includes the Sabbath observance in the ceremonial part of the law, which passed away with the coming of Christ: "Therefore do not let anyone judge you by what you eat or drink, or with regard to a religious festival, a New Moon celebration or a Sabbath day. These are a shadow of the things that were to come; the reality, however, is found in Christ" (Colossians 2:16–17). The Sabbath day is placed alongside the other rituals and celebrations of the ceremonial law. If we should continue to observe the ceremonial aspect of the Sabbath, why ought we not to practice the other required Sabbaths: the Sabbath every seventh year for the land and a Sabbath Year every fiftieth year, when prisoners are freed and all debts are canceled?

But none of this, including the Sabbath day, is commanded in the New Testament. Jesus Christ is the rest for the people of God, and even the land will enjoy His eternal rest and be "liberated from its bondage to decay and brought into the glorious freedom of the children of God" (Romans 8:21). These Sabbaths pointed to Christ, and in His advent, death, resurrection, ascension, and future return, we find a fulfillment so complete that we no more need the Sabbath as a sign than we need sacrifices or a temple. According to Hebrews, Christ is all three of these: Sabbath, sacrifice, and temple.

That being said, even though the ceremonial part of the Sabbath (i.e., the observance of an actual day) is no longer in force, the reality of that shadow is indeed. If people do not trust in Christ and cease relying on their own efforts, God will swear in His anger that they, like the lost generation, will not enter His rest. "There remains, then, a Sabbath-rest for the people of God; for anyone who enters God's rest also rests from his own work, just as God did from his" (Hebrews 4:9–10). Those who do not trust Christ will find themselves in the same difficulty as those whom God cursed in the wilderness and those who were executed for breaking the Sabbath in the Old Testament, with one exception: the rejection of Christ leads to eternal loss, not merely to one's death in this world.

IS THERE ABSOLUTELY NO PRACTICAL APPLICATION TO US TODAY, THEN?

Even though I have argued for the fulfillment and, therefore, passing, of the Sabbath commandment in terms of ritual observance, I do maintain that much of the practical activity of the Sabbath (separating one day of the week for meditation, prayer, fellowship, Word, and sacrament) continues to be the main activity of the church (Acts 2:42–47). Although we are not to demand that Sunday be elevated for spiritual or theological reasons (that would be to make it a ceremonial or ritual observance), there is every reason to elevate it for practical reasons.

American Christians are often amazed to see how seriously Europeans take Sundays as far as shop-keeping and commerce. In fact, the "Keep Sunday Special" campaign launched by evangelicals in Britain was supported by a wide cross-section of the general public. It is good for families, for workers, for unions, for employers, and for those in service-related professions, such as the police, fire, and public utilities, who would also have to work on Sundays, if public shops were open. Great Christian spokespersons, such as Sir Fred Catherwood, a member of Parliament, have defended closing down public shops and companies on Sunday on pragmatic grounds, and many non-Christians have found their arguments convincing for the general good of society.

The same could be said of other European countries. In fact, Sunday closing has actually been written into the legislation of the European Community. It has become that much of a public institution and has for so long borne fruit in better relationships and greater productivity. As I mentioned at the beginning, although none of God's commandments were given for their usefulness, they end up serving useful ends, and that is true of the Sabbath. We would do well to give our land and resources periods of rest as well (this is already practiced in the form of "crop rotation" in many places). And we may even want to consider applications of the Jubilee principle. We could set nonviolent criminals free or enroll them in community service projects instead of putting them in prison, or perhaps we could consider canceling debts through some creative and ingenious method of restitution. But while we may find wisdom and inspiration in these laws, they do not come to us in the New Testament in the form of a command. They were there to rule a geopolitical nation that served to foreshadow a spiritual nation, an eternal kingdom consisting of "men for God out of every language and people and nation" (Revelation 5:9).

Besides the usefulness of setting Sunday aside for society, it serves an even greater practical purpose for the church to have one day set apart for believers and their families to concentrate on God's Word and refocus themselves on Him for the coming week. As a pastor, I could come up with a long list of people I have known who thought they could get by on irregular church attendance. Sadly, most of them are no longer active church members, and many have left the church altogether.

We are not as strong as we think. We desperately need to hear God's Word proclaimed and have that Word of promise confirmed through the sacraments on a regular basis. If we are not learning, growing, and being constantly reminded of our basic convictions, we are not standing still, but moving backwards. There is no such thing as standing still in the Christian life. The early church had an effective way of coming together on the first day of the week, every week, for public worship, and that has served the advancement of Christ's kingdom for almost two thousand years. Because it is an ancient practice that conforms to God's Word and makes a singular opportunity for exercising believers in that which He does clearly command, the regular attendance of public worship on Sunday ought to be retained. But it ought not to be observed as a divinely ordained, sanctified day. For the believer, every day is a Sabbath; having entered into God's eternal rest, the Christian sets every day apart unto the Lord. The Heidelberg Catechism points to this:

> 103 Q. What is God's will for us in the fourth commandment?
> A. First, that the gospel ministry and education for it be maintained, and that, especially on the festive day of rest, I regularly attend the assembly of God's people to learn what God's Word teaches, to participate in the sacraments, to pray to God publicly, and to

bring Christian offerings for the poor. Second, that every day of my life I rest from my evil ways, let the Lord work in me through his Spirit, and so begin in this life the eternal Sabbath.

Following the interpretation of the early Fathers, Calvin also sheds some light on this point:

But there is no doubt that by the Lord Christ's coming the ceremonial part of this commandment was abolished. For he himself is the truth, with whose presence all figures vanish; he is the body, at whose appearance the shadows are left behind. He is, I say, the true fulfillment of the Sabbath. "We were buried with him by baptism, we were engrafted into participation in his death, that sharing in his resurrection we may walk in newness of life." For this reason the apostle elsewhere writes that the Sabbath was "a shadow of what is to come; but the body belongs to Christ," that is, the very substance of truth, which Paul well explained in that passage. This is not confined within a single day but extends through the whole course of our life, until, completely dead to ourselves, we are filled with the life of God. Christians ought therefore to shun completely the superstitious observance of days. . . . Although the Sabbath has been abrogated, there is still occasion for us: (1) to assemble on stated days for the hearing of the Word, the breaking of the mystical bread, and for public prayers; (2) to give surcease from labor to servants and workmen. There is no doubt that in enjoining the Sabbath the Lord was concerned with both. . . .

Why do we not assemble daily, you ask, so as to remove all distinction of days? If only this had been given us! Spiritual wisdom truly deserved to have some portion of time set apart for it each day. But if the weakness of many made it impossible for daily meetings to be held, and the rule of love does not allow more to be required of them, why should we not obey the order we see laid upon us by God's will. . . . For we are not keeping it as a ceremony, with the most rigid scrupulousness, supposing a spiritual mystery to be figured thereby. Rather, we are using it as a remedy needed to keep order in the church.[3]

CONCLUSION

Once the people of God settled in Canaan, God commanded the Israelites to give a number of towns to the Levites, the priest-line of Israel. And of those towns, six were to be "cities of refuge" to which murderers could legally flee to escape execution (Numbers 35:11). "They will be places of refuge from the avenger, so that a person accused of murder may not die before he stands trial before the assembly" (v. 12). In our last chapter, concerning the third commandment, we saw what it meant to "call upon the name of the Lord," and why it was so essential, therefore, that God's name be protected from blasphemy. Similarly, to call upon the name of the Lord is to enter into His Sabbath rest, or, to use another rest-metaphor from this passage in Numbers 35, to flee to the city of refuge from the avenger. On this hill, God is both the avenger and the protector, both the just and the justifier of the wicked. Here there is rest and peace.

But to flee to this hill, this city of refuge, we must recall the war that brought us this peace. We must remember how the Son of God was cruelly and savagely torn by the same human race He created and how His war brought us peace; how His agony brought us deliverance, and how His toil brought us rest. For here, in the city of rest and refuge, we find the Lord of the Sabbath stretching His scarred arms toward us in peace: "Come to me, all you who are weary and burdened, and I will give you rest... [For] a bruised reed he will not break, and a smoking candle he will not snuff out" (Matthew 11:28; 12:20).

NOTES

1. Geerhardus Vos,. *Biblical Theology* (Grand Rapids: Eerdmans, 1948), 139.
2. John Calvin, *Institutes of the Christian Religion*, 2.8.28–29.
3. Ibid.

CHAPTER SIX

HONOR TO WHOM HONOR IS DUE

Honor your father
and your mother.

"I was somebody once," Marguerite announced in a broken Swiss accent. Like many of the elderly folks at the rest home my parents owned while I was growing up, Marguerite had a life that included glamor and excitement. A hairdresser to European royalty, she had a million stories and told each in a low voice, as though she were leaking forbidden information anonymously to the press. Helen spent most of her life as a missionary in Brazil and founded a school there. At 102 years old, Millie had a catalog of stories about her days working for the Pony Express in Washington territory, before it gained statehood. My own grandmother—"Bigmama," as we called her—could tell similar stories about the Oklahoma territory before its entrance into the Union.

When did we ever get this notion that our elders have little to offer society? The years of practical experience, the knowledge of past events for first-hand historical accounts, and the wisdom for dealing with problems they faced before us have given the elderly the role of Wise One or Sage in most cultures around the world. But in our self-centered, individualistic, now-oriented culture, we can leave our debts from the past in a nursing home and our debts for the future to our children. But for now, it's Miller Time.

The Reggae singer Ziggy Marley wrote a song a few years ago about Americans, whom he called "tomorrow people." Americans, he said, have thrown away their past and therefore have no future. We are known around the world as an optimistic, fast-paced, aggressive, and ambitious people. That has been our strength and weakness. It has given us the ability to create wealth, but at the same time, to the degree that we have downplayed the spiritual wealth of our own people—men, women, and children, who are more than consumers and producers —to that degree we are little more than spoiled children with too many toys for our own good.

There has been a great deal of discussion about the fact that the elderly population in this country is increasing, and is likely to continue to do so. Yet, though it may be difficult for many of us to ache as we pass a homeless person waiting on the street corner for a job, one would think that at least we could take care of our immediate families, but apparently not, according to recent polls. Barely half of the American public believe it is the children's responsibility to look after their parents. No wonder half of the forty-five-and-over population said they didn't think their children would take care of them in their old age.

But we're Christians. That means that we're supposed to treat our elders—not just our own parents, but our elders in general—with respect and dignity, as the revered tutors of the home, the academy, and the culture. One of my most vivid memories of growing up in a rest home environment is of pastors and church workers depositing their parents there and not even visiting them at Christmas or Easter. Christmas after Christmas I watched my mom shop for the only gifts these sad souls would get that year. One year my mom typed a letter to the pastors in the surrounding area, inviting them to visit the old folks during the holidays. In spite of the fact that over half of the residents were parents of evangelical Protestants, it was the Catholic and Episcopal churches that responded, and they already had an on-going visitation schedule established at our place. Out of thirty evangelical churches, not one accepted my mom's invitation. I suppose the Singing Christmas Tree program was more important.

Reports have been growing concerning the abuse of the elderly in our society by con artists, inefficient government bureaucracies, pharmaceutical companies, and the children themselves. *Newsweek* magazine reported a disturbing trend of turning hospitals into "a dumping ground for Granny." Abandonment of the elderly in emergency rooms appears to be more usual than we would imagine: 38 percent of hospitals responding to a survey by the Senate Aging Committee reported "as many as eight elderly patients dumped on their emergency wards every week."[1]

According to *USA Today* "more than one in 10 of us are over 65. And that will grow to one in five in the next 45 years."[2] With a rising percentage of our population being elderly, the burden of caring for these neighbors, parents, and grandparents is sure to fall on someone's shoulders. Our response to the elderly is, I believe, part of a larger picture. But before we consider that larger picture, let us gain a better understanding of the fifth commandment itself.

WHAT DOES GOD REQUIRE
IN THE FIFTH COMMANDMENT?

The Heidelberg Catechism explains, with scriptural proofs, what is meant by this decree: "That I show honor, love, and faithfulness to my father and mother and to all who are set in authority over me; that I submit myself with respectful obedience to all their careful instruction and discipline; and that I also bear patiently their failures, since it is God's will to govern us by their hand."

The first four commandments concern our relationship to God: We must worship Him alone, in the way He has prescribed, taking utmost diligence in bringing honor and glory to His name. Now the commandments turn from our duty to God directly to our duty to God indirectly—that is, to our duty to our neighbor, who is created in God's image. And who is our neighbor? First in priority are the members of our own family. This is why the "second table" of the law, concerning human relationships, begins with the command to "honor your father and mother." Out of respect for the dignity and worth of God our heavenly Father and in view of the honor due His name, we are moved to submit ourselves to those whom He has placed over us in a similar relationship.

Therefore, the family forms the foundation of all human relationships. This principle has, of course, been demonstrated also in the behavioral sciences. Psychologists have made a great deal (I would argue, too much) of the determinative character of our families. Those who are abused in that environment themselves often abuse, whereas those who come from strong, loving, and supportive backgrounds are less likely to commit the crimes associated with the rest of the Ten Commandments that follow.

As the apostle Paul reminds us, this commandment has two aspects: a command and a promise. In his seventeenth-century commentary on this commandment, Zacharius Ursinus (principal author of the Heidleburg Catechism) writes, "The design or end of this commandment is the preservation of civil order, which God has appointed in the mutual duties between inferiors and their superiors. Superiors are all those whom God has placed over others, for the purpose of governing and defending them. Inferiors are those whom God has placed under others, that they may be governed and defended by them." Thus, a "superior" includes parents, tutors/guardians, schoolmasters, teachers, and ministers of the gospel; local, municipal, state, and federal officials, and the elders in society generally.

So Ursinus, like most Christian thinkers of his time, saw society as a family. The family of God, of course, was the church—the body of Christ. And yet the civil society, influenced by Christianity, ought to mirror this heavenly family. There must be order; at the same time, the superiors have two duties: to govern and to defend. A ruler—whether a parent, guardian, public official, employer, teacher, or minister—may never exercise rule as a matter of power or pointless force. There is no place for tyrants or authoritarian personalities, since the duty is to govern *and* to defend. As a father exercises his duty by looking out for the best interests of his children, so other superiors in society must seek the good of those they serve. The best rulers are servants; those who govern best defend those within the scope of their authority.

This is consistent with Paul's teaching in Ephesians 6:1–4: "Children, obey your parents in the Lord, for this is right. 'Honor your father and mother'—which is the first commandment with a promise—'that it may go well with you and that you may enjoy long life on the earth.' Fathers, do not exasperate your children; instead, bring them up in the training and instruction of the Lord." Children are commanded to obey their parents, but parents are also responsible to their children. They must not exasperate their children, but must teach them patiently and carefully. To provoke their children to wrath is to govern without defending, to rule without serving.

In verses 5–9, Paul turns to slaves and masters. When we read these terms, we tend to think of slavery in terms of selling African men, women, and children who had been kidnapped from their homeland at gun-point. What Paul has in mind has more to do with relationships between employees and employers, since slavery in his time was a matter of economic justice and not racial injustice. One can argue with the ancient Greco-Roman practice, but it was an institution that actually allowed many indebted families to serve their way to freedom. If a person could not pay his debts, he simply entered the service of the creditor until the debts were paid. To be sure, the institution could be—and was—abused, as Paul's admonition would imply. Nevertheless, we must not imagine that Paul was condoning the type of slavery with which we are most familiar. That is why I suggest we substitute the terms *employee* and *employer* for the terms *slave* and *master* in Ephesians. The modern terms do not fully express the meaning of the terms Paul used, but they are certainly closer to what Paul is talking about than a literal translation would be.

At any rate, employees are to obey "with respect and fear, and with sincerity of heart, just as [they] would obey Christ" (6:5). Paul commands, "Obey them not only to win their favor when their eye is on you, but like slaves of Christ, doing the will of God from your heart. Serve whole-heartedly, as if you were serving the Lord, not men, because you know that the Lord will reward everyone for whatever good he does, whether he is slave or free" (vv. 6–8). To serve our earthly superiors is to serve our heavenly Superior; therefore, our attention, efficiency, and diligence are to be motivated not by whether the boss shows enough respect for our work, but by the fact that God our heavenly Father is pleased when we help build a good car or house, use our time at work efficiently, or read and pray with our family. We can endure many of the frustrations of working conditions when we realize that the dignity of our work is measured by God's satisfaction, not merely by our employer's.

But duty does not end with the employee any more than with the child. "And masters," Paul commands, "treat your slaves *in the same way.* Do not threaten them, since you know that he who is both their Master and yours is in heaven, and there is no favoritism with him" (6:9, italics added). As employees are to show respect to their employers out of reverance to God, so employers are to show respect for their employees "since you know that he who is both their Master and yours is in heaven, and there is no favoritism with him." Every parent, employer, minister, and ruler has a higher authority. Never does the buck stop with a human being; every human authority may come under God's judgment if it becomes tyrannical or unjust. The fact that God Himself does not distinguish between slave or free, employer or employee, clergy or laity in His judgments renders Him an impartial judge. He does not take sides before the trial but judges the evidence on its own terms.

Christian attitudes in this regard tend to polarize. On one end are those who favor egalitarianism, a sort of leveling of the playing field so that there are no "superiors" and "inferiors." The spirit of the French revolution is reflected in such attitudes, which democratize human relationships to the point where every decision must be made by the people—not only on election day, but in the office, the home, and the schools and universities. This can create so much bureaucracy that, ironically, the people become separated from the process; it overwhelms them. Furthermore, it contributes to a suspicion of every kind of authority, rendering an entire society a feeble cacophany of demands. Chains of command in society restrain the damage self-will can create.

On the other end are those who heavily favor hierarchy, often in reaction against the former extreme. Decisions have to be made without cumbersome red tape, so strong leaders get away with a good deal in the political process. Pastors and laypeople, wearied of committee meetings and votes, find it easier to invite a strong-willed, aggressive leader to take charge. Employees know that their CEO is making more money than the GNP of some nations, but he's the boss and he has, after all, done much to turn the company around. Weary of weak, ineffective bureaucracy masquerading as democracy, many Americans are ripe for strong political, social, and religious leaders who can sing and dance their way to the top.

In the church we have seen both tendencies toward extremes. Egalitarianism has so weakened pastoral authority in some churches that job security depends on how well the pastor can tickle his congregation's ears. If he exercises church discipline of a popular parishioner, the backlash can be enormous. Calvin faced similar problems in his pastorate. After throwing off the tyrannical shackles of an authoritarian bishop, Geneva was not about to let its Reformed pastors exercise even normal disciplinary functions. When Calvin refused to give Communion to popular and wealthy citizens who refused the church's discipline over major offenses, he was exiled.

But we have the authoritarianism, too. In *Churches That Abuse,* Ronald Enroth surveys this pressing problem within mainstream evangelical churches, not merely among the Pentecostal groups. The irony is that just as legalism breeds antinomianism, so authoritarianism breeds anarchy, and vice versa. The same groups that mock mainline traditionalism and offer a grass roots, populist appeal, rejecting the authority of denominations, creeds, and confessions, end up concentrating power in the hands of a new elite very quickly. In fact, because over the years denominations have learned to place checks and balances on the power of leaders, they are usually much less prone to authoritarianism. I remember not long ago receiving a tongue-lashing from a brother about my belonging to "churchianity" because I am ordained in a mainstream denomination that requires adherence to creeds and confessions. And yet he is associated with a church that has spawned numerous offshoots, each naming itself after the mother church, where the pastor has the last word not only in that congregation, but in the daughter congregations as well. Seeking to eliminate authority, these groups usually succeed only at creating new forms of tyranny.

The fifth commandment is, therefore, rich in wisdom for every sphere of our lives. If we do not have clear lines of authority to which we submit, there will be anarchy; and if there is anarchy, tyranny is close behind. At the same time, authority must be tempered by the duty rulers have to serve and defend.

That being the definition of the fifth commandment, what is it in our society and in our own lives that undermines our sensitivity to honoring it?

YOUTHISM

Travel to London or Lisbon, Prague or Peking, Nairobi or Nepal, and you will find a common respect for the elders of society. While mobility, technology, entertainment, and other factors of modern life have surely been felt around the world, nowhere have these forces more solidly combined to create a cult of youth than in the United States.

According to a *USA Today* analysis of trends, "The images attached to old age—especially in the youth-oriented '60s and the yuppie-oriented '80s—have not been flattering ones. At best we imagined old age as a relief from the grind of having to get up early every morning. At worst we considered it a time of having no real reason to get up at all. About the best thing anyone had to say about old age is that "it wasn't so bad, once you considered the alternative."³ If make-overs, facial operations, hair loss treatment centers, and similar consumer goods and services are any indication, our era is consumed with a passion for youth. Our society places a premium on youth, probably not so much for efficiency and commitment to hard work (previous generations seem to have more going for them in that department), but for image. To be sure, the workplace is always changing and it is sometimes risky to hire and retrain older employees rather than training younger ones for the long-term success of the company, but with the mobility we experience anyway, and the higher level of commitment many older workers feel to their workplace, it is at least conceivable that there would be more value in the long run in retraining one's own loyal workers. Nevertheless, retirement is enforced—not by law but by circumstances. Whereas in older cultures, the skill and acumen of a craftsperson, merchant, banker, doctor, lawyer, parent, or grandparent grew with age, these virtues are often overlooked today in the headlong pursuit of the successful image.

It must be said that in many cases the elderly are all too willing to take on this new role, abandoning the office of "sage" to more traditional eras. Retirement age is getting younger and younger as people spend their energies trying to climb the ladder of success in order to retire in luxury at an early age. Many older Americans have bought into the youth-culture themselves by spending their children's inheritance on holidays and entertainment. Fun, fun, fun: If you can't beat 'em, join 'em. In only four decades, the number of men in the work force over sixty-five has dropped by 50 percent.[4] I am not arguing that retirement is wrong or that enjoying one's retirement is wrong, but we have to see what youthism is doing to the fabric of our own lives as Christians and in society at large.

We in the "Pepsi generation" ought to ask ourselves: If we undervalue our elders today, what will our place be in society when we reach the golden years?

NOWISM

After two bloody world wars, anxiety about the future has hung like a fog over the West. Existentialism has taken our focus off of the big questions of life and our relationship to the big picture (God, the family, the community, the past and future), demanding an answer to questions concerning the meaning of personal, individual existence: Who am I? Why am I here? How can I find meaning to my own existence?

But today we have moved beyond existentialism to despair, as Francis Schaeffer observed. We don't really see any deeper meaning to life than making money, friends, and deals. We want to make a lot of money, spend it, and live for today. This is as true for Christians, unfortunately, as it is for non-Christians, as we will see in following chapters. Our attitude toward the elderly in the society at large and in the church in particular is indicative of a general attitude toward the past and the future. Following the existential culture, we find ourselves burdened with our own personal happiness and peace of mind and cannot seem to root ourselves in the past or prepare ourselves for the future.

Yet as Christians we have the answer to this problem. Ours is a religion committed to history. From the creation and preservation of humanity to the drama of redemption, climaxing in the self-sacrifice and resurrection of a Jewish carpenter who was God incarnate, the biblical story is synonymous with true time-and-space history. It is not a tale spun by cultures reflecting on their existential context. Fishermen and prostitutes are not known for inventing new philosophical and religious reflections on the meaning of life for their communities. Christianity depends not on pious *expressions* of divine love and forgiveness, mercy and atonement, but on divine *acts* of love and forgiveness, mercy and atonement, and these acts are rooted in history, particularly in the events surrounding the life and times of Jesus of Nazareth in Palestine nearly two thousand years ago.

But that's not all. Christianity also provides a vision for the future, because its eschatology sweeps past and present into one continuous flow of God's redemptive story. God is sovereign over the future as well as over the past, and each of us is an actor on the stage. To waste one's life sitting in the audience is to dishonor God, who makes the whole creation cry out in praise if His people will not. Christians ought to see every day at work as an opportunity to "glorify God and enjoy him forever," anticipating the day when Christ returns and makes all things new. A great God, a great plan, a great past, and a great future: these all add up to provide believers with a context in which to place the honor due to those in our society who link us to the past, even as we link them to the future through our own children.

PRETENTIOUSNESS

When the forebears of the colonists came to America, they were escaping the tyranny of a church that ejected them. Nevertheless, the Separatists and Puritans were hardly anarchists. The former formed a civil community on board the Mayflower, and the Massachusetts Bay Puritans formed a community with closely knit communal ties. They were committed to the Bible, to the historic creeds, and to the confessions of the Reformation. Church discipline was exercised, for the most part without serious challenge. Regardless of how we may view the situation today, the majority of New England citizens did not complain of tyranny or authoritarianism.

The founding fathers had among their number, however, many who had embraced the spirit of the Enlightenment and the revolutionary impulse of Rousseau and other French activists. These individuals were not merely opposed to tyrannical authority but showed a distaste for authority in principle. By the time of the Jacksonian era (late eighteenth to early nineteenth centuries), many Christians rejected the creeds and confessions, together with the liturgies and traditions of their various Old Word churches. They were going to chart their own course and interpret the Bible from scratch.

There is an incredible arrogance in that way of thinking. When the Reformers championed the translation of the Bible into the language of the people so that they could read and understand it themselves, they never meant to suggest for one moment that individuals could believe whatever they wanted to believe, so long as they could find a verse for it. But that is what *sola Scriptura* (only Scripture) came to mean to many Americans. Our generation is unique. After all, my grandparents rode in a covered wagon to their parcel of land in the Oklahoma Land Rush and flew the same distance a number of times on a DC-10. From traveling on horseback to viewing the lunar landing on television, their lifetimes spanned one of the most revolutionary technological ages in human history. Inspired by such confidence, many Bible teachers have emphasized the uniqueness of this "terminal generation," as if ours was the only truly important generation—we are the ones who will see all of the events of biblical prophecy come together. And again, there is a certain arrogance in all of this, disregarding the past and the future.

This arrogance undermines our attention to honoring those who have preceded us and defending those who will follow. The immediate practical import of the attitude is illustrated in the intolerable evil of our national debt, whose interest alone exceeds the GNP. As child abuse and granny dumping rise on a personal level, preoccupation with ourselves tears the fabric of our national life as well.

In fact, we ought to think of the federal debt we are leaving to future generations as a kind of child abuse.

In the church, this mentality has created Flip Wilson's "Church-Of-What's-Happening-Now," where the latest and greatest drowns out the tried and tested. The church's equivalent of granny dumping in theological terms is its ignorance or outright rejection of creeds and confessions, in an effort to create the First Church of Youth. Its equivalent of child abuse is its failure to catechize and instruct the children in the great truths of Scripture, preferring to spend the majority of the time competing with video games and rock concerts. According to Gallup, one of the reasons many young people give for leaving the church is its failure to provide profound answers to their deepest questions in its headlong pursuit of marketing success. They have MTV already. What they need is a church that answers their questions.

Third, we see this mentality in the workplace, where people often find it difficult to submit to someone else's authority. In a sense, one of our greatest gifts as Americans is our skepticism. We don't want to believe what everybody else believes just because everybody else believes it. We like to question established norms, customs, and ideas. Nevertheless, this skepticism can make us poor employees if we are not careful. We began as children asking, "Why?" every time Mom or Dad gave us a command. "But I don't want to," we whined. Eventually we are supposed to grow out of that whining stage, but our generation is given, it seems, to prolonging the juvenile response to every form of authority.

ME-ISM

Along with the tendency to reject everything old and established, simply on the basis that it *is* old and established, is the propensity toward individualism. Paul warned Timothy, "But mark this: There will be terrible times in the last days. People will be lovers of themselves, lovers of money, boastful, proud, abusive, disobedient to their parents, ungrateful, unholy, without love, unforgiving, slanderous, without self-control, brutal, not lovers of the good, treacherous, rash, conceited, lovers of pleasure rather than lovers of God—having a form of godliness but denying its power" (2 Timothy 3:1–5). Notice the close connection Paul makes between narcissism, arrogance, individualism, materialism, hedonism, and "disobedience to parents." Rejection of legitimate parental authority is a sign of a weakness in character, not strength. Again, when the Puritans came to New England, their goal was to form a new community, not to disband and form independent societies of individual people. "That saying, 'Each man for himself and God for us all,' is a most devilish one," snapped one Puritan divine.

But we are living at a time when this "most devilish" saying is the most popular motto in society and, it seems, also in the church. When people act like brutes, the church is supposed to be the institution to remind them that they are human beings, created in God's image, with responsibilities having to do not only with themselves, but with each other. There are many ways a Christian can get involved and a variety of positions a Christian might take in terms of political and personal strategies, but the aim must be shared by every Christian.

That means that before we even talk about what is done in Washington, D.C., we have to take inventory of our own lives. Those who leave their able-bodied parents in nursing homes without visiting them ought not to discuss what the government should do to care for the elderly. People who do not exercise mercy and compassion when they see a neighbor in need in everyday circumstances ought not to raise their voices in protest over a lack or an excess of government intervention. Those who insist that the church should do more to care for the poor and the elderly must ask themselves what they are doing in this regard. After all, what is the church but the people of God gathered for worship and scattered for service?

In short, people violate the fifth commandment, according to Ursinus, in the following ways. First, it is a violation for parents

not to seek or provide the support and nourishment necessary for their children, or to bring them up in luxury and
extravagancc; not to protect them from injuries, or not to
accustom them to patience and gentleness . . . ; not to edu-
cate their children . . . ; to raise their children in idleness
and licentiousness; or not to correct them when necessity
requires it; or to chastise them with greater severity than
duty or the nature of the offense demands, and so to alien-
ate their affections by too great severity and cruelty.

Second, the office of schoolmaster and teacher "requires them faithfully to teach and instruct . . . ; to rule
and govern with proper and suitable discipline."
Third, the office of magistrate

may be reduced to these heads, to require from their subjects obedience and external propriety . . . ; to enforce the
precepts of the Decalogue, by defending those who yield
obedience to it, and punishing such as are disobedient; to
enact certain positive laws for the maintenance of civil order . . . ; the execution of the laws which they prescribe
from time to time.

For the magistrates fail when they do not enact laws necessary for civil order, "or in not defending the innocent from
the wrongs which may be inflicted upon them. . . ." Yet,
"the other extreme is tyranny, which consists cither in demanding from their subjects what is unjust; or in not punishing those who sin; or in punishing them more severely
than the offense which they have committed calls for."
The duty for masters is not to command works "such
as are unlawful, impossible, oppressive, or unnecessary; to
afford them proper food and reward them for their labor;
to rule and govern them with such discipline as is suited to
their case." And in advice similar to that of Calvin's, Ursinus offers an application that would have been considered quite liberal and revolutionary in his day: "The whip,
fodder and burdens belong to the ass; bread and correc-
tion to the servant." Further, the masters violate this commandment when they "indulge their slaves in idleness,

147

slothfulness and licentiousness, . . . command things which are unjust, and oppress them by exacting too much from them, withhold from them proper food and wages, or exasperate their household by the exercise of too much rigor and severity."

Finally,

> the duty of elders, and others who excel in wisdom and authority, is to govern and assist others by their examples, counsels and admonitions. These persons sin and act contrary to the duties of their calling, 1. When they are guilty of folly, or of giving improper counsels. 2. When they show levity and a want of gravity in their manners, and present a bad example to others. 3. When they neglect by their counsels and authority to reprove and correct others who are under them when they see them sin and do that which is wrong.

CONCLUSION

Once again we are reminded of the wisdom of past ages, in particular the Reformation. Luther and Calvin—especially Calvin—advocated views that were considered radical for their day. Medieval society mirrored the medieval church, and both were as tyrannical as they were disordered and antiauthoritarian. Calvin defended not only the rights of the ruler from this commandment, but the rights of the ruled as well. In fact, even if it is a bit overstated, Dietrich Bonhoeffer, the German theologian, a leader in the resistance against Hitler, wrote of the differences between the American and French revolutions:

> The American democracy is not founded upon the emancipated man but, quite the contrary, upon the kingdom of God and the limitation of all earthly powers by the sovereignty of God. It is indeed significant when, in contrast to the [French] *Declaration of the Rights of Man*, American historians can say that the federal constitution was written by men who were conscious of original sin and of the wickedness of the human heart. Earthly wielders of authority, and also the people, are directed into their proper bounds, in

due consideration of man's innate longing for power and of the fact that power pertains only to God. With these ideas, which derive from Calvinism, there is combined the essentially contrary idea that comes from the spiritualism of the Dissenters who took refuge in America,[5]

a spiritualism that saw moral obligations in terms of private taboos rather than in terms of public responsibilities for one's neighbor.

However, Bonhoeffer sees the modern world as a rejection of all submission to legitimate authority, an overthrow of the sovereignty of God, which alone places every other authority under its supervision.[6]

We live in a day when parents abandon children, children abandon parents (or sue them); when there is very little sense of loyalty to a company or to one's employees. Instead of looking to others, particularly to the government, to care for our neighbors, we ought to begin with ourselves. Doug Bandow, an evangelical and a senior fellow at the Cato Institute in Washington, D.C., challenges us on this point:

> The nation's moral climate is obviously not good. The majority of Americans may call themselves Christians, but a large number of them live by anything but Christian tenets. It probably isn't surprising, then, that many Christians see political action as a way to make things right. The religious left, carried away with the "social gospel," has long been a vigorous advocate of forced income redistribution. But many conservative evangelicals and fundamentalists, while resisting economic collectivism, now advocate an expansive state in the social arena. Indeed, many of the strongest opponents of government economic intervention have pressed for social intervention through antipornography prosecutions, tougher drug enforcement, and prayer in public schools. And they have done so without addressing or even recognizing any contradiction between their positions.[7]

Similarly, Congressional aide John Palafoutas tells the story of Richard Halverson, U.S. Senate chaplain, speaking before a group of evangelical leaders who were demanding prayer in public schools. "Dr. Halverson asked the crowd of 300 to answer a question. 'How many of you have prayed with your children this month, outside of church?'" Palafoutas reports: "Response: none."[8]

We ought to care for those closest to us in terms of relatedness. After our immediate family, we ought to pursue our calling diligently as employees and provide just incentives (perhaps through profit-sharing) and reasonable care for our workers as employers. We should seek the wisdom of teachers and elders in society and look to them for leadership, while rejecting their folly when it is discerned. We must put our children and their education, both at home and in school, before our own entertainment, pleasure, and success. We ought not to tolerate insolence or haughtiness in them; nor ought we to punish them too severely, but should lead them as good teachers, by example and patient instruction.

And finally, we must care for our parents and for the generations that have passed if we are to properly value the present and the future. "Lord, have mercy, and incline our hearts to keep this law."

NOTES

1. *Newsweek*, 23 December 1991, 64.
2. *USA Today: Tracking the Trends,* ed. Anthony Casale (Kansas City: Andrews, McMeel, and Parker, 1986), 151.
3. Ibid., 150.
4. Ibid., 153.
5. Dietrich Bonhoeffer, *Ethics* (New York: Collier, 1986), 104–5.
6. Ibid.
7. Quoted by Doug Bandow, in *Tabletalk*, September 1992, 11.
8. Ibid., 10.

CHAPTER SEVEN

HOW PRO-LIFE ARE WE REALLY?

You shall not murder.

Theologians usually distinguish between theology and ethics—or, at least, that's what they're supposed to do. In other words, although our behavior can undermine our confidence in Scripture or our sense of obligation to God, one may engage in even serious sins without altering one's view of God, oneself, and salvation. When that occurs, the sin does not point to heresy but to disobedience.

But, as I say, there are exceptions. Abortion is one such exception. In order to engage in this serious sin, a Christian must actually deny a cardinal doctrine of the Christian faith. He or she must deny that God is the Sovereign author of life who alone has the power and right to give and take away human breath, and he must also deny the creature, destroying his or her dignity as an image-bearer of God Himself.

In Christian belief, the significance of human beings over all other species of animal life resides in the image of God *(imago Dei)* stamped on each person, as an artist signs his masterpieces. Furthermore, Christians have *always* opposed abortion on that ground (cf. *The Didache*, etc.). Although God created all things, only humans bear His likeness, and they bear it from conception. As Calvin put it, "Though the primary seat of the divine image was in the mind and the Heart, or in the soul and its powers, there was no part even of the body in which some rays of glory did not shine."[1] Bavinck, the great Reformed dogmatist, argued that "as long as Man remains Man, he bears the image of God," however tarnished and effaced.

If this doctrine is lacking in the church, surely it will be lacking in society. Before the late Francis Schaeffer, a Reformation thinker, reminded the evangelical and fundamentalist world of this biblical doctrine, there was virtually no response from the evangelical church to the atrocity of abortion. The Roman Catholics opposed abortion, of course, based on theological grounds, but their position was obscured by their rejecting birth control as well as abortion. Today, thanks to the efforts of the Schaeffers and their many colaborers, a wide cross section of the evangelical movement supports the protection of human life in its most vulnerable phase.

Clearly, humanity is determined by the *imago Dei*, not by concepts such as "viability." Nevertheless, because we evangelicals over the last two centuries have been given to feverish activity without much theological reflection ("Don't bother me with all that 'head stuff'—let's just get out there and get it done!"), we are single-issue people. We can only handle one issue at a time. As important as the abortion debate is, the anger that people like Francis Schaeffer felt in response to it was motivated by a theological conviction—the same well-spring that produced anger at the pollution of the environment (cf. his freshly released *Pollution and the Death of Man*), outrage at the racism rampant in evangelical circles, and frustration over the injustices of the powerful over the weak.

The abortion debate has been led, as were the abolitionist and civil rights movements, as a protest against oppression of the weak by the strong, picking up on the rich biblical language: "Blessed is he who has regard for the weak" (Psalm 41:1); God "will deliver the needy who cry out, the afflicted who have no one to help. He will take pity on the weak and the needy and save the needy from death. He will rescue them from oppression and violence, for precious is their blood in his sight" (Psalm 72:12). And yet, although many evangelicals oppose abortion, there is a curious silence on nearly every other issue where the pro-life ethic, commanded by Scripture, is at risk. A cursory glance at a concordance will reveal how concerned God is about the treatment of the homeless, the poor, the weak, the minorities ("aliens and strangers"), and others too often marginalized.

The Scripture is replete with condemnation of those who "oppress," and it levels barbs against "you cows of Bashan on Mount Samaria, you women who oppress the poor and crush the needy and say to your husbands, 'Bring us some drinks!'" (Amos 4:1). "'I will tear down the winter house along with the summer house; the houses adorned with ivory will be destroyed and the mansions will be demolished,' declares the LORD" (3:15). The people of God are entrusted with a special obligation to social justice: "Defend the cause of the weak and fatherless; maintain the rights of the poor and oppressed. Rescue the weak and needy" (Psalm 82:3-4). God hates oppression with the same intensity with which He hates abortion, but are we as consistent in our righteous indignation?

Like abortion, apartheid is a theological as well as ethical question. To deny life and justice to the unborn or to the unwhite is not only a serious sin (such as selfishness or racism) but a deliberate system, complete with biblical proof texts twisted beyond recognition. Whereas those committed to being faithful to the Christian creeds and Reformation confessions have declared apartheid in South Africa a heresy, evangelicals here at home have shown more ambivalence. Although Jerry Falwell and other leaders of the Christian Right have courageously defended the human rights of the unborn, Falwell returned from a trip to South Africa declaring that Archbishop Desmond Tutu, whose pleas for a peaceful transition from apartheid to democracy have kept South Africa from bloodshed thus far, was "a phony" and urged Christians to oppose economic sanctions. In the face of American apartheid during the fifties, Falwell declared, "The Christian is nowhere called upon to reform society,"[2] and when the Christian Right, including Jerry Falwell, abandoned this pietistic separation from the world, it seemed surprising to many that God's will coincided almost identically with the conservative Republican agenda.

In the meantime, Jessie Jackson expressed outrage at then 1992 Democratic presidential nominee Bill Clinton's criticisms of a rap song encouraging black violence against whites. There is a general suspicion these days, not unfounded, that white evangelicals will support one agenda and nonwhite evangelicals will support another, but both in the name of God, both claiming proof texts for support. In short, Christian involvement in the public square these days is predictable—not because the increasingly secular society knows its Bible, but because it knows which secular "powers that be" each side of the Christian divide answers to.

What we need in our day is a fresh encounter with the Word of God, and in particular, with this commandment: "You shall not murder." On the face of it, it is hardly an earth-shattering decree; and yet from this single commandment a stream of biblical themes are woven from Genesis to Revelation. By returning to these rich biblical themes, we may be able to gain the wisdom necessary to transcend the reductionistic worldview of our politicized culture and love our neighbor in a distinctively Christian manner.

BEYOND SINGLE-ISSUE POLITICS

Christians are called to be captive to the Word of God, not to the passing ideologies of this world. In the sixties, the mainline churches took the prohibition against murder as a direct verdict on the Vietnam War. It was as though there was no other application of the commandment, certainly not to abortion, in the wake of *Roe v. Wade*. But many of the conservative evangelical churches since the seventies have treated the sixth commandment as though abortion were the only application. Since most readers of this volume will be sensitive to the concerns over abortion-on-demand, I want to argue a broader biblical understanding of this commandment.

Think of other issues involving the doctrine of the image of God. It is the motivation behind our concern for the victim of a savage murder; our horror at seeing children searching for food in garbage bins behind a restaurant while their mothers hold up signs that read "Will Work for Food and Diapers." It is that conviction that breaks our heart when we see a prostitute selling her body to keep alive, while others (including those who participate in the same industry through pornography and other forms of sexual entertainment) pour shame and contempt on them. It is that conviction, that religious belief, that binds us to our neighbors and to their interests, regardless of whether they are believers or share our values or our ethnic, cultural, or linguistic heritage.

Evangelicals in other parts of the world are often baffled by the political agenda of some of their American brothers and sisters: pro-life and pro-family, yet opposed to any restrictions on fire arms and generally unsympathetic to the problems of the inner cities. In America, the wealthiest nation on earth, one child in five is poor. We may be anti-abortion, but are we really pro-life?

Evangelicals rightly protest the murder of the unborn and decry the silence of those who refuse to defend those who have no voice to defend themselves. Nevertheless, silence hovers over the same impassioned group when children die senselessly after they're born. Shouldn't this be an outrage of equal proportions? Isn't life *life*? Or are we just caught up in the glitz and glamor of political debates? *Are we pro-life?*

In the nation that prides itself on being the most religious, church-going country, violent deaths are twenty times that of Western Europe and forty times that of Japan. The United States has won the dubious title "Most Violent Nation on Earth." These contradictions exist, at least in part, because there is an underlying contradiction in our own thinking as Christians. We believe that religion has to do merely with external morality and codes of conduct, not with responsibilities to one's neighbor. Thus, while white evangelicals claim to be "pro-life," they are more likely than any other group to oppose living next door to a nonwhite person.[3] When listing their causes in order of importance, they support the right of every person to own even sophisticated automatic weapons above the concern for basic human rights,[4] and many place concern for social justice and environmental stewardship at the bottom of the agenda, something reserved for radicals and extremists.

Until Christians put their theology first, their activism will be little more rationally motivated than that of Hare Krishnas passing out flowers in airports. We will be moved along, one issue at a time, by charismatic and energetic talk-show hosts, politicians, and religious leaders, and our internal contradictions (such as calling ourselves "pro-life" when in truth we rarely speak up for the poor and oppressed after they're born) will not win for evangelicalism respect in the eyes of the world even for having the courage of its convictions. What convictions? Activism, agendas, ideology: In the sixties, these were left-wing and called the "social gospel"; in the nineties they are right-wing and called "discipleship." Activism, agendas, and practical involvement mean nothing without convictions, and convictions come from deeply held beliefs about God and ourselves. And that is theology.

The authors of *The Day America Told the Truth*, after exhaustive surveys, concluded, "Americans wrestle with these questions in what often amounts to a moral vacuum. The religious figures and scriptures that gave us rules for so many centuries, the political system that gave us our laws, all have lost their meaning in our moral imagination."[5] Each special interest vies for public support, including the evangelical community, and there is little sense anymore of what God requires of us in terms of our relationships.

That is why we must begin, not with social issues, but with biblical themes. Instead of deciding on a set of core issues and then going to the Bible for support, we must develop a concern for God's concerns and search the Scriptures to find where He places the heaviest emphases. We must discern our role in personal and practical—not just political and ideological—terms and must distinguish clearly between the role of the church (purely Word and sacrament) and that of the individual Christian. Finally, we must begin to see our duty in one-on-one terms, not just in political categories.

WHAT IS THE SIXTH COMMANDMENT?

Martin Luther, a former monk, was no friend of the monastic way of life. When he was released from the bondage of climbing the ladder to heaven by piety, he saw his place in the world as one of service—not to himself, but to his neighbor. Instead of trying to save his own soul, he was now concerned with issues beyond himself. The monks, however, lived in their own subculture, wasting much of their time on their own private spirituality. Godliness, Luther insisted, was not a self-serving, individualistic pursuit, but a means of glorifying God by serving others. That is why the German reformer explained the sixth commandment in the following manner:

> This commandment is violated not only when a person actually does evil, but also when he fails to do good to his neighbor, or, though he has the opportunity, fails to prevent, protect, and save him from suffering bodily harm or injury. If you send a person away naked when you could clothe him, you have let him freeze to death. If you see anyone suffer hunger and do not feed him, you have let him starve. Likewise, if you see anyone condemned to death or in similar peril and do not save him although you know ways and means to do so, you have killed him. It will do you no good to plead that you did not contribute to his death by

word or deed, for you have withheld your love from him and robbed him of the service by which his life might have been saved. Therefore, God rightly calls all persons murderers who do not offer counsel and aid to men in need and in peril of body and life. He will pass a most terrible sentence upon them in the day of judgment, as Christ himself declares: "I was hungry and thirsty and you gave me no food or drink, I was a stranger, and you did not welcome me, I was naked and you did not clothe me, I was sick and in prison, and you did not visit me." . . . But everyone should see how the monks mock and mislead the world with a false, hypocritical show of holiness, while they have thrown this and the other commandments to the winds, regarding them as unnecessary, as if they were not commandments but mere counsels. Moreover, they have shamelessly boasted and bragged of their hypocritical calling and works as "the most perfect life," so that they might live a nice, soft life without the cross and suffering. (Large Catechism)

I fear that we modern Christians come perilously close to deserving Luther's criticism. We have abandoned the world in our pursuit of "holiness"—a style of holiness about which God could care less. Fleeing to our evangelical subculture, with its own music, symbols, bumper stickers, activities, and even Christian cruises, we are able to avoid at least some of the suffering and need of our unbelieving neighbors. Our "holiness" is individualistic and selfish, like the monks' of Luther's day, with the greatest attention given to the commandments of men (dancing, drinking, smoking, movie-going). But God's holiness concerns relationships. In other words, my abstinence from secular entertainment may help me, but what does it accomplish for my neighbor?

Biblical holiness is concerned with getting us to love God and neighbor in tangible acts of self-giving, not with entangling us in a web of worries and doubts over whether we have done our duty to a rule. God is more concerned about our care for a neighbor who is hungry than with our making sure we prayed in the restaurant "as a testimony." For the Pharisees, too, had such a set of priorities in their holiness (Matthew 6:5).

Therefore, biblical holiness is a matter of loving God and our neighbor, not of doing homage to a rule. This is why we must only prescribe what God has commanded.

John Calvin spoke in similar terms, referring to the dangers of focusing so much on one's own salvation that the salvation and welfare of one's neighbor is overlooked.[6] Because we are justified by grace through faith alone, apart from works, the question of acceptance before a holy God is settled once and for all. We can get on with the tasks at hand simply out of gratitude rather than fear and slavery.

The Reformers, therefore, saw the Ten Commandments as the prophets and apostles, and our Lord, saw them: as both negative and positive in scope. Negatively, the sixth commandment insists that we not kill another person by thought, word, gesture, or speech, much less in action. But we must not think that just because we have not murdered someone, we have obeyed this commandment. After all, positively, the commandment requires us to do everything in our power to see to the health and welfare of our neighbor. The Heidelberg Catechism asks, "Is it enough then, if we do not kill our neighbor in any of these ways? No; for when God condemns envy, hatred, and anger, he requires us to love our neighbor as ourselves, to show patience, gentleness, mercy, and friendliness toward him, to prevent injury to him as much as we can, and also to do good to our enemies."

But where do we get these definitions? Were the Reformers justified in expanding the sixth commandment beyond the mere taking of another life by physical violence?

THE BIBLICAL IDEA

In the Sermon on the Mount, Jesus clarified the commandment. "You have heard that it was said to the people long ago, 'Do not murder, and anyone who murders will be subject to judgment.' But I tell you that anyone who is angry with his brother will be subject to judgment. Again, anyone who says to his brother, 'Raca,' is answerable to the

Sanhedrin. But anyone who says, 'You fool!' will be in danger of the fire of hell" (Matthew 5:21–22). Pushing the definition even further, Jesus tells the people not to do their temple duties until they are reconciled to their brothers and to settle legal disputes out of court (vv. 23–26). But that is to say nothing of outright enemies. "You have heard that it was said, 'Love your neighbor and hate your enemy.' But I tell you: Love your enemies and pray for those who persecute you, that you may be sons of your Father in heaven" (vv. 43–45). Of course, nowhere in the Old Testament is it written, "Love your neighbor and hate your enemy"; the people had been told this by the religious leaders in their interpretations of the law. Jesus, therefore, was overturning Jewish tradition, not Scripture.

Nevertheless, there was much in the Old Testament to lead the people of God to believe that their enemies and God's were one and the same. Surrounding nations are destroyed by Israel at God's behest because of their false worship and immorality. The Psalmist's "imprecatory" psalms calling fire down on his enemies, too, lend credibility to this tradition of loving one's neighbor but hating one's enemy. A neighbor, then, is someone who is friendly. But Jesus redefines "neighbor" to *include* enemies. Is Jesus at odds with the Old Testament here? Not at all. There are various theocracies (lit., "God-reigns") in redemptive history. In Eden, God rules both worship (vertical) and culture (horizontal) through one representative, Adam. When He establishes Israel as a nation, God rules both spheres once again through one representative, the king. It is the king who cleanses the land of God's enemies and ensures the propriety of divine worship. But apart from these theocracies, God rules through providence rather than miracle, and the two spheres are separated. The City of God is in no way identified or confused with the City of Man, although both interact and contribute to each other in different ways.

Throughout the gospels Jesus announces the dissolution of the Jewish theocracy. The kingdom of God is no longer identified with one single nation. This is the point of many of the parables.

The Gentiles who are grafted into the kingdom of God may be Johnny-come-latelies, but they receive the same promise because it is based on a gift, not on wages (Matthew 20:1–16). One morning, Jesus, being hungry, found a fig tree that had no fruit, and He cursed it: "'May you never bear fruit again!' Immediately the tree withered" (21:18–19). The disciples were fascinated with the miracle, but it clearly pointed to the the nation of Israel. For, in another parable, Jesus says, "A man had a fig tree, planted in his vineyard, and he went to look for fruit on it, but did not find any," so the owner orders, "Cut it down! Why should it use up the soil?" The gardener replied, "Leave it alone for one more year, and I'll dig around it and fertilize it. If it bears fruit next year, fine! If not, then cut it down" (Luke 13:6–9). In other words, the promise of the kingdom is not on the basis of national or ethnic identity any more than a fig tree is safe in the vineyard simply because it is a fig tree. It must produce fruit. There must be faith and repentance, or one is not a child of the promise regardless of his or her race.

In the parable of the two sons (Matthew 21:28–32), the first begins the day in defiance of his father's command to work in the vineyard, but later changes his mind, whereas the second says, "Yes, Father," but does not end up making it to the vineyard. "Jesus said to them, 'I tell you the truth, the tax collectors and the prostitutes are entering the kingdom of God ahead of you'" (v. 31). Those who previously had not received mercy now receive it, while those who simply took it for granted that they were members of God's kingdom are left out of it. And on we could go through the parables of the kingdom.

The point of all of this is to say that Jesus was announcing during His ministry that the kingdom of God had come. If it had come with His arrival, then it could not have been around just prior to that arrival. Its coming presumes its prior absence. In fact, when Micah prophesied that the Messiah would be born in Bethlehem, he added that Israel would be given up "until the time that she who is in labor has given birth; then the *remnant* of His brethren shall return to the children of Israel" (Micah 5:3–4 NKJV, italics added). As I mentioned above, Israel was a theocracy, where both worship (sacrifices, prayer, thanksgiving, religious feasts and celebrations) and culture (politics, the arts, the courts) were bound together in one nation-state, where the City of God and the City of Man were one and the same, ruled by God's representative king. But when Jesus, the King of kings arrived, He declared, "My kingdom is not of this world" (John 18:36). As Abraham and the patriarchs looked for a better land even when they were in Palestine (Hebrews 11:14–16), so Jesus is a better king than David. A heavenly king and a heavenly land, foreshadowed by earthly types: The Old Testament makes sense in the light of the New.

This is how we must explain the apparent contradiction between Jesus and the Old Testament. In the theocracy, where every war was a "holy war," not merely a "just war," the enemies of God were to be driven from the New Eden—Israel. Adam, as the Lord's king in Eden, should have driven the serpent out of the garden, but instead he allowed him to seduce Eve and then himself. God ordered Saul, as His king in Israel, the new theocracy, to destroy the Amalekites, but Saul spared the heathen king Agag and made him a friend of the court. Therefore, God rejected Saul as king (1 Samuel 15:7–26).

But when Jesus brings His kingdom from heaven, all of the earthly types and shadows are fulfilled. The "holy war" this king wages against God's enemies is postponed until He judges and subdues all of His enemies at the end of the age. That is why we read in Revelation 11:15 the angel's announcement "The kingdom of the world has become the kingdom of our Lord and of his Christ, and he will reign for ever and ever." Thus, the kingdom of God began with Christ's first coming, as a mustard seed, and will be consummated at His second coming, when the two kingdoms will merge into one, as Eden and Israel fore-shadowed.

Once we see this distinction between the types and shadows on the one hand, and the reality fulfilled in Christ on the other, we can understand that our Lord was not contradicting the Old Testament. He was simply saying that His kingdom is one of salvation, not of judgment—at least for the time being. So He offers the parable of weeds. An enemy sowed weeds among the wheat in a farmer's field. "When the wheat sprouted and formed heads, then the weeds also appeared." The workers asked the farmer, "Do you want us to go and pull them up?" "'No,' he answered, 'because while you are pulling the weeds, you may root up the wheat with them. Let both grow together until the harvest. At that time I will tell the harvesters: First collect the weeds and tie them in bundles to be burned; then gather the wheat and bring it into my barn'" (Matthew 13:24–30).

In other words, Christ's kingdom is not like David's. It is, for the time being, a kingdom in spiritual rather than physical conflict. There is a struggle for the redemption of men and women, and it is the time for salvation, not judgment (John 3:17). Even in the kingdom, the church, there will be both wheat and weeds, but we are to leave the final judgment to Christ our King at the end of the age. For now, unbelievers and believers must grow up beside each other even in the church, much less in society. Therefore, Jesus is not the "good God" of the New Testament at odds with the "bad, vengeful, violent God" of the Old Testament. Rather, He is the same God, but this is the day of salvation. It is, after all, this same Jesus Christ about whom John the Baptist prophesied:

> And do not think you can say to yourselves, "We have Abraham as our father." I tell you that out of these stones God can raise up children for Abraham. The ax is already at the root of the trees, and every tree that does not produce good fruit will be cut down and thrown into the fire. I baptize you with water for repentance. But after me will

come one who is more powerful than I, whose sandals I am not fit to carry. He will baptize you with the Holy Spirit *and with fire* [judgment]. His winnowing fork is in his hand, and he will clear his threshing floor, gathering up his wheat into the barn and burning the chaff with unquenchable fire. (Matthew 3:7–12, italics added)

The same one who said, "For God did not send his Son into the world to condemn the world, but to save the world through him," said in the very next breath, "But whoever does not believe stands condemned already because he has not believed in the name of God's one and only Son" (John 3:17–18).

Therefore, judgment is inevitable and imminent, but until that final day, it is an era of salvation. That is why Jesus commands us to follow His example of showing love to our neighbor *whether or not that person is an enemy of God's or of ours.* On that last day, all of Christ's enemies will become our enemies and we, like the children of Israel, will be sent out on war horses in a "holy war," with Christ Himself as our military King. But until that day, it is inappropriate to speak or act in terms of victory over God's enemies. This is the age, not of hostility or judgment, but of civility and evangelization; an age of conversion, not of war. If this is not understood, there can be no way of understanding the importance of what Christ said when He commanded His followers to love not only their friends and God's, but even their enemies. And why is this? Jesus Himself explains: "He [God] causes his sun to rise on the evil and the good, and sends rain on the righteous and the unrighteous" (Matthew 5:45). This is the age of common grace, where God rules in *providence* rather than *miracle;* in *mercy* rather than *judgment.*[7] That does not mean that God is overlooking sin, but that He is postponing His sentence. In the meantime, He provides oxygen, food, water, clothing, pleasure, and success to believer and unbeliever alike, without distinction, regardless of how sharply one curses God or of how immorally one lives. That is why Jesus tells us to imitate our heavenly Father's perfection in this matter.

One wonders whether we have moved the Day of Judgment up a bit and taken the matter of pulling up the weeds into our own hands. But this is the brief respite from God's wrath, when even secular humanists are warmly and lovingly called to faith and repentance to join the growing family of God around the table.

If we are really going to love our neighbor, which is the intention of the sixth commandment, we are going to have to love our enemies and the enemies of the gospel. We are going to have to demonstrate that love in tangible ways, not only to brothers and sisters in the faith but to aliens and strangers outside the kingdom, even to those who would just as soon see the church buried. This is the true test. After all, asks Jesus, "If you love those who love you, what reward will you get? Are not even the tax collectors doing that? And if you greet only your brothers, what are you doing more than others? Do not even pagans do that?" (Matthew 5:46–47). In other words, every group looks out for its own kind; each minority group looks after its special interests. Our society is becoming increasingly dominated by special interest groups, each vying for its own piece of the pie, often to the extent that people forget their duty to the whole society. Jesus confronts us here as Christians and says, in effect, "Isn't that the sort of love the pagans have? The kingdom of God commands an attitude much more selfless and far less bigoted than that."

Jesus pushed the point even further in the parable of the Good Samaritan in Luke 10:25–37. A religious leader wanted to know what one must do to receive eternal life, and Jesus, knowing that the leader was an expert in the law who saw the law as a means of achieving righteousness before God, put him to the test by asking him, "What is written in the Law? How do you read it?" We are to love God and our neighbor, the leader replied; that's the law. "'You have answered correctly,' Jesus said. 'Do this and you will live.'"

But of course the point of the encounter was to drive the person to realize that he had not really loved God or his neighbor, and consequently the conversation continued. "But [the leader] wanted to justify himself, so he asked Jesus, 'Who is my neighbor?'" In other words, the leader knew that there were people he did not love as he loved himself, so he reached for the traditional distinction between neighbor and enemy. A neighbor was a friend, someone who was worth being treated well. When the leader asked Jesus, "Who is my neighbor?" it was a rhetorical question, not a genuine one to which he expected a direct answer. It was as though he said, "Sure, but, I mean, who is my neighbor? When you really analyze it, are those people I despise so much really *neighbors?*" By limiting the field of who constituted a neighbor, the leader could fool himself into thinking he had conformed to the law simply because he loved his friends. But as we have seen, Jesus saw that as no different from what pagans do all the time, without the law. It is not love; it is just looking out for the tribe.

Therefore, Jesus told a parable that explained what He meant by "neighbor." A man was traveling from Jerusalem when he was mugged and left for dead. "A priest happened to be going down the same road, and when he saw the man, he passed by on the other side. So too, a Levite, when he came to the place and saw him, passed by on the other side." Jesus did not even have the decency in His parable to include a layperson, so cynical was He concerning the attitudes of the religious leaders toward the needy. "But a Samaritan, as he traveled, came where the man was; and when he saw him, he took pity on him. He went to him and bandaged his wounds, pouring on oil and wine. Then he put the man on his own donkey, took him to an inn and took care of him. The next day he took out two silver coins and gave them to the innkeeper. 'Look after him,' he said, 'and when I return, I will reimburse you for any extra expense you may have.'"

Jesus then asked, "Which of these three do you think was a neighbor to the man who fell into the hands of robbers?" The expert in the law responded, "The one who had mercy on him." This would be similar to a wealthy white person from the suburbs who despised minorities being mugged and beaten up in his own community and a black person from the inner-city looking after him as people in the suburban community, even pastors, passed by. The Samaritans were regarded as half-breeds, partly Jewish and partly Gentile. The irony is that it is the Samaritan, not an orthodox, full-blooded Jew, who is the heroic neighbor in Jesus' parable. This must have been rather offensive to the religious leader.

Thus, again our Lord calls us to understand the wider scope of the commandment. As Luther said, just because we did not mug our neighbor and leave him or her for dead does not mean that we loved the person. "Thou shalt not kill" means much more than the negative, keeping ourselves from physical violence. It also means that we look after the physical and spiritual well-being of our neighbor, a person who may even be an enemy.

HOW IS THIS COMMANDMENT VIOLATED TODAY?

As the Heidelberg Catechism tells us, "In forbidding murder God means to teach us that he abhors the root of murder, which is envy, hatred, anger, and the desire for revenge, and that he regards all these as hidden murder."

In Paul's epistles, this is placed in the categories "Fruit of the Spirit" and "Fruit of the Flesh," because the Holy Spirit is the author of the former and our own fallen, sinful nature is the source of the latter. Not long ago I had a conversation with a Jewish rabbi who said to me, "You know, one of the greatest differences between our two religions is this idea that you've committed a sin just by desiring or thinking it. We believe you have to actually commit the physical act before it's really sin. Otherwise," he concluded with an incredulous chuckle, "we'd be sinning all the time!" "We *are,*" I replied. "That's the whole point." But it is quite natural for us to think legalistically: Because I have not engaged in a violent act, I must be free of this violation.

In the church, these forms of "hidden murder" are tolerated, while we write our own unpardonable sins. Right up there with sexual immorality, idolatry, and witchcraft are "hatred, discord, jealousy, fits of rage, selfish ambition, dissensions, factions and envy" (Galatians 5:19). And yet, it is precisely these sour apples that create the greatest divisions in the body of Christ, destroy relationships, and leave our neighbors in distress. Again, it is relationships that concern God, not rules *as* rules. The commandments are absolutes, but only because they are always and everywhere the only way of regulating human relationships. We owe love to God and to our neighbor, not to our character and to our code of ethics. It is not for ourselves and for our own personal piety that we embrace these commandments, but for the glory of God and good of others.

Therefore, we disobey the sixth commandment by tolerating whatever attitude might produce either active injury or passive apathy toward our neighbor's good. But there are some issues that need to be particularly addressed because of the wide scale on which this commandment is violated by us as Christians in this time and place.

ABORTION-ON-DEMAND

Simply stated, murder is prohibited by law. Even apart from special revelation, natural revelation written on our conscience tells us that it is wrong to take someone else's life. Therefore, the only question is whether the human fetus is a person. That, of course, is the point where the debate becomes heated. On one side, it is argued that the fetus does not enjoy the status of personhood (and is, therefore, unprotected by the Bill of Rights) until it can survive outside the mother's womb. Pro-lifers, however, insist that the fetus is a human being at the moment of conception, when the 23 male and 23 female chromosomes are joined.

From Scripture we have some important hints in answering this question. The moment Adam had consciousness was the moment when the Lord created his soul. Furthermore, according to Israel's civil law, if a pregnant woman or her fetus was injured, it is "life for life, eye for eye, tooth for tooth, hand for hand, foot for foot, burn for burn,

wound for wound, bruise for bruise" (Exodus 21:23–25).
The fetus was treated as possessing the basic human qualities that placed it under the same legal protection as the
mother. In other words, both had an equal right to life.
That caused a moral dilemma, of course, in the cases where
the mother's life was in danger. In those cases, according to
Jewish interpretation of the civil law, the life of the mother
was always a higher priority than the life of the fetus.

Nevertheless, that is comparing life to life. In the case
of abortion-on-demand, all but a small percentage are performed when the comparison is not between life and life,
but between life and a lesser value, such as personal happiness, material well-being, and even psychological health.
Of course, these are difficult decisions to make, but the tragedy of the circumstances never justifies the highest act of
violence—murder.

HOMELESSNESS AND STARVATION

That, of course, does not mean that abortion is the
only way in which we participate in murder. Too often, we
evangelicals these days are inconsistent on this matter of
being pro-life. We rightly struggle for the oppressed *before*
they are born, but surely they are not less human *after* they
are brought into the world. As Luther said, "If you send a
person away naked when you could clothe him, you have let
him freeze to death. If you see anyone suffer hunger and do
not feed him, you have let him starve" (Large Catechism).
This, of course, is the force of our Lord's remarks in Matthew 25, where the sheep and goats are separated, the former placed on the King's right hand, the latter on his left:

> Then the King will say to those on his right, "Come,
> you who are blessed by my Father; take your inheritance,
> the kingdom prepared for you since the creation of the
> world. For I was hungry and you gave me something to eat,
> I was thirsty and you gave me something to drink, I was a
> stranger and you invited me in, I needed clothes and you
> clothed me, I was sick and you looked after me, I was in
> prison and you came to visit me."

Then the righteous will answer him, "When did we see you hungry and feed you, or thirsty and give you something to drink? When did we see you a stranger and invite you in, or needing clothes and clothe you? When did we see you sick or in prison and go to visit you?"

The King will reply, "I tell you the truth, whatever you did for one of the least of these brothers of mine, you did for me."

Then he will say to those on his left, "Depart from me, you who are cursed, into the eternal fire prepared for the devil and his angels. For I was hungry and you gave me nothing to eat, I was thirsty and you gave me nothing to drink, I was a stranger and you did not invite me in, I needed clothes and you did not clothe me, I was sick and in prison and you did not look after me."

They also will answer, "Lord, when did we see you hungry or thirsty or a stranger or needing clothes or sick or in prison, and did not help you?"

He will reply, "I tell you the truth, whatever you did not do for one of the least of these, you did not do for me."

Then they will go away to eternal punishment, but the righteous to eternal life. (vv. 34–46)

First, notice that Jesus so identifies with the needy that whatever is done to or for them, He considers as something done to or for His own person. It is not because there is a "spark of divinity" or a bit of Jesus in everybody; nor is it because the poor are somehow more righteous than the rich. Rather, it is because Jesus regards Himself as the lord and liberator of all aspects of human life, not just that narrow strip we call "spiritual" or "religious" life. He does not merely want to save our soul but, as the resurrection guarantees, intends to save our bodies as well for all eternity.

Notice also from this text that both groups have failed to make the connection between their duty to their neighbor and their duty to God. Nevertheless, the sheep, regenerated by God's Spirit, have been enabled to love their neighbor, whereas the goats, although they claim to be disciples of Christ, have not seen love of their neighbor as an aspect of their Christian discipleship. Discipleship for them was merely commitment to tithing, prayer circles, accountability and Bible study groups, witnessing and other "spiritual" activities. That is why the "goats" are so surprised at the Lord's words. They thought they had pulled it off; they thought their discipleship was enough to earn them right-standing with God. It is a scene not unfamiliar to those who had heard our Lord's statement earlier, in Matthew 7:21–23:

> Not everyone who says to me, "Lord, Lord," will enter the kingdom of heaven, but only he who does the will of my Father who is in heaven. Many will say to me on that day, "Lord, Lord, did we not prophesy in your name, and in your name drive out demons and perform many miracles?" Then I will tell them plainly, "I never knew you. Away from me, you evildoers!"

Discipleship, for these people who really believed they were serving the Lord, was a matter of great, spectacular displays of spiritual power and zeal, including prophesying, driving out demons, and performing miracles in the name of Jesus. And yet, this is not where God's heart lies in terms of true discipleship. In Isaiah 58, God takes Israel to task for setting aside the commandments requiring service to neighbor, even while religious services and zeal flourish. "'Why have we fasted,' they say, 'and you have not seen it? Why have we humbled ourselves and you have not noticed?'" (v. 3). We are prone to setting up our own acts of piety and spiritual devotion and wonder sometimes why God is not "blessing" us for our extraordinary discipleship. But God answers, in verse 4, "Yet on the day of your fasting, you do as you please and exploit all your workers. Your fasting ends in quarreling and strife, and in striking each other with wicked fists. You cannot fast as you do today and expect your voice to be heard on high." And then, as though God were coaxed into laying His frustrations on the line, He declares:

Is this the kind of fast I have chosen,
  only a day for a man to humble himself?
Is it only for bowing one's head like a reed
  and for lying on sackcloth and ashes?
Is that what you call a fast,
  a day acceptable to the LORD?

Is not this the kind of fasting I have chosen:
to loose the chains of injustice
  and untie the cords of the yoke,
to set the oppressed free
  and break every yoke?
Is it not to share your food with the hungry
  and to provide the homeless with shelter—
when you see the naked, to clothe him,
  and not to turn away from your own flesh and
    blood? . . .

If you do away with the yoke of oppression,
  with the pointing finger and malicious talk,
and if you spend yourselves in behalf of the hungry
  and satisfy the needs of the oppressed,
then your light will rise in the darkness,
  and your night will become like the noonday.
                              (vv. 5–7, 9–10)

I cannot help but take this to heart at a time when there is so much talk about culture wars between Christians and non-Christians in this nation. Since when is Christianity a culture? It is at its best when it is "salt" and "light," and at its worst when it is a culture. A cursory glance at church history will bear that out. Like the Israel of Isaiah's prophecy, we engage in fasts God has not chosen, while we ignore "the yoke of oppression" and engage in "the finger-pointing and malicious talk" that keeps us from spending ourselves "in behalf of the hungry" and satisfying "the needs of the oppressed." Why is our witness so bleak and dark right now? Of course, it is, before all else, a failure to proclaim the biblical gospel clearly and faithfully. But it is also because we have not chosen God's path of discipleship and have created our own values and priorities.

Why does the world show so much contempt for the church right now? Is it because of the gospel? Why is the culture so devoid of values? It is not because we do not have prayer in schools, when we hardly pray with our own children at home, and not because we do not have the Ten Commandments in the classrooms, when most evangelicals themselves cannot name half of them. "If you do away with the yoke of oppression, with the pointing finger and malicious talk, and if you spend yourselves in behalf of the hungry and satisfy the needs of the oppressed, *then* your light will rise in the darkness, and your night will become like noonday" (vv. 9–10, italics added).

Two things are required for reformation in our church and the transformation of our society. First, the gospel. This comes when people stop trusting in any and every form of law-keeping, discipleship, or whatever they want to call it, as a means of establishing peace or fellowship with God. As we have seen, Christ's demands for salvation-by-discipleship are so high that only the most self-deluded soul would attempt it. But having been saved by Christ's discipleship, death, and resurrection alone, we do enter that high calling of discipleship ourselves. So first we need the gospel, to truly bring us into a right relationship with God. Apart from the gospel, the law can only condemn, oppress, and threaten. But once we are justified by grace apart from obedience, that same grace gives us the power to live a new life—not a perfect life, but a new life. What we need, then, is a recovery of the greatness of God's law, first, to cut our foolish pride off at the pass and cause us to despair of our own efforts at pleasing God, and then, second, to remind us of what true discipleship really is once we become God's children by His free adoption. For both our justification and our sanctification we desperately need to recover *God's* idea of holiness, *His* standard for right relationships, because, quite frankly, it seems to bear only slight resemblance to the personal and social piety of evangelicals in America today.

"HIDDEN MURDER"

The Heidelberg Catechism spoke of the "fruit of the flesh," in Galatians, as "hidden murder." Gossip, slander, back-biting: these are often tolerated in Christian circles where the slightest off-color joke would bring reprisals. Instead of bearing each other's burdens, we seem too often to revel in them. That, of course, is part of our fallen nature: to take some secret delight in the misfortune of others, perhaps to comfort ourselves.

Nevertheless, this commandment challenges us to pull this weed up by its roots. And one way we do this, again, is by appealing to biblical theology. First, we are all (non-Christian and believer alike) created in God's image, and this means that we must regard each other as possessing a divinely assigned dignity that does not depend on personal character or actions. James observes, "With the tongue we praise our Lord and Father, and with it we curse men, who have been made in God's likeness" (3:9). How can we, in one breath, make some racist slur or gossip about our neighbor and then sing hymns to the God who created those very people in His own image? Isn't it hypocritical to use the same lips to recite John 3:16 that we use to judge our neighbor? This is why I was disturbed, but not surprised, to see the Gallup report indicating that evangelicals were the most likely of all religious groups to object to black or Hispanic neighbors.[8]

We all think more highly of ourselves than we ought; and we extend this to our family, then to our group, then to our race, until we have created rings of collective narcissism. We all do that, regardless of whether we are black, white, Hispanic, Asian, rich or poor, old or young. It is part of original sin to form cliques where we not only share the comfort of things in common, but the evil of shared self-love. Calvin wrote,

> Say that your enemy does not deserve even your least effort for his sake; but the image of God, which recommends him to you, is worthy of your giving yourself and all your pos-

sessions. Assuredly there is but one way in which to achieve what is not merely difficult but utterly against human nature: to love those who hate us, to repay their evil deeds with benefits, to return blessings for reproaches (Mt. 5:44). It is that we remember not to consider men's evil intention, but to look upon the image of God in them. . . .[9]

After all, Calvin concluded,

Our neighbor bears the image of God: to use him, abuse him, or misuse him is to do violence to the person of God who images himself in every human soul, the Fall notwithstanding. . . . Not only do I despise my flesh when I wish to oppress someone, but I violate the image of God which is in me."[10]

A second doctrine to which we must appeal in this regard is the Fall. Christians are sinners before and after their conversion. Gossip, therefore, misunderstands the basic fact that every one of us has something that could be the matter of public gossip on any given day, were it out in the open. Think of some of the sins you have committed just this week in thought, word, deed, and desire. What if they were played on a giant screen for all of your friends and neighbors to view? Every time we engage in gossip, we are presuming a weakness in others that we do not regard in ourselves, and that is a failure to take our own sin seriously enough.

Third, redemption must be seen as a corrective teaching in this area. Christ is in the business of conforming us to His image and of restoring the original image of God in us, not of destroying us. Redemption, in this sense of progressive sanctification, is never final until we stand before God glorified. We are always "simultaneously justified and sinful." Therefore, "Do not judge, or you too will be judged. . . . Why do you look at the speck of sawdust in your brother's eye and pay no attention to the plank in your own eye?" (Matthew 7:1, 3). Gossip, slander, and other roots of "hidden murder" depend largely on how we *view* other people. That, in turn, determines how we *relate* to them.

If we recovered the doctrine of the priesthood of all believers, we might gain a greater level of integrity in our relationships. I like to gossip just as much as the next guy, but when we get the urge to let our tongues run wildly, passing on the latest news, we should remember our calling and the duty required by ministers. Like psychologists, priests have a unique relationship of confidentiality, recognized even by the courts in the case of a client or parishioner committing a crime. No wonder we do not let others bear our burdens and confess our sins to each other these days—it could be devastating! But if we had a sharp and abiding sense that we were priests to each other, perhaps that would curb our tongues and recover a sense of duty to confidentiality in our relationships.

CONCLUSION

This commandment reminds us once more that God is much more concerned with how we relate to others than with codes of conduct. His law is concerned more with how we help others grow, than with how we help ourselves grow. Our spiritual and physical well-being is included, but subordinated to the good of God and neighbor.

Those of us who think that we can conform to God's righteousness must only see Christ's radical demands as the "impossible dream." These demands ought to make us squirm in our seats and cause us to give up trying to please God. But for those who have given up on using these demands as a means of achieving righteousness (that is, right standing) before God, the sixth commandment, with all of its implications, becomes a challenge that the indwelling Holy Spirit takes up with delight and pleasure.

The Reformers remind us that being set right with God leads to radical liberation of human relationships as well. Many white Christians in South Africa realized that they could not share communion with their black brothers and sisters on Sunday and then sit silently by as these same brothers and sisters were victims of systematic oppression and violence. We cannot, ultimately, separate our relationships in church from our relationships in general. We stand in solidarity with suffering people of every race, class, and creed—Christian or not—because this is God's will, and for no other reason. In the words of one of the leading Reformed advocates of justice in South Africa, John de Gruchy, "The liberating Word of justification and the liberating Word of justice are thus brought together in Jesus Christ in such a way that while they are not confused, neither are they separated."[11]

Although we will fail and will never conform to the law perfectly in heart, mind, and action, the new life God has secured for and has given to us in Christ is not merely a potentiality for the believer that he or she must somehow actualize. The same faith through which we were justified communicates to us all of the spiritual blessings of Christ. In Him we were crucified, buried, and raised to newness of life (Romans 6), and in spite of failure the believer has the certainty that a different kind of life belongs to him or her than that which he or she possessed before. Loving our neighbors in a radical way that causes the world to seek out the source of our liberation—the impossible dream? Only if we are seeking peace with God by it. For, in Christ, it is a dream come true. Let us not just *tell* our cynical, hostile neighbors; let us *show* them.

NOTES

1. John Calvin, *Institutes of the Christian Religion*, 1.15.3.
2. George Gallup and James Castelli, *The People's Religion* (New York: Macmillan, 1989), 188.
3. Ibid.
4. James Patterson and Peter Kim, *The Day America Told the Truth* (New York: Plume, 1992), 32.
5. Ibid.
6. John Calvin, in *A Reformation Debate*, ed. John Calvin and Jacopo Sadoleto (Grand Rapids: Baker, 1976), 84.
7. Gallup and Castelli, *The People's Religion*, 188.
8. Calvin, *Institutes*, 3.7.6.

9. Quoted in John Leith, *Calvin's Doctrine of the Christian Life* (Grand Rapids: Baker, n.d.), 191.

10. John W. De Gruchy, *Liberating Reformed Theology: A South African Contribution to an Ecumenical Debate* (Grand Rapids: Eerdmans, 1991), 86.

CHAPTER EIGHT

'TIL DEATH US DO PART

*You shall not
commit adultery.*

Every age since the Fall in Paradise has been able to say, with Dickens, "It was the best of times; it was the worst of times." Whereas there has never been an era so bleak that there were no signs of God's common grace and providence, there has yet to be an age so noble and heroic that could be justly regarded as a Golden Age. In the supposed "Golden Age" of ancient Greece, abortion, violent crime, poverty and excessive luxury, political and judicial corruption, and sexual license were standard fare. At the dawning of the Reformation, the evangelical Reformers lamented the moral corruption of medieval life, locating the source of the cesspool in the cell of the monk who had supposedly escaped the world's entanglements and carnal passions in his pursuit of a false holiness. And the Puritans cried out against the misuse of the very gifts of that Reformation for private ambition within a church they saw as only "halfly reformed."

In our own time, justly celebrated for its technological and scientific advances, we have proved once again that cleverness and knowledge, mastery of technique and mastery of self, sophisticated use of tools and sophisticated use of wisdom do not always require each other's company. Now, there is a great deal of talk about a moral revival and a return to "traditional American values," although the precise nature of those values remains somewhat undefined. And no wonder there is such talk. More than half of our nation's men and a third of the women engage in extramarital affairs. And yet, once again, we have to ask some searching questions of our own Christian community. Just as the monks complained about the immorality of those who lived in "worldly, secular occupations" at the same time they, as a group, were viewed as immoral, we must be sensitive to the ironies our secular contemporaries see in our moral behavior. There is, of course, no use in dragging up the memory of the scandals of the televangelists, which seem to be ongoing. Nevertheless, we seem to forget that, from Sister Aimee Semple McPhereson to Billy James Hargis to the current affairs of average preachers all across our nation, there is a general perception that those who do the most talking about morality and spend the most time finger-pointing are among the most corrupt in their private lives.

Ironies abound. George Barna reports, "Over the years, surprisingly little research shows evidence that the lifestyles of born-again Christians differ from those of nonbelievers, apart from involvement in religious activities. . . . In nonreligious activities, the profile was nearly identical among believers and nonbelievers."[1] In fact, even though MTV, in addition to offering hours of mindless images, exhibits some of the most sexually explicit eroticism on television, surveys indicate that Christian young adults watch more of this network's programming than non-Christians.[2] Once again, it would appear that the very group that is the most vocal about "traditional values" in the public arena is itself confused as to what those values are. For instance, two-thirds of Christians surveyed by Barna saw divorce as "a reasonable solution to a problem marriage," and "nearly half (45 percent) of the Christians interviewed stated that the children produced by unhappy marriage partners should not serve to keep the family intact."[3] Thus, Barna observes, "although Christians believe that marriage is intrinsically an important institution, they are buckling under the social and economic pressures that have challenged marital relationships and child-rearing obligations."[4]

Earlier I mentioned how it is often the case that Christians themselves are at least perceived as those who prescribe one rule for society and another for themselves. We all violate God's commandments, but the statistics reveal that many modern believers do not even know what those commandments involve or why they consider such relationships so essential. Perhaps we should get our own house in order before launching campaigns against worldliness in the world. These surveys reveal much more than moral failure; it is a shift in basic attitudes and beliefs. Therefore, it is vital that we recover the essence of the seventh commandment: its nature, purpose, and far-reaching implications. Before we change the way we act, we must change the way we think.

WHAT IS ADULTERY?

Like those of our Lord's day, many Christians today think of sin in legalistic, technical terms. It is something I *did* on such-and-such-a-day. Growing up in fundamentalism, we would sometimes tell each other about teenage sexual exploits with the caveat, "But we didn't actually have sex." Alas, we didn't cross that technical line from clinical virginity to "immorality." When I went to an evangelical college, I heard the same stories. "Where do *you* think the line is?" we would ask each other. And most often, we would offer the answer that happened to coincide with the limits of our own experience. Legalists are concerned about "lines," whereas Scripture regards sin, first and foremost, as a *condition* and only secondarily as an *act*.

Beyond "lines," then, adultery is a matter of the heart.

That being the case, who among us can stand when this commandment is read? Legalists are concerned with keeping their record intact, but the biblical definition of adultery renders that a self-righteous pipe dream for all of us. As Calvin commented regarding this commandment, "the hypocrisy" of the monks "is quite stupid—to make lust no sin, until assented to by the whole heart. But there is no wonder that the sin is so watered down by them, for you would expect that sort to be unintelligent and careless in reckoning sins, who ascribe righteousness to the merits of works."[5] In other words, those who place their confidence in their own righteousness eventually have to rationalize their sin and downplay its seriousness.

Once again, we are transported to the hill where Jesus gave His famous sermon.

> You have heard that it was said, "Do not commit adultery." But I tell you that anyone who looks at a woman lustfully has already committed adultery with her in his heart. . . . It has been said, "Anyone who divorces his wife must give her a certificate of divorce." But I tell you that anyone who divorces his wife, except for marital unfaithfulness, causes her to become an adulteress, and anyone who marries the divorced woman commits adultery. (Matthew 5:27–28, 31–32)

As with the other commandments on which our Lord elaborated, here He is not at odds with Moses but with the Pharisaical and scribal tradition of interpretation. What did God actually command in the Old Testament prohibition of adultery and divorce?

In Deuteronomy 24, the guidelines are clearly defined:

> If a man marries a woman who becomes displeasing to him because he finds something indecent about her, and he writes her a certificate of divorce, gives it to her and sends her from his house, and if after she leaves his house she becomes the wife of another man, and her second husband dislikes her and writes her a certificate of divorce, gives it to her and sends her from his house, or if he dies,

then her first husband, who divorced her, is not allowed to marry her again after she has been defiled. That would be detestable in the eyes of the LORD. Do not bring sin upon the land the LORD your God is giving you as an inheritance.

If a man has recently married, he must not be sent to war or have any other duty laid on him. For one year he is to be free to stay at home and bring happiness to the wife he has married. (Deuteronomy 24:1–5)

We often think of the Pharisees as one unified group, set against the more liberal Sadducees. But by the time of Christ, the Pharisees had divided into two schools: the Shammai and the Hillel. According to the Shammai school, this passage from Deuteronomy should be interpreted to exclude all divorce except in the case of adultery, whereas the Hillel Pharisees broadened the possibilities of divorce to include any dissatisfaction the husband might have with his wife. We must be careful to note that this was a one-way street: the husband could divorce the wife for any reason, but the wife enjoyed no such privilege, according to the Hillel tradition. It is obvious from our Lord's response to the Pharisees on this point that the Hillel interpretation had gained the upper hand by this time. Therefore, what Jesus was challenging was not the commandment in Deuteronomy, which requires "uncleanness" or "indecency"—in other words, sexual infidelity—to be the only ground of divorce. During Moses' time, men were divorcing their wives for any reason at all, leaving them on the streets, to be victims of ridicule or even of stoning, since this was the prescribed civil penalty for adultery and, without a certificate of divorce, a rejected wife had no legal defense.

Martyn Lloyd-Jones comments in this regard:

In those days, you remember, the men generally had a very low and poor view of women, and they had come to believe that they had a right to divorce their wives for almost any and every kind of frivolous and unworthy reason. . . . The Mosaic legislation, therefore, was introduced in order to regularize and control a situation that had not only become chaotic, but was grossly unfair to women, and which, in addition, led to untold and endless suffering on the part of both women and the children. . . . All the various excuses which men had been using and bringing forward were now prohibited. Before he could obtain a divorce, a man had to establish that there was some very special case, described under the title of uncleanness. He not only had to prove that, he had also to establish it in the sight of two witnesses. Therefore, the Mosaic legislation, far from giving a number of excuses for divorce, greatly limited it.[6]

Furthermore, as Jesus pointed out later when the Pharisees questioned Him again on divorce, "Moses permitted you to divorce your wives because your hearts were hard. But it was not this way from the beginning. I tell you that anyone who divorces his wife, except for marital unfaithfulness, and marries another woman commits adultery" (Matthew 19:8–9), rooting marriage in the original covenant between Adam and Eve: "Haven't you read that at the beginning the Creator 'made them male and female,' and said, 'For this reason a man will leave his father and mother and be united to his wife, and the two will become one flesh'? So they are no longer two, but one. Therefore what God has joined together, let man not separate" (vv. 4–6).

The legalistic Pharisees were concerned with bits of paper—legal documents, which a husband could easily obtain with their permission for almost any reason, the Hillel tradition ruling the day. What Jesus is opposing is this legalistic view of marriage. Adultery may dissolve a marriage because sexual intercourse is God's ordained means of joining two flesh into one. Sexual infidelity breaks the bond between a husband and wife, but apart from this unfaithfulness, the union is intact and cannot be dissolved simply because of dissatisfaction or incompatibility. Therefore, a more important question than "What is adultery?" is "What is marriage?"

THE MARRIAGE COVENANT

As we have seen, God relates to us *covenantally*. That

is, He makes unconditional promises to us and, based on *His* resolve and commitment to that covenantal relationship, we submit ourselves to Him in love and obedient service. So strong is this covenantal bond that, "If we are faithless, he will remain faithful, for he cannot disown himself" (2 Timothy 2:13). "I will be their God," He declares, "and they will be my people" (Ezekiel 37:27).

Likewise, God calls us to enter into covenantal relationships with other human beings, the foundational among them being marriage. If there is a breakdown on this level, it is sure to have a ripple effect throughout other social relationships. Here, community and self-giving commitment to our neighbor begins. As charity begins at home, so also does vice.

However, marriage is not a sacrament, as the Roman Catholic Church teaches. It is a *creation*, not a *redemption*, ordinance. It was given to all of humanity at creation, not merely to Christians. Sometimes this fact is obscured by the practice of having weddings in church buildings. Although there is nothing wrong with that practice, it must not be allowed to give us the impression that somehow Christian marriages are in a different class.

Although we must not confuse the common (creation) with the holy (redemption), the New Testament itself illustrates the relationship of the church to Christ by reference to marriage (Ephesians 5). Similarly, we might say that just as earthly gifts such as bread, wine, and water become signs and seals of the covenant God made on our behalf, so too sexual intercourse is the gift God has given for the purpose of sealing the covenant of marriage. This is why Paul demands, "Do you not know that your bodies are members of Christ himself? Shall I then take the members of Christ and unite them with a prostitute? Never! Do you not know that he who unites himself with a prostitute is one with her in body? For it is said, 'The two will become one flesh.'" Therefore, Paul warns, "Flee from sexual immorality. All other sins a man commits are outside his body, but he who sins sexually sins against his own body" (1 Corinthians 6:15–16, 18).

For Christianity, the body is very important. It is neither to be mistreated by severe denial of earthly pleasure, nor to be misused by excessive indulgence. In fact, in his commentary on the Heidelberg Catechism on this very commandment, Ursinus notes that this demand requires temperance, but that intemperance is not merely drunkenness, orgies, and immorality but "*extremes* of temperance . . . , or *too great* abstinence, and such as does not agree with our nature, as the temperance of hermits and superstitious fasts."[7] As monks would commit gluttony before and after a spiritual fast, and engage in some of the most perverted sexual acts while condemning marriage, the Reformers called upon Christians to accept with gratitude the divinely ordained gifts God created for us, by nature, to enjoy. Marriage was God's gift for experiencing the deepest relationship of humanity, and sexual activity outside of this institution is an attempt to enjoy the *pleasure* of this covenant without the *responsibility* of the covenant. The irony, of course, known all too well to those who have been promiscuous, is that the gift itself becomes an empty thing apart from the covenant it is meant to seal.

Thus, the emphasis of Jesus and Paul in these texts, in sharp contrast to the legalistic outlook of the Hillel Pharisees, falls on the covenantal relationship involved with the two individuals becoming "one flesh." In fact, Paul does not even allow for divorce in the case of a Christian married to an unbeliever (1 Corinthians 7). As Lloyd-Jones points out, we ought to take that to heart at a time like ours, when, similar to Moses' and Jesus' day, divorce over incompatibility is so common. If ever there were an argument for incompatibility, surely it would be the case of the believer married to an unbeliever. And yet the Scriptures clearly forbid it as a proper grounds for divorce. Remember, marriage is a covenant of creation, not of redemption. Therefore, a Christian is just as much "one flesh" with an unbeliever as two married believers would be.

Therefore, just as the legalistic approach to fornication is, "How far can I go, technically, without sinning?" so the legalistic attitude in this matter of divorce is, "What legal grounds can I find?" In both cases, God demands that we look beneath the surface, beyond legalistic codes, to the sanctity of relationships, to the divine ordination of covenantal bonds between human beings. Instead of asking "How far can I go?" one should ask, "Am I relating to my neighbor (in this case, my girlfriend, boyfriend, or spouse) as a person created in God's image? Am I honoring this person's body? Am I loving him or her as I would myself?"

"How far can I go?" is a selfish question. It asks, in typical legalistic fashion, "What can I get?" instead of the covenantal question, "What can I give?" If our orientation is legalistic, we will always justify our sin in technical and clinical jargon; if it is covenantal, we will discover that adultery in one case might be a husband confiding in a female friend at work instead of sharing his problems with his wife; in another, giving oneself to one's work to the practical abandonment of one's marital and parental responsibilities. Some unmarried people will discover that they cannot even engage in romantic kissing without it involving lust, whereas another will kiss his or her date in order to express a sense of commitment to and love for that person. Sin is a condition first, then an attitude; only then does it become an action or series of actions. If we view relationships covenantally instead of legalistically, we will at least in principle be better prepared to form proper relationships toward others, rather than merely getting what we legally may from other people.

HOW DO WE VIOLATE THIS COMMANDMENT?

Again, we find ready commentaries on this commandment in the evangelical catechisms. Luther notes the admirable arrangement of the commandments. "First they deal with our neighbor's person. Then they proceed to the person nearest and dearest to him, namely, his wife, who is one flesh and blood with him." In one sense, the seventh commandment is an extension of the previous one: "Thou shalt not kill," which was interpreted as anything that causes injury or fails to protect a neighbor from injury.

Whenever we commit adultery, we sin against God, our own body, the partner in the affair, our spouse, and the partner's spouse. In all, that involves five relationships, if we include ourselves. If the moral law is concerned chiefly with "right relationships," surely this is a form of murder itself. Adultery is not wrong because of the act itself, as though the very fact that we crossed the line were the crime, but because it violates covenants; it destroys relationships established by a good God for our pleasure and thanksgiving.

Thus, Luther adds, "Inasmuch as there is a shameful mess and cesspool of all kinds of vice and lewdness among us, this commandment applies to every form of unchastity, however it is called. Not only is the external act forbidden, but also every kind of cause, motive, and means. Your heart, your lips, and your whole body are to be chaste and to afford no occasion, aid, or encouragement to unchastity. . . . In short, everyone is required both to live chastely himself and to help his neighbor do the same" (Large Catechism).

Calvin concurred: "And let him who does not touch a woman not flatter himself, as if he could not be accused of immodesty, while in the meantime his heart inwardly burns with lust."[8] As Paul advised, it is "better to marry than to burn" (1 Corinthians 7:9). The monks had flattered themselves, like the Pharisees, that they had not "crossed the line." They were, therefore, not adulterers. They, after all, were still, technically speaking, virgins at the time they married. And yet, Jesus makes it clear that inward lust on one single occasion during our lifetime renders us adulterers and strips away from us any confidence in our moral purity, regardless of how tenaciously we have clung to our virginity.

The Heidelberg Catechism offers a number of ways in which we violate the seventh commandment:

108. Q. What does the seventh commandment teach us?
      A. That all unchastity is condemned by God, and that we should therefore detest it from the heart,

and live chaste and disciplined lives, whether in marriage or in single life.

109. Q. Does God forbid nothing more than adultery and
such gross sins in this commandment?
A. Since both our body and soul are a temple of the
Holy Spirit, it is his will that we keep both pure and
holy. Therefore he forbids all unchaste actions, ges-
tures, words, thoughts, desires, and whatever may
excite another person to them.

Once again, however, the Bible assumes a positive as
well as negative aspect to each commandment. As with
murder, where we are commanded not only to refrain
from violence, but to do everything we can to look out for
our neighbor, so with adultery; we are not only to abstain
from sexual immorality, but to remember that before it has
anything to do with us, it has to do with our neighbor. The
Westminster Shorter Catechism asks, "What is required in
the seventh commandment? A. The Seventh Commandment requireth the preservation of our own and *our neighbor's* chastity, in heart, speech, and behavior" (italics
added). Again, the legalist is self-centered, always asking
whether he or she is "in bounds," instead of asking whether he or she is leading the *other person* out of bounds. "Am I
honoring myself?" or "Am I honoring this rule?" is not the
primary question, from the biblical point of view. Even if
we ourselves are acting in a way that does not violate our
conscience, are we leading someone else to violate his or
her own?

Ursinus once again comes to our aid. Positively, the
seventh commandment calls us to (1) mutual love; (2) con-
jugal [sexual] fidelity; (3) community of goods, together
with sympathy in each other's sorrows and misfortunes; (4)
the training and education of children; (5) bearing each
other's infirmities with a desire to remove them.

First, then, there is mutual love. Calvin and other reformers created scandal when they declared that young
people could refuse an arranged wedding. There must be
mutual love for a marriage. It is not merely a legal ar-

rangement, but a union of two people in one flesh. The Scriptures, though not romanticizing or sentimentalizing love and marriage, certainly do not represent it as a Stoic matter of social convenience.

Second, there is sexual fidelity. The Reformers and Puritans interpreted this to mean not only that each spouse had to refrain from extramarital dalliances, but that each owed the other sexual intercourse. Most even considered "sexual abandonment" (a spouse's refusal to engage in sexual intercourse) a form of adultery and allowed for divorce in such cases. Of course, this does not command the temperature of romance in the bedroom. There are obviously happy marriages that do not require tremendous sexual passion, but to deny each other sexual intimacy is to dissolve the covenant in practice, if not in theory. Men are "to love their wives as their own bodies" (Ephesians 5:28), and vice versa.

Third, there is a community of property and sympathy. The wedding service in the older Book of Common Prayer puts it like this: "For better or for worse, for richer or for poorer, in sickness and in health, until death us do part." In some marriages, one partner simply refuses to share—either in the case of material possessions or personal interests, concerns, dreams, problems, hopes, and fears. This can become eventually a form of desertion. Though the husband and wife are both physically present, there is an absence of partnership and genuine covenantal interaction. This is particularly difficult in cases where both partners are strong-willed and put their careers first. The ambition for success and fear of failure makes it dangerous to let one's guard down, for fear of losing the admiration of those closest to oneself. But marriage is one relationship in which we can be free to express ourselves in success and failure, to give ourselves to each other in body *and* soul, in time *and* possessions. In short, "mine" becomes "ours" in marriage, the only form of communism commanded in Scripture. Not only does one's property become the possession of the other person; one's very body belongs to the other.

Fourth, marriage calls for the training and education of children. Ursinus brought this up under the fifth commandment, but raises it again here. Marriage was instituted not only to provide for a proper bond between men and women, but for social reasons as well. A well-run family contributes a certain order and integrity to the broader social relationships. We do, of course, have to be careful here, since there are some fine single parents who have raised their children and provided them an excellent education, but it is difficult to argue with the notion that a caring family environment, with both parents, is the most conducive to the productive education and rearing of children. We even refer to situations in which divorce has tragically disrupted the family as "broken homes."

According to *Newsweek*'s Joe Klein,

> There is a high correlation between disrupted homes and just about every social problem imaginable. According to research compiled by Zinmeister, more than 80 percent of the adolescents in psychiatric hospitals come from broken families. Approximately three out of four teenage suicides "occur in households where a parent has been absent." A 1988 study by Douglas A. Smith and G. Roger Jarjoura showed that "the percentage of single-parent households with [teenage] children . . . is significantly associated with rates of violent crime and burglary.". . . There are other effects. The ability to learn is impaired, especially for boys growing up without fathers.[9]

In committing themselves to each other in covenant, the parents together commit themselves to the joint welfare and education of their children.

Fifth, there is the bearing of each other's infirmities with a desire to remove them. Once again, as adultery is a form of murder, so marriage is a form of protection from injury. Each spouse looks out for the other, with an interest in not only sympathizing with the other's problems, but with a determination to actually do something about them. The husband or wife should not be able to bear to see the other disturbed, troubled, brokenhearted, or unhappy. Adultery may be committed not only by sexual infidelity, but by being preoccupied with someone or something else to the extent that the marriage suffers.

CONCLUSION

Having said all of this, we must return to our opening remarks. Believers must take stock of their own personal lives before they point their fingers at the unbelieving world. Lloyd-Jones warns, "We must start with ourselves; we must start at the beginning, we must observe the law of God in our own personal, individual lives. And then, and then only, will we be entitled to trust nations and peoples, and to expect a different type of conduct and behavior from the world at large."[10]

The "traditional values" campaign of many evangelicals today is at risk of making some serious mistakes, in my estimation. First, it risks confusing the gospel with so-called family values. As we learned, the family was instituted as a creation ordinance, not as a redemption ordinance. There are many happy Mormon families and Hindu, Jewish, Muslim, and agnostic homes. There are also many happy Christians who, for one reason or another, are not married; they must not be regarded as second-class Christians, particularly in the light of New Testament teaching (Matthew 19:11–12; 1 Corinthians 7:32–38).

Second, it risks creating unrealistic expectations of Christian marriages. While I was a student at an evangelical college, we learned from the counseling department that the divorce rate among students who married from the college was higher than the national average. I have witnessed a number of Christian marriages fall apart, and more times than not it has been due, at least in part, to unrealistic expectations. Christians need to be reminded again and again that there is no such thing as "a marriage made in heaven," because we ourselves are all sinners. Christians, as well as non-Christians, should expect the normal sinful attitudes and actions of fallen men and women even in the marriage relationship. The Christian family must not be glorified; there is nothing that makes a Christian home immune to the same insidious sins encountered by non-Christian families. In fact, I have seen a number of cases in which a "traditional Christian family" brought forth neurotic children who had lifelong hang-ups because of an overly strict parent with perfectionistic and performance-oriented expectations. Traditional values, though important, cannot guarantee a healthy environment.

At a time when many Christians in his own country yearned for a Victorian spirituality, C. S. Lewis warned against mistaking traditional values for the actual presence of a healthy environment. In the "The Sermon and the Lunch," in *God in the Dock,* Lewis tells us of an experience he had during lunch at a vicar's house.[11] "'And so,' said the preacher, 'the home must be the foundation of our national life. It is there, all said and done, that character is formed. . . . It is there that we retreat from the noise and stress and temptation and dissipation of daily life to seek the sources of fresh strength and renewed purity . . .'" Lewis observes the reaction:

> And as he spoke I noticed that all confidence in him had departed from every member of that congregation who was under thirty. They had been listening well up to this point. Now the shufflings and coughings began. Pews creaked; muscles relaxed. The sermon, for all practical purposes, was over; the five minutes for which the preacher continued talking were a total waste of time—at least for most of us. . . . I was thinking . . . , 'How can he? how can *he* of all people?' For I knew the preacher's own home pretty well. In fact, I had been lunching there that very day, making a fifth to the Vicar and the Vicar's wife and the son (Royal Air Force) and the daughter (Auxiliary Territorial Service), who happened both to be on leave.

Lewis lays out the conversation before us: The father, the vicar, keeps interrupting the other members of his family; the children protest that he doesn't know what he is talking about and they have logic and the facts on their side. "The father storms; the mother is (oh, blessed domestic queen's move!) 'hurt'—plays pathos for all she is worth. The daughter becomes ironical. The father and son, elaborately ignoring each other, start talking to me. The lunch party is in ruins." And this is all only hours before the vicar's excursus on the romanticism of family life. Lewis comments on the entire episode:

> He [the father, the preacher] keeps on talking as if "home" were a panacea, a magical charm which of itself was bound to produce happiness and virtue. The trouble is not that he is insincere but that he is a fool. He is not talking from his own experience of family life at all: he is automatically reproducing a sentimental tradition—and it happens to be a false tradition. That is why the congregation have stopped listening to him. If Christian teachers wish to recall Christian people to domesticity—and I, for one, believe that people must be recalled to it—the first necessity is to stop telling lies about home life and to substitute realistic teaching. Perhaps the fundamental principles would be something like this. Since the Fall no organization or way of life whatever has a natural tendency to go right. In the Middle Ages some people thought that if only they entered a religious order they would find themselves automatically becoming holy and happy: the whole native literature of the period echoes with exposure of that fatal error. In the nineteenth century some people thought that monogamous family life would automatically make them holy and happy.

The family is, after all, a community of sinners and communicates no innate, magical powers of moral improvement. "But it is the place where there is unconditional love," the preacher prated. Lewis responds, "I do not think this aspect of affection is nearly enough noticed by most popular moralists. The greed to be loved is a fearful thing. Some of those who say (and almost with pride) that they live for love come, at last, to live in incessant resentment." After all, if the need to be loved is our idol, who will be our high priest for that religion? Christian recovery books talk about our being "love cups" that need to be filled, but isn't this the very dangerous kind of language Lewis is pointing out here? A Christian home can become a deeply dysfunctional place where there are unrealistic demands for love, obedience, respect, and sincerity from fellow-sinners. As Lewis concludes, "There is *nowhere* this side of heaven where one can safely lay the reins on the horse's neck." We will always be fighting with our own sins and those of others, especially the sins of those with whom we come into daily and even hourly contact.

Therefore, the home is essential, but is not the panacea for the woes of secular society. There are many very strict, moral, traditional families that are simply unhealthy and unbearable environments. "Home schooling," for some families, may actually contribute to social and psychological damage, while it may be a vastly superior education for others. But we must beware of locating sin in the secular institutions and almost divinizing the home, an institution of creation, not of redemption. When we view the home with the realism our biblical doctrine of sin demands, it can become a place where even sinners such as ourselves can find a web of covenantal relationships and contribute to human community at its most local level.

By the standards of the seventh commandment, none of us is left standing. Fantasizing about a body one sees on the beach; ignoring one's spouse or denying him or her our full sympathy and devotion; using a date as an object rather than a person—we all want to justify ourselves with technical and clinical definitions, but by our Lord's standard, none of us passes the test. Of course, there are other readers who may have actually engaged in the physical act of adultery or who may even now be living in a sinful relationship or series of relationships. We tend to think, partly because of the importance God attached to sexual relationships in creation, a knowledge stamped upon our conscience, that sexual sins are somehow unpardonable, the really unforgivable sins. And yet, while the damage done to relationships—which is the measure of a sin's greatness—is more severe in sexual transgressions, God always has more grace than we have sins (Romans 5:20). Lloyd-Jones offers us a fitting conclusion:

> On the basis of the Gospel and in the interest of truth I am compelled to say this: Even adultery is not the unforgivable sin. It is a terrible sin, but God forbid that there should be anyone who feels that he or she has sinned himself or herself outside the love of God or outside His kingdom because of adultery. No; if you truly repent and realize the enormity of your sin and cast yourself upon the the boundless love and mercy and grace of God, you can be forgiven and I assure you of pardon. But hear the words of our blessed Lord: "Go, and sin no more."[12]

NOTES

1. George Barna, *The Barna Report 1992–93* (Ventura: Regal, 1992), 128.
2. Ibid., 124.
3. George Barna and William Paul Mackay, *Vital Signs: Emerging Social Trends and the Future of American Christianity* (Westchester, Ill.: Crossway, 1984), 13.
4. Ibid.
5. John Calvin, *Commentary on Matthew*, 5:28.
6. Martyn Lloyd-Jones, *Studies in the Sermon on the Mount* (Grand Rapids: Eerdmans, 1984), 254.
7. Zacharius Ursinus, *The Commentary Upon the Heidelberg Catechism* (1852; Phillipsburg, N.J.: Presb. & Ref., n.d.), 592.
8. John Calvin, *Institutes of the Christian Religion*, 2.8.43.
9. Joe Klein, in *Newsweek*, 8 June 1992, 20.
10. Lloyd-Jones, *Sermon on the Mount*, 261.
11. C. S. Lewis, *God in the Dock* (Grand Rapids: Eerdmans, 1957), 284–86.
12. Lloyd-Jones, *Sermon on the Mount*, 261.

CHAPTER NINE

TRUSTING GOD'S PROVISION

You shall not steal.

In the first four commandments, called the First Table of the law, our duty to God is spelled out. We are to honor His name, defend His worship, and proclaim His gospel. And yet, as our Lord's summary proves, our duty to God and our duty to our neighbor are bound together in one common obligation: "'Love the LORD your God with all your heart and with all your soul and with all your mind.' This is the first and greatest commandment. And the second is like it: 'Love your neighbor as yourself.' All the Law and the Prophets hang on these two commandments" (Matthew 22:37–40).

When we misuse God's name or withhold from Him the honor that is due it, when we turn God-centered worship into human-centered entertainment, or when we fail to tell the whole gospel, we steal from God that which properly belongs to Him. But because human beings are created in His holy image, the principle of giving to God His due is carried over to our neighbor. As Calvin pointed out, we owe our neighbor righteousness and justice in our dealings, even if he or she is an enemy, by virtue of the divine image every person bears.[1]

Further, each commandment governing our relationships to our neighbors sets out to protect them. From the biblical point of view, the emphasis falls on responsibilities rather than on the modern obsession with rights. In today's world, every special interest group vies for its rights, even if one group's rights threaten the community or other groups. It is interesting to read Henry Grunwald's remarks in *Time* magazine about our needing "a new psychological climate" based on responsibilities instead of rights. Grunwald makes these suggestions in an article on life in the year 2000 and the need for a revival of faith.[2] The Ten Commandments stress what each of us owes his or her neighbor, not what each of us has a right to expect from them. So, when God commands honor to parents and all in authority, as well as concern for those committed to our charge, he is protecting the value of authority. Without a chain of command, beginning with the family institution, there can be no order. Hence, as C. S. Lewis pointed out, "the alternative to rule is not freedom but the unconstitutional (and often unconscious) tyranny of the most selfish member" of the family.[3] The same, of course, could be said for all social institutions.

The prohibition of murder defends the value of human life; God forbids adultery in protecting the value of marriage and the family; and here the decree against theft requires us to respect our neighbor's right to private property.

THE BASIS OF THIS COMMANDMENT

The Right to Private Property

The prohibition of theft presupposes the right of private property. If it is a crime to take something that belongs to someone else, then surely the offended party has a right to own that which has been unlawfully taken. Nevertheless, we are not left to inferences in this regard. The Bible specifically argues the case for private property as a right that is rooted in creation, not in the benevolence of others, including the state.

In Exodus 22, where we have the application of the Ten Commandments to social relationships, the discussion of private property occupies a prominent place:

> If a man steals an ox or a sheep and slaughters it or sells it, he must pay back five head of cattle for the ox and four sheep for the sheep.
>
> If a thief is caught breaking in and is struck so that he dies, the defender is not guilty of bloodshed; but if it happens after sunrise, he is guilty of bloodshed.
>
> A thief must certainly make restitution, but if he has nothing, he must be sold to pay for his theft.
>
> If the stolen animal is found alive in his possession . . . he must pay back double.
>
> If a man grazes his livestock in a field or vineyard and lets them stray and they graze in another man's field, he must make restitution from the best of his own field or vineyard.
>
> If a fire breaks out and spreads into thornbushes so that it burns shocks of grain or standing grain or the whole field, the one who started the fire must make restitution.
>
> If a man gives his neighbor silver or goods for safekeeping and they are stolen from the neighbor's house, the thief, if he is caught, must pay back double. But if the thief is not found, the owner of the house must appear before the judges to determine whether he has laid his hands on the other man's property. In all cases of illegal possession . . . , both parties are to bring their cases before the judges. The one whom the judges declare guilty must pay back double to his neighbor. (vv. 1–9)

Although we must remember that the civil law (the case-law application of the Ten Commandments to political and judicial affairs) was an aspect of the Jewish theocracy and passed away (along with the ceremonies) with the passing of that theocracy, we may nevertheless learn a great deal here about the value God places on private property.

First, there is the case of outright theft. The principle of restitution is not merely "an eye for an eye," since the thief must pay not only an ox for an ox but also "five head of cattle for the ox and four sheep for the sheep" if the stolen ox or sheep had been slaughtered and sold. Again, these are applications for a specific situation—a theocracy that was primarily agrarian and rural. Farmers and ranchers, and all of the many people they employed, depended on their livestock for their very survival. What capital, stocks and bonds, market investments, savings accounts, IRAs, and Social Security are to modern American society, livestock and agriculture were to the ancient Near East. There were no retirement accounts and no insurance policies one could depend on against theft. Therefore, to steal one's property was to threaten the life of the victim and those who depended on him for their livelihood. Hence, not only did the thief owe *distributive* justice (an ox for an ox, a sheep for a sheep), but *retributive* justice as well. The thief must pay dearly for his violation of his neighbor's right to private property. If the thief could not afford such reimbursement, he became an involuntary employee of the victim—a debtor-slave, until he made full restitution.

The principle involved here is instructive for us. In our modern system, justice is rarely satisfying to the victim. That is due, at least in part, to the fact that we have lost the relational character of justice. It is justice *between neighbors,* not merely the satisfaction of economic claims, that the Bible commands. Biblical justice sought to bring the victim and the criminal into close proximity, face-to-face, so the relationship could be restored. That is not to say that the two parties had to "kiss and make up," or become friends. It was not a sentimental "live and let live" policy. The goal was to mend broken relationships in society.

Imagine a thief breaking into your home, stealing your major appliances. If this happened at night and you really believed your life and that of your family to be immediately threatened, and if in the process of confronting the thief you killed him, you would not be "guilty of bloodshed." However, if the incident happened in broad daylight, where

you had your full wits about you, the self-defense plea would not apply, since life is a higher value than property. You would be guilty of murder (v. 2). Life is too high a price to pay for theft. Hence, the law protected both the victim of theft as well as the life of the thief.

But not all loss of property is due to outright theft. A fire, for instance, whether due to arson or negligence, could destroy one's property and livelihood. In this case, the one who started the fire must make restitution, with the assumption, once again, that if he could not make such restitution immediately, he would become a debtor to the victim until repayment had been made. In today's system, it is too often the case that payment is made to lawyers and insurance companies rather than to victims, removing the parties involved from the process and leaving the impression that justice has not really been served.

The principle involved here ought to make us rethink some of our legal approaches and attempt to bring the parties involved into closer proximity, bringing a sense of satisfaction to the victim as well as to the criminal. The thief must also sense, at the end of the day, that he has made restitution, so that he may go on with his life. And there must be some ethical connection between violating the rights of another person and the punishment that is inflicted. After all, the thief does not owe the state satisfaction, but the injured party. The state is there, not to preserve its own rights or authority, but to use its authority to enforce justice on behalf of the parties involved.

Therefore, the first principle requiring this commandment against theft is the value of private property. No one has the "right" to invade another person's property, use or remove another person's possessions without permission or in any other way deny the rights of others to life, liberty, or property. God has given each of us more than he or she deserves, even if that is no more than "our daily bread." His common grace loans us the very breath we use to curse Him, to complain about His provisions, and to enjoy the fruit of our labor, whether one is a believer or an unbeliever. Therefore, to violate our neighbor's

right to privacy and property is to steal not only from our neighbor, but from the God whose gifts they are.

The Principle of Stewardship

The prohibition against theft rests not only on the value of private property, but also on the principle of God's sovereignty over all that He has created. That means, of course, that our ownership is never ultimate, but derives from God's kind permission.

In the beginning, God placed Adam over the created world, not as a tyrant, but as a steward. Adam was not given Paradise in any sense of ultimate ownership. We must remember that this was in the state of innocence and, had sin not entered the world, there would have been no need to protect rights or mark boundaries of ownership. There would have been no such thing as protecting private property. Only in a perfect world would collectivism be possible, where each person worked together solely for the glory of God and the common good. However, sin necessitated the marking off of boundaries and the institution of civil government to keep neighbors from theft, vandalism, and trespassing.

"The LORD God took the man and put him in the Garden of Eden *to work it and take care of it*" (Genesis 2:15, italics added). It has become a favorite pastime of many environmentalists to blame the exploitation of the earth on classical theism, and in particular, on the cultural mandate God gave Adam to "rule over the fish of the sea and the birds of the air, over the livestock, over all the earth, and over all the creatures that move along the ground" (1:26). God even commanded Adam to "be fruitful and increase in number; [to] fill the earth and subdue it" (v. 28). Does this not justify human exploitation of the creation? On the contrary. The goal of the human reign over creation is "to work it and take care of it" (2:15). Although vegetable and animal life are at human disposal, man is to preserve the integrity of the creation over which God has placed him. The purpose of his dominion is to subdue and rule the

created order the way a parent cultivates the obedience of a child—by looking out for the child's best interest.

This intention is carried right on through the Old Testament. The land itself is to be given a rest from its labor, and God impressed Jonah with His interest in the salvation of Nineveh because "Nineveh has more than a hundred and twenty thousand people who cannot tell their right hand from their left, and many cattle as well. Should I not be concerned about that great city?" (Jonah 4:11). One must assist a donkey under its burden, even if it belongs to an enemy (Exodus 23:5); animals must be allowed to rest as well on the Sabbath (v. 12); the ox must not be muzzled so that it cannot eat some of the corn it treads (Deuteronomy 25:4); and Proverbs 12:10 declares that "a righteous man cares for the needs of his animal."

In Hosea 4, God includes in His charges against Israel the pollution of the waters to the point where the fish are dying. In fact, secular historians, such as Oxford's Keith Thomas, have described those who have taken the biblical tradition seriously also as those who have taken a special interest in and responsibility for the natural world. Thomas observes that the Presbyterian minister John Flavel wrote of a tired horse in 1669,

> What hath this creature done that he should be
> Thus beaten, wounded and tired out by me?
> He is my fellow creature.

In fact, Thomas argues that the Puritans had a much higher view of creation and the environment than their more secular contemporaries, such as Thomas Hobbes. There was a new emphasis upon gardens instead of cloisters: "In post-Reformation literature the enclosed garden was a symbol of repose and harmony. Its flowers and trees were emblems of spiritual truths, its walks and arbours a sort of outdoor cloister. The garden thus became the accepted place for spiritual reflection, in life no less than in literature." For example, Roger Crabb wrote, "When I was in my earthly garden a-digging with my spade, I saw into the Paradise of God from whence my father Adam was cast forth."⁴ Calvin writes of this "dominion" given to man, that

> the custody of the garden was given in charge to Adam, to show that we possess the things which God has committed to our hands, on the condition, that being content with a frugal and moderate use of them, we should take care of what shall remain. Let him who possesses a field, so partake of its yearly fruits that he may not suffer the ground to be injured by negligence; but let him endeavour to hand it down to posterity as he received it, or even better cultivated. Let him so feed on its fruits, that he neither dissipates it by luxury, nor permits it to be marred or ruined by neglect. Moreover, that this economy, and this diligence, with respect to those good things which God has given us to enjoy, may flourish among us; let every one regard himself as the steward of God in all things which he possesses. Then he will neither conduct himself dissolutely, nor corrupt by abuse those things which God requires to be preserved.⁵

Thomas notes of Calvin that he followed both biblical ideas: human lordship over the lower creation and stewardship. "When God placed the beasts 'in subjection unto us,' he explained, 'he did it with the condition that we should handle them gently.'" In fact, "God will not have us abuse the beasts beyond measure," the Reformer wrote, "but to nourish and take care of them." "And if a man says, 'Tush, I care not for it is but a brute beast,' I answer again, 'Yea, but it is a creature of God.'"⁶ Although the Puritans were not against hunting for sport, they insisted that there must be moderation, in order to prevent waste and mismanagement of natural resources; and violence for violence, such as bearbaiting and cockfighting, they outlawed in the Commonwealth.

Although our track record on stewardship of nature may be lacking in this century, the case often made by modern environmentalists against the alleged negative influences of Christianity cannot be maintained. To fail in our stewardship, either in our duty to our neighbor or in our duty to God on behalf of our environment, is to steal from God, from ourselves, from each other, and from future generations.

E. Calvin Beisner was not far off of the mark when he wrote, "Calvin's insights into Scripture's teaching on stewardship became key elements in the transformation of the Western world, enabling it to become more productive—and so to alleviate poverty more fully—than any other civilization in history. Building and conserving an inheritance for descendants, an idea Calvin stressed, was particularly important."[7]

Again and again, God reminds the Israelites that they do not really "own" anything as far as He is concerned, even though there is such a principle neighbor-to-neighbor. When they followed their own texts, the Jews had a profound sense, in sharp contrast to their pagan neighbors, that the whole earth belonged to God and that they were merely custodians. This stewardship applied to fellow-humans and also to fellow-creatures. At the end of every seven years, all debts were canceled. This is because "there should be no poor among you" (Deuteronomy 15:1–4). Again, then, the priority of life over property emerges. "But," one might object, "you have just explained the importance of private property and ownership, and now you're contradicting yourself: If debts are canceled before they are paid, isn't that theft?" And here again God interjects with this second principle: His own sovereignty over all property. Entering into debt with no intention to pay is strictly forbidden, and yet an Israelite is not to be a slave in the land God has given to all His people.

Once again, however, we must see the purpose of the civil and ceremonial laws. These are not given to us as absolute civil commandments for modern democracies, but to the nation of Israel as a theocracy. Their purpose was not merely to organize civil life, but to point to the great redemptive themes they foreshadowed. As there are not to be any slaves in the Promised Land, so too, Paul instructs believers, "You did not receive a spirit that makes you a slave again to fear, but you received the Spirit of sonship. And by him we cry, 'Abba, Father'" (Romans 8:15). We are not slaves, but coheirs of the Promised Land with Christ (vv. 16–17). Our debts have been canceled; we are living in the land, "seated . . . in the heavenly realms in Christ Jesus" (Ephesians 2:6).

Although we ought not to regard the civil legislation as directed to nations other than ancient Israel, we can learn not only from their theological use, but also from their moral implications. The principle in these laws is that God owns the land and all that grows, lives, moves, and works upon it. He will not hold guiltless those who, raising themselves above Himself, rule as tyrants instead of as custodians.

HOW IS THIS COMMANDMENT VIOLATED?

With these two principles guiding our discussion of the eighth commandment, what are some of the principle ways in which we violate it today?

In his Large Catechism, Luther comments that this commandment is violated by "taking advantage of our neighbor in any sort of dealing that results in loss to him." In other words, "a person steals not only when he robs a man's safe or his pocket, but also when he takes advantage of his neighbor at the market, in a grocery shop, butcher stall, wine-and-beer-cellar, work-shop, and, in short, wherever business is transacted and money is exchanged for goods or labor." Luther includes those "who act high-handedly and never know enough ways to overcharge people and yet are careless and unreliable in their work." Luther lamented, "If we look at mankind in all its conditions, it is nothing but a vast, wide stable full of great thieves. These men are called gentlemen swindlers or big operators. Far from being picklocks and sneak-thieves who loot a cash box, they sit in office chairs and are called great lords and honorable, good citizens, and yet with a great show of legality they rob and steal."

But this general condition of great thieving is not the province of the high and mighty alone. Even artisans and people we hire for various jobs

act as if they were lords over others' possessions and entitled to whatever they demand. Just let them keep on boldly
fleecing people as long as they can. . . . The same fate will
overtake those who turn the free public market into a car-
rion-pit and a robbers' den. Daily the poor are defrauded.
New burdens and high prices are imposed. Everyone mis-
uses the market in his own willful, conceited, arrogant way,
as if it were his right and privilege to sell his goods as costly
as he pleases without a word of criticism.

In the tradition of the biblical prophets, Luther adds, "We
shall put up with those of you who despise, defraud, steal,
and rob us. . . . But beware how you deal with the poor, of
whom there are many now." To this end, the civil government must do all within its legitimate power "to establish
and maintain order in all areas of trade and commerce in
order that the poor may not be burdened and oppressed."

Similarly, the Heidelberg Catechism summarizes the
evangelical interpretation of this commandment:

God forbids not only those thefts and robberies which are
punishable by the magistrate, but he comprehends under
the name of theft all wicked tricks and devices whereby we
design to appropriate to ourselves the goods which belong
to our neighbor; whether it be by force, or under the appearance of our right, as by unjust weights and measures,
fraudulent merchandise, false coins, usury, or by any other
way forbidden by God; as also all covetousness, all waste
and abuse of his gifts.

Let us, then, briefly touch on the various ways in
which we violate the eighth commandment, just as surely
today as in any other age since the Fall.

Outright Theft

We often humor ourselves that we are not thieves,
since we have never broken into another person's house or
deliberately planned an illegal scheme. And yet, we even
engage in outright theft in a number of ways.

First, by fraud. I shall never forget a lesson my father taught me when I was eleven years old. I had agreed to clear a neighbor's property of accumulated rubbish and stack wood that had been strewn from one corner of the lot to the other. In the course of the first day, this neighbor watched my every move and looked for every opportunity to criticize my work. Exasperated, I walked off the job on the second day. "If you don't like what I'm doing, Mr. Hanson, you can find someone else to do it!" I said directly. Returning home, expecting to find some sympathy for my protest, I instead found myself being commanded to go back, apologize to Mr. Hanson, and finish the job. "You don't have a right to walk off the job like that," my father said sternly. "You made a deal and he has already paid you for your work." "I'll give him the money back," I replied, but my father was set on this "a deal's a deal" thing and said, "Son, it doesn't matter how difficult he is—you're responsible for *your work,* not for *his attitude.*" Reluctantly, I returned to our neighbor's lot, by now something akin to an escaped convict's returning to a prison camp voluntarily. Mr. Hanson was as difficult as ever, but I finished the job and was rewarded with a sense of having done the right thing.

I wish I could say I have followed my father's advice as closely down through the years, but this is what God requires of us: to fulfill our obligations, to be faithful to our contracts, to pay our debts, and to honor our word. Anything short is fraud, regardless of how much we think the other party "deserves" what we owe.

This brings up the issue of credit-card debt. The postwar generation was enormously productive. The average worker was a saver more than a spender; leisure was simpler, due in part to less technology; and the emphasis fell on work rather than play. Work had meaning in and of itself, not merely as a means to the end of having money to spend for leisure. Credit was viewed as a necessary evil and was considered an extension of the person's name and character. To have poor credit was to have a poor name. Today, in the wake of the credit-card party of the eighties, it has become fashionable to live beyond one's means. The nouveaux riches (new rich) are distinguished from old money families by their ostentatiousness and their colorful display of newfound status.

But to live beyond one's means, one must actually charge items for which one does not expect to pay. Oh, sure, there is the realization that the company will not let the bill go forever, but we will enjoy it now and worry later. This, too, is a form of theft. The creditor assumes that when we charge something, we intend to pay off the debt; but if that responsibility is not assumed by the debtor, there is a breech of contract—fraud, or, if you will, theft. It is not really our hard-earned cash that paid for the item, but the money loaned to us by the creditor. To default on our loans, of course, does not mean merely that we fail to pay for the item, but that we are requiring someone else to pay for it.

The subject of debt is difficult and complicated, and as the Old Testament made provisions for debtors to secure a decent future, so we must not seek to enslave forever those who, for one reason or another, have been unable to meet their obligations. After all, not all unresolved debt is a matter of theft. Sometimes it is due to tragedies (such as medical catastrophes), to ignorance (mismanaged funds), or to unforeseen circumstances (loss of a job and income). But it is essential that we see the economic duty we have to preserve just relationships with our neighbors, even if they seem to us to be uncaring, impersonal corporations.

We can also defraud our neighbor by unjust sales. Charging more than a product is worth has been considered theft in the Christian tradition. And yet, we seem to think that a just price is whatever the market allows. If, for instance, the supply is scarce for a particular item and the demand is high, there is no moral difficulty in charging the top dollar. It's simply "good business," we hear these days —even from Christians. Nevertheless, what may be legal— and even sanctioned by the reigning economic theories of the day—is not necessarily just and right by biblical standards.

Recently I watched an exposé on television of a large retail chain known for its defense of "traditional American values" using child labor in Bangledesh and smuggling more than its trade quota into the States. Christians are obligated to do the right thing, even if the wrong thing isn't illegal. Luther said that the Christian cobbler had a special duty "to make a good shoe and sell it at a fair price." Let not Christians be found among those who gouge the public and charge more than the product is worth, just because they may.

In our discussion of adultery we distinguished between the legalist's concern over lines—what one may get away with, and the Bible's concern with relationships—what one owes the others involved. So here, the question is not, "How much can I get for this item?" but "How much should I charge for this item?" How much is it worth? That does not mean that it is immoral to test market conditions or to include the going price in one's decision on price-setting. But it does mean that one may not charge more than a product or service is reasonably worth simply because "it's the going price."

When the biblical ethic was practiced, it was possible for an average, middle-income person to purchase even fine clocks, furniture, homes, and expect good service at fair wages. Today, comparable goods and services are regarded as delicacies for the rich.

Finally, the Heidelberg Catechism gives us yet another way we commit outright theft, according to Scripture: "Excessive interest." Here again, we are led to believe that if we simply leave the economy to the laws of the market, there will be freedom and justice for all, or at least for most. Yet in recent years there have been times when interest rates were so high that the children of the postwar generation—that is, the children of factory workers who were able to buy their own home—wondered if the American Dream is just that, only a dream. There is a history to the discussion of interest in the Christian church.

Throughout the Middle Ages, most churchmen thought it was a sin to charge interest on any and all loans, based on Exodus 22:25–26:

> If you lend money to one of my people among you who is needy, do not be like a moneylender; charge him no interest. If you take your neighbor's cloak as a pledge, return it to him by sunset, because his cloak is the only covering he has for his body. What else will he sleep in? When he cries out to me, I will hear, for I am compassionate.

This meant, of course, that loaning money was not a lucrative venture for bankers, and only the most daring transgressed the medieval suspicions. Calvin, therefore, forbade interest on loans to the poor and needy but opened the door to minimal interest on loans. The key word is *minimal;* Calvin even established the interest rate in Geneva, since it was considered a moral and theologial issue. The rate was high enough that loaning institutions began springing up in the region, and those who would never have had the possibility of obtaining enough capital to start a small business were given new opportunities. It was justice, not charity. The principle remained, however: the bank must never take advantage by charging high rates of interest simply because of the urgency of a borrower's need.

This is why usury or excessive interest was considered such a crime, not only by the biblical writers, but also by the Reformers. It was taking advantage of a divine gift and was an abuse of liberty by using one's freedom to bring another person into bondage.

STATISM

Regardless of one's political or economic philosophy, there is no doubt that the burden placed on taxpayers in the United States in this last quarter of the twentieth century is driving middle-income individuals into poverty—the very poverty against which higher taxes are supposed to insure taxpayers. The national debt hangs like an albatross around our necks, bound to constrict tighter with the coming generations, as the interest alone on our debt exceeds our current Gross National Product (GNP). All of the evangelical catechisms make some reference to going into debt with no arrangement for reimbursement as a form of theft. The state is instituted by God to preserve order, to maintain public services and defense, and to direct justice. Although the state is authorized to exact taxes, it is no more authorized to steal from taxpayers of today or future generations than is any individual the state is expected to punish for a similar infraction.

The conservative economist M. Stanton Evans notes: "The principal beneficiaries of the money absorbed and dispensed by government are not poor blacks in ghettos or Appalachian whites or elderly pensioners receiving Social Security checks. . . . The major beneficiaries, instead, are the *employees of government itself*—people engaged in administering some real or imagined service to the underprivileged or, as the case may be, the overprivileged."[8] Evans argues that "the gross effect of increased government spending is to transfer money away from relatively low income people—average taxpayers who must pay the bills— to relatively high income people—Federal functionaries who are being paid out of the taxpayer's pocket." As evidence for this, Evans refers to the fact that "the two richest counties in the United States are . . . Montgomery County, Maryland, and Fairfax County, Virginia—principal bedroom counties for Federal workers in Washington, D.C."[9] Ronald Nash, referring to the statement of the prominent black economist Walter E. Williams, that in 1979 the U.S. was spending $250 billion annually "just to fight poverty," responds: "Had this amount of money been distributed equally to all families below the poverty level, each of them would have received an annual payment of $34,000."[10]

In other words, taxes collected for one purpose (the amelioration of suffering and poverty) are actually used for another (the self-perpetuation of a well-paid bureaucracy). That constitutes theft on a national scale.

I am not opposed to government intervention in the break-up of monopolies and trusts, or in legislating and enforcing justice. I believe that the government has not only a negative function (restraining evil), but a positive one as well (assisting in the retraining of the unemployed or unskilled, creating incentives for good business, guaranteeing the basic security of life to the elderly, poor, and disabled). Both negative and positive functions seem clear from Romans 13:1–7, where Paul insists that Christians are to respect even pagan governments. "This is also why you pay taxes, for the authorities are God's servants, who give their full time to governing. Give everyone what you own him: If you owe taxes, pay taxes; if revenue, then revenue; if respect, then respect; if honor, then honor" (vv. 6–7).

The idea of taxation itself is not immoral. Nevertheless, we live at a time when (a) the people presumably determine, through their elected representatives, how their tax dollars will be spent; and when (b) the interest of the people in having their revenues assist the underprivileged is undermined by that money's actually going to the members of a vast overprivileged bureaucracy. Christians must continue to obey the government, but misdirection of public funds (a euphemism for theft) ought to be a matter of some concern to us all.

The Christian walks an ethical tightrope between the right of private property and ownership on the one hand, and the duty of stewardship on the other. Both principles are laid down in Scripture, and both must be given equal attention.

Theft by Implication

As the Catechism pointed out, we not only commit outright theft by "cheating, swindling our neighbor by schemes made to appear legitimate, such as: inaccurate measurements . . . , fraudulent merchandising; counterfeit money, and excessive interest," but by implication as well, through "greed and pointless squandering of his gifts."

"Merchandising," or what we would today call "marketing," is not a dishonorable profession; nevertheless, it seems to have become an increasingly cynical and unscrupulous profession in recent decades. And even when it is entirely above board, there seems to be an obsession with consumerism in our day. C. S. Lewis complained, "I wish we didn't live in a world where buying and selling things (especially selling) seems to have become almost more important than either producing or using them."[11] Historically, evangelicals since the Reformation have seen it as their duty to be productive members of society. Hence, the Heidelberg Catechism, in answering the question, "What does God require of you [positively] in this commandment?" replies, "That I do whatever I can for my neighbor's good, that I treat him as I would like others to treat me, and that I work faithfully so that I may share with those in need (Is. 58:5–10; Mat. 7:12; Gal. 6:9–10; Ephesians 4:28)."

A Christian in business ought to ask, "Am I attempting to create a desire for something that is unnecessary or even harmful to the consumer?" In business, as in any other occupation, we are rendering a service to the community. A society cannot last long once it has adopted the view that the community exists to serve the individual. The Christian idea of the commonwealth is taken from the imagery of the body of Christ, each part supplying its unique role in supporting the whole, no part being despised, regardless of how diminished its role may be, compared to other parts of the body.

Sometimes we act as though, since the local manifestation of the body of Christ is the local church, it is there that we must maintain charity and justice in our relationships. If one is a Christian auto mechanic, special attention is taken to provide good service to a fellow believer, while the general public complains of poor service and poor workmanship. And yet, in a very real sense, it is the unbeliever who ought to be impressed with the quality of our work first of all (1 Thessalonians 4:12). The English Reformer, Thomas Bacon, wrote of the eighth commandment, "They that exercise themselves in merchandise . . . ought so to travail . . . that they may deal truly and faithfully with all men, having ever an eye not so much unto their own private profit, as to the commodity of the country wherein they dwell; remembering also, that we be not born for ourselves, but to do good to other and to serve other."

Furthermore, landlords have a Christian duty to rent their apartments at reasonable prices. Market competition assists in this, since free trade often means more choices for the consumer and the possibility of lower prices. Nevertheless, sometimes that same market creates "bloodclots," such as monopolies and trusts, and it is the duty of the magistrate, or government, to break up the "clot" and get things circulating again for the good of the many, not just of the few.

Exploitation and unjust business dealings have been the staple of reporters, with a marked rise during the greedy eighties. The eighth commandment forbids greed; the apostle Paul warned that "the love of money is a root of all kinds of evil" (1 Timothy 6:10). Yet even a former President of the United States expressed the sentiment often found in evangelical circles these days, that there is really nothing wrong with greed since it turns the engines of the market.[12] Perhaps never before in our nation's history has greed received such accolades, and we saw the fruit of such menacing notions in scandals of greed in business, government, and religion. Greed is *not* good; it is a *sin,* one of the most pernicious vices in the life of an individual and a society. It is not only immoral; it is the wellspring of debt and exploitation.

Whenever we try to find transcendent answers for human conduct in society, we are always brought back to two competing moral interests: freedom and justice. Absolute freedom, in a sinful world, would be anarchy and disorder, resulting in the dictatorship of a person or group capable of ruling a mob. But absolute justice, in a sinful world, would eliminate liberty and the variety that enables us to make meaningful choices. So long as we live as sinners in a sinful world, we ought to seek a balance of the two concepts. With any degree of freedom, there will be injustices;

likewise, if there is to be any justice in society, certain freedoms must be curtailed (particularly the freedoms of criminals). But greed is never good, either for a government
that overtaxes for the feathering of its own nest; or for an
individual, who also forgets to feel pain at the sight of debt.
John Murray, the staunch, conservative Reformed theologian, wrote,

> The evils of capitalism are not to be spared. Perhaps few
> weaknesses have marred the integrity of the witness of the
> church more than the partiality shown to the rich. The
> church has compromised with their vices because it has
> feared the loss of their patronage. Its voice has been si-
> lenced by respect of persons and discipline sacrificed in
> deference to worldly prestige.

After quoting James 2:1–4, Murray concludes,

> Respect of persons! It has warped the judgment of judges
> and equity could not enter. It has also invaded the sanctuary
> of God's house, and the vices of the rich—high-mindedness,
> oppression, voluptuosity, worldliness—have enjoyed im-
> munity from censure and the rich themselves a patronage
> of 'distinction' which has brought into the church itself the
> reproach of worldliness."[13]

Although capitalism and a market economy may be
the best means of creating wealth in a fallen world, it must
never be treated as though it were an amoral, blind, merely
economic system. No system is without its set of moral priorities and objectives, and no system merely creates wealth.
Those who start out with advantage and capital, not surprisingly, become the new feudal lords, with the exception
that in a democracy, unlike an aristocracy, new money
rules, and there is no chivalry or sense of obligation for the
community that comes with newfound, democratic wealth.
One Puritan snapped, "That saying, 'Each man for himself
and God for us all' is a most devilish saying." It would appear, however, that it is the most popular attitude in mod-

ern America, even among Christians. *Newsweek* ran a story on values that argued that

> the Republicans won not only the political argument but the right to indulge in their own egregious obsession with the mystical healing powers of the market. "Greed is good" was the '80s analogue to the '60s "Do your own thing" (and the '70s "You can have it all"). Many of the icons of the Reagan boom are now bankrupt or on parole. Their most visible legacy is the $4 trillion national debt that stands as a metaphor for the *moral* deficit incurred during the nation's 30-year spree. "Both ends of the spectrum say the same thing: 'As long as I get mine, the hell with everyone else,'" says Paul Weyrich, a leader of the religious right. "This was Ronald Reagan's failing as president. He was great in the international arena, but I don't think history will treat him kindly when it comes to domestic issues or value questions."[14]

The tragedy is that, as in recent decades, the "Christian" position ends up being confused with materialism, greed, and selfishness. Of course, it is no better for the "Christian" position to be confused with collectivism or shame for having achieved financial success. Nevertheless, I doubt very seriously that the latter is a greater plague than the former in contemporary evangelicalism.

One need not advocate an alternative economic system simply because there are flaws. Even with its inequities, capitalism has created more wealth for more people than any other system in modern history. Therefore, what we need is not a new system, perhaps, but a new moral sensitivity. We must stop thinking that economics somehow is beyond the pale of biblical criticism and be willing to challenge the "free, invisible hand" of the marketplace when freedom for the few means injustice for the many—or, indeed, for any.

The Word of God has never been against the rich *as rich*; nor did God tolerate partiality in judgments to be shown to the poor (Exodus 23:3). Every person is jealous for the prosperity of another, and the poor, if they fell into sudden wealth, would end up exploiting the rest of society to their own private advantage, given the chance. We all have the desire; the powerful and wealthy have the means. Hence, every prophet included exploitation of the poor and social injustice as a major factor in God's judgment; our Lord condemned greed, showed a special interest in the poor, and warned the rich about the difficulty of their entering the kingdom. James declared,

> Listen, my dear brothers: Has not God chosen those who are poor in the eyes of the world to be rich in faith and to inherit the kingdom he promised those who love him? But you have insulted the poor. Is it not the rich who are exploiting you? . . . If you really keep the royal law found in Scripture, "Love your neighbor as yourself," you are doing right. But if you show favoritism, you sin and are convicted by the law as lawbreakers. (James 2:5–6, 8–9)

A further way in which we violate this commandment is by laziness and waste. Work is not a necessary evil in the Scriptures, but an institution of creation. God gave Adam a calling in the Garden of Eden *before* the Fall, so we ought to value work as a gift, not as a curse. In Ecclesiastes 5:18–19, we are reminded, "Then I realized that it is good and proper for a man to eat and drink, and to find satisfaction in his toilsome labor under the sun during the few days of life God has given him—for this is his lot. Moreover, when God gives any man wealth and possessions, and enables him to enjoy them, to accept his lot and be happy in his work—this is a gift of God." Furthermore, to be "called by God" does not mean merely to be called to the foreign mission field or to church-related occupations; all men and women are called by God, even non-Christians, in the sense that they are gifted with natural abilities, desires, and opportunities to take their post in society. Again, this calling or vocation is rooted in creation, not in redemption. Therefore, there is no such thing as "Christian work" and "secular work," as the Reformers were anxious to remind the medieval church.

Thus, the apostle Paul urges, "Whatever you do, work at it with all your heart, as working for the Lord, not for men" (Colossians 3:23). Paul also tells the struggling Thessalonians, "Make it your ambition to lead a quiet life, to mind your own business and to work with your hands, just as we told you, so that your daily life may win the respect of outsiders, and so that you will not be dependent on anybody" (1 Thessalonians 4:11–12). Notice two objectives here.

First, the believer is to work in order to win the respect of unbelievers for his or her excellence and pleasure in his or her calling. Although every person receives a calling or vocation by virtue of being an image-bearer, only believers can really enjoy their calling as a gift of God and see it as an opportunity to reflect God's own excellence. The second objective of work for a believer is to make sure that he or she does not depend on others. An able-bodied believer who could work, but chooses not to because of laziness, brings reproach to the Christian faith. Therefore, "If a man will not work, he shall not eat" (2 Thessalonians 3:10). Of course, this did not include those who, for one reason or another, were unable to work, since this same apostle was taking collections for the poor in the Jerusalem church. What it did mean was that able-bodied people living off of the fruit of other people's labor constituted theft. There is yet a third reason Paul gives elsewhere for a believer to take special interest in his or her calling: "He who has been stealing must steal no longer, but must work, doing something useful with his own hands, *that he may have something to share with those in need*" (Ephesians 4:28, italics added).

At the same time, "the worker deserves his wages" (Luke 10:7; 1 Timothy 5:18), and the worker is not to be taken advantage of by the employer. Honest work for honest wages is a principle of biblical justice all the way through, from the prophets to the apostles. At least one way in which some Christians in particular transgress this commandment is by leaving a tract instead of a tip after being served in a restaurant.

Secular historians lament the loss of the so-called Protestant work-ethic, sometimes known also as the Calvinistic or Puritan work-ethic. Yet it is Christians themselves who have lost the sense of the worth and dignity of work. How many of us, like the world, are working for the weekend? Perhaps the weekend activities to which we are looking forward differ somewhat from the world, but the toll this mentality takes on excellence in work is devastating. We have become a nation of consumers and debtors rather than producers and savers. Instead of using our vocation as an opportunity to glorify God, to gain independence, and to give to those in need, we so often see it as a means of making money in order to spend it on luxuries, dropping a check every now and then in the offering plate. We need to realize that the purpose of work is not even to make money in order to give to the church but to fulfill our destiny, to find an avenue of giftedness through which we may bring honor and praise instead of shame and mockery to our Redeemer's name. There was a time when even the cynic had to admit that Christians were the most trustworthy businesspersons, clients, customers, borrowers, and lenders. People were known more by what they did and made than by what they bought and sold.

If we are to restore the tarnished splendor of the eighth commandment, we must recover something essential to it—the value of work. Economic factors of employment and diverse conditions prevalent in a fallen world may take their toll on our ability to discover, refine, and pursue our calling with excellence. Sometimes a "job" is a necessary prelude to a "calling." But there must be no theft, either by relying on the labor of our neighbor's calling when we could work ourselves or by taking advantage of our workers. Labor and management must find ways of working together in order to assist each other in the pursuit of each person's calling for the good of all, rather than seeing how much each side can take from the other for private advantage.

Finally, there is a matter about which we as Christians must be especially sensitive. We steal from our employers even in the exercise of what we consider spiritual tasks. Complaints abound about workers reading their Bibles, praying, or witnessing on company time, reducing productivity. After all, the thinking is, Jesus is coming back, and this business will be burned up with everything else. We need to remember Paul's advice: "Mind [our] own business, working quietly with [our] hands, so that [we] may win the respect of outsiders" by the quality of our work. We must earn the right to share the gospel, and we cannot win respect for our faith if it is perceived to corrupt our obligations. Someone asked Luther what he would do if he knew the Lord were coming back tomorrow. The Reformer replied, "I'd plant a tree."

CONCLUSION

According to the authors of *The Day America Told the Truth,* some who responded to the surveys on American attitudes mentioned things such as:

"Our night manager steals from the company nightly. We call him The Burglar."

"Everybody steals supplies out of the warehouse."

"Coworkers take money out of the cash register."

"My boss has taken money and given merchandise away."

"Bosses often ask someone to say a job's done when we haven't even started."

"Cheating people out of pay."

"Leaving work without finishing the job."

"Shameful misuse of company materials and company time."

"Cover-ups for jobs not done."

"Falsification of a lot of sign-in sheets which get billed."

A growing position within larger companies is "Vice-President for Loss Prevention," with the testing of employees for theft growing by 20 percent annually.[15]

And yet, once again, evangelical Christians do not think that they violate this commandment. "Despite reports that petty larceny and other forms of theft have reached record proportions in our country," George Barna tells us, "86 percent of *all adults* claim that they are completely satisfying God's command regarding abstinence from stealing"; only nine percent of the evangelicals polled said they had fallen short of God's glory on this one.[16] Once again it is apparent that our definitions of sin have more in common with the Pharisees' than with our Lord's.

All it takes for us to be guilty of theft is one misspent hour at work; one item we "forgot" to return from the office; one personal long-distance phone call we made at the company's expense; one overpriced item in our store. We see our sinless Lord, crucified for thieves not unlike the one hanging next to Him. Here was one person who never took what did not belong to Him, and who fulfilled all His obligations and paid debts He did not owe, and yet He hangs here next to a common thief, bearing His shame and guilt before God as though He had committed the crime. The thief crucified next to our Lord may have experienced the wrath of Rome that dark Friday afternoon, but because of the crucifixion of a Man just feet from him, he would not have to endure the wrath of heaven. All thieves who trust in Christ can expect to hear those same words on their death-bed from the spotless Lamb: "Today you shall be with me in Paradise."

NOTES

1. John Calvin, *Institutes of the Christian Religion*, 3.7.6.
2. *Time*, 30 March 1992, 74.
3. C. S. Lewis, *God in the Dock* (Grand Rapids: Eerdmans, 1957), 286.
4. Quoted in Keith Thomas, *Man and the Natural World* (New York: Pantheon, 1983), 237.
5. Calvin, *Commentary on Genesis 2*.
6. Thomas, *Man and the Natural World*, 154.
7. E. Calvin Beisner, *Prosperity and Poverty* (Westchester, Ill.: Crossway,1988), 235 n 36.

8. M. Stanton Evans, quoted by Ronald Nash in *Economic Justice and the State*, ed. John A. Bernbaum (Grand Rapids: Baker, 1986), 19–20.

9. Ibid., 517.

10. Ibid.

11. C. S. Lewis, *Letters to an American Lady* (Grand Rapids: Eerdmans, 1967), 50.

12. Ronald Reagan, quoted in the *Los Angeles Times*, 1 February 1984.

13. John Murray, *Principles of Conduct* (Grand Rapids: Eerdmans, 1991), 90–91.

14. *Newsweek*, 8 June 1992, 19.

15. James Patterson and Peter Kim, *The Day America Told the Truth* (New York: Plume, 1992), 156–57.

16. George Barna, *The Barna Report 1992–93* (Ventura: Regal, 1992), 117.

CHAPTER TEN

TELL THE TRUTH!

*You shall not give false
testimony against your neighbor.*

During the 1992 presidential race, *Time* ran a cover story
on lying.[1] From politicians to close family members, it
seems we would sooner lie than tell the truth these days—
even when there doesn't seem to be an obvious payoff. "Is
anyone telling the truth in this campaign?" Paul Gray
asked in that issue. According to one poll conducted during that campaign, "Sixty-three percent [of Americans]
have little or no confidence that government leaders talk
straight. Seventy-five percent believe there is less honesty
in government than there was a decade ago."[2] After sur-
veying the many relationships in which deceit often rears
its head, the essay takes its cue from the commandment
under consideration in this chapter:

> The injunction against bearing false witness, branded in
> stone and brought down by Moses from the mountaintop,
> has always provoked ambivalent, conflicting emotions. On
> the one hand, nearly everybody condemns lying. On the
> other, nearly everyone does it every day. How many of the

Ten Commandments can be broken so easily and with so little risk of detection over the telephone? Hence the never-ending paradox: some bedrock of honesty is fundamental to society; people cannot live together if no one is able to believe what anyone else is saying. But there also seems to be an honesty threshold, a point beyond which a virtue turns mean and nasty. Constantly hearing the truth, the cold, hard, brutal unsparing truth, from spouses, relatives, friends and colleagues is not a pleasant prospect. "Human kind," as T. S. Eliot wrote, "cannot bear very much reality." Truth telling makes it possible for people to coexist; a little lying makes such society tolerable.[3]

We all want people to tell us the truth, to come clean with us and shoot straight, even though we often justify our failure to do the same for others. *Time*'s essay makes a good point: Who wants to be told the truth *all the time*? "Gee, what an ugly tie." "Martha, you didn't actually pay for that haircut, did you?" "Frankly, Ted, I think your lack of creativity and basic intelligence is going to render you a penniless slob to be cared for by the state for the rest of your life." Brute honesty is just that, brutish, but surely our relationships break down when we sabotage them at the most basic level of communication.

Our greatest problem in this matter today is probably our willingness—indeed, enthusiasm—at the prospect of being lied to by others: "I'm OK, you're OK." "Guilt is not of God." "Sure it costs more, but you're worth it." We don't *really* believe it, but it will do. E. Christian Kopff, a classicist at the University of Colorado, observes,

As our society sinks into the hungry quicksand of bankruptcy and ruin, we pretend that there is some technical, political, or social solution. Our situation cannot be due to a moral defect in us. Anyway, we did not make up that story. We are just repeating a joke Jay Leno told us last night. If we asked for a reference for the remark, it might look rude. We believe in a kindhearted God. He gives us C's when we deserve F's and awards us A's when our work is barely worth a B. He would not condemn a soul, or a city, or a so-

ciety because it had ceased to care about truth, because in carelessness or malice it bore false witness against its neighbor. Would He?[4]

As we have seen God's concern about His own name, worship, and gospel as well as His commandments for just relationships with regard to our neighbor's life, property, and welfare, so here we will consider God's concern for protecting our neighbor's name, as well as his or her right to know the truth.

THE BASIS FOR THE COMMANDMENT

There are at least three reasons why God commanded us to take care in this matter. First, the value of a person's name; second, the value of a person's word; and third, the value of truth itself. First, the value of one's name.

You'll remember the commandment, "Thou shalt not take the name of the LORD thy God in vain" (Exodus 20:7 KJV). God's name was regarded among the Jews as so sacred that they would never even write out His full name. But since humans were created in His image, they too ought to have their names protected against deceit and slander. In the ancient world, one's name was essential to one's survival. A bad name ended one's career, spoiled the farmer's trade, and promised a life of hopeless penury. Much depended on a good name. Solomon writes, "A good name is more desirable than great riches; to be esteemed is better than silver or gold. Rich and poor have this in common: The Lord is the Maker of them all" (Proverbs 22:1–2).

We find it so easy to dig up some piece of news on somebody else—gossip, slander, backbiting, and vicious rumors that not only injure our neighbor, but demoralize the family, the church, and the society. According to recent surveys, modern Americans see lying as a means to an end. Most are not even sure any more that it is wrong, so long as it achieves its goal. Lie now, pay later, is a common practice. Of course, the simple ethical value of telling the truth is enough reason for us to hold our tongue, but remember, the Ten Commandments are not concerned primarily with the ethical value of these commandments in and of themselves, but with regulating just relationships. When truth is replaced by deceit in any relationship, that relationship loses its value.

Second, there is the value of one's word. Communication is one of the divine gifts we often take for granted. As James so eloquently pointed out, the tongue is capable of the most exhilarating praise and the most devastating cruelty. It is not the tongue itself—communication—that is the problem, but the direction in which sinful men and women, even those sinners redeemed by Christ, choose to twist, distort, exaggerate, or confuse the truth. Our Lord said, "What goes into a man's mouth does not make him unclean, but what comes out of his mouth," which is to say, that which is already in his heart, and then vocalized by his hearth, is that which "makes him unclean" (see Matthew 15:11). Words are symbols of a person's spiritual condition, a barometer of the storms we all encounter, and the measure of our responses to them.

Even before God created Adam and Eve, Satan had been endowed with the gift of speech. Notice that this was not given to other animals. In this respect we are like God, sharing His ability to communicate. In heaven's sacred halls, Lucifer—the angel of light—entertained the royal court day and night and led all of the heavenly hosts in Magnificats and Te Deums. Nevertheless, the gift of communicating praise and wonder at God's majesty may also become a tool of diabolical pride, hatred, slander, and deceit.

By contrast, God's word always is fulfilled. He keeps His promises, in spite of the failures of the second party to keep theirs. His people trust Him precisely because He has always been reliable in His communication. We are to mirror that concern for the written or spoken word.

Third, the value of truth itself. The Ten Commandments direct not only our individual relationships, but also our corporate lives. Harvard was founded as an academy for training in the great truths of Scripture as well as in philosophy, art, science, and the humanities. Its motto was, and still remains, *Veritas,* "Truth." Yet as Allen Bloom pointed out so decisively in *The Closing of the American Mind,* what goes on inside those hallowed halls these days is far from the search for ultimate truth. Modern men and women are being told that there is no such thing: only personal preferences, calculated to give us the most bang for our buck.

Is the church really any different, though? What place does truth have in a church that has had Benny Hinn at the top of a best-seller list for months? Where does truth rate in a church that pushes theology—the study of God—aside in order to sell God to self-seeking consumers? How can we talk about being truthful in our personal relationships, rooting out that ecclesiastically acceptable sin of gossip and slander, if we are not first of all concerned with defending truth at the most precious level? We speak often of the relativism of secular culture while we relativize truth in our own Christian circles. Surely it is here where truth-telling begins, with the most important issues involved and the highest stakes imaginable.

Granted that the basis for the ninth commandment is the honor we owe to our neighbor's name as well as to the truth itself, what exactly is forbidden and commanded in this decree?

Martin Luther, following Augustine, distinguished between three classes of lies: the humorous, the helpful, and the harmful. The humorous lie was nothing more than a joke, such as "Two men were walking down the street and one said to the other . . ." when the conversation never took place in reality. Actors, especially good ones, can be said to deceive their audiences by their performance. But, of course, these are not sinful "lies," since they are not meant to be taken seriously as truth. The second class, the helpful lie, is told for the benefit of one's neighbor. Rahab's lie fits into this category. Other examples could be cited from 2 Samuel 15:34 and 17:20. Luther said, "Therefore, it is improperly called a lie. It is rather a virtue and remarkable prudence by which the fury of Satan is hindered, and the honor, life, and interests of others are served as well." During the Second World War, Corrie ten Boom and her family hid Jews from the Nazis, lying to the soldiers when they came asking if there were any Jews in the house. Luther would have considered this, like Rahab's lie, "remarkable prudence by which the fury of Satan is hindered," and, therefore, not, properly speaking, a lie.

The Reformed tradition departs from Luther at this point, however. Ursinus writes, "Nor are those lies which are uttered for politeness sake excused, because we may not do evil that good may come." Yet "we may here remark that we should not be too severe and rigid in passing sentence upon the actions of the saints; neither should we make an apology for those things which need none." Even though Rahab and others lied, "God did not bless them because they lied, but because they had reverence toward God." In other words, a lie, even in the interest of a greater good, is always a sin, even though one might be required by one's conscience to lie in order to, for instance, save a neighbor's life. Here, a lie is still evil, but a lesser evil compared to murder.

Ursinus lays out for us, once again, a marvelous outline of this biblical commandment, both its negative and positive aspects. As the author of the *Time* cover story mentioned above noticed, too much truth-telling can damage relationships. Ursinus observes that an untimely profession of the truth can undermine relationships when we say something that is true and honest to a neighbor but at the wrong time or in the wrong context: "He who admonishes at the wrong time injures." In addition, curiosity may masquerade as truth-seeking, whereas it is in fact simply butting in on the business of others. What then, according to the author of the Heidelberg Catechism, does the commandment require?

CANDOR

Following Luther's interpretation, Ursinus argues that the ninth commandment leads us, positively, to "put the best construction upon such things as are doubtful," so that we do not "entertain suspicions, or indulge in them, although there might be sufficient cause for so doing." It requires us to never "base any actions upon these suspicions, nor resolve anything in consequence thereof," so that we are always "hoping that which is good" about our neighbor. It includes giving our neighbor the benefit of the doubt, even when he or she has done something wrong, that the person is capable of changing his or her mind. After all, we can never finally condemn a person because "the inmost recesses of the human heart are never brought fully to light."

In opposition to candor, Ursinus argues, are calumny and suspiciousness. "Calumny is not only to incriminate and find fault with the innocent, where there is no reason for it, but it is also to put the very worst construction upon things spoken indifferently, or to propagate and coin that which is false." Meanwhile, "Suspiciousness is to understand things, spoken correctly or ambiguously in the worst light, and to suspect evil things from those who are not guilty of the crime; or to entertain suspicions where there is no just cause for so doing; and where there are even reasons for so doing, to indulge in them to too great an extent." This does not mean, of course, that we are to be naive or to ignore the obvious, but that we are not to indulge our curiosity or suspect the worst of our neighbor.

How this is so easily undermined in our day. Candor has suffered setbacks, not only at the hands of sensationalistic rags for "inquiring minds," but at the hands also of inquisitive Christians who are too eager to accept gossip about the sins and shortcomings of their neighbors. What is our first response when we hear a report about a brother or sister caught in a sinful act? Do we immediately presume the person's innocence, or the person's guilt? Our evangelical forebears are calling us here, based on the clear teaching of Scripture, to assume our neighbor's innocence until all the facts are sorted out by the proper authorities.

All too often today, perhaps because of the frequency of moral scandals even on the part of church leaders, our first reaction is to believe every report we hear. How quickly one's reputation, honor, and name can be destroyed by false rumors. Instead of being busybodies, Paul commands, "Make it your ambition to lead a quiet life, to mind your own business and to work with your hands" (1 Thessalonians 4:11). God has appointed leaders among us, called out by the congregation, to guard against disorder and scandal in the body of Christ, and it is with them, not with us and our curiosity, that this responsibility lies.

This is particularly important at a time when we are, as a society and as a church, given to conspiracy theories. Though we must be discerning, I have heard of ministries' being destroyed because they used terms or phrases some people regarded as New Age, humanistic, or liberal to address modern audiences with the timeless gospel message. Similarly, although they disavowed any connection with such errors, some individuals have nevertheless been caricatured as being part of one of the many scenarios for end-time conspiracies. We all have a right to know the truth about what people believe and teach, but we must be eager to put the best face on the statements as well as the actions of those who may not have intended what we suspiciously assumed. I find it interesting, in fact, that Ursinus says that we engage in suspiciousness not only when we have insufficient grounds, but even when we have sufficient grounds but indulge our suspicions "to too great an extent." Candor requires us to be civil and courteous, to give our neighbor the benefit of the doubt in all questionable circumstances.

But candor also requires us to be direct and honest, not to hide our true beliefs or attitudes under the guise of something else. It is inevitable for those who move in academic circles to learn of numerous cases in which professors at Christian colleges and seminaries were actually told by their employers that it did not matter whether they disagreed with the doctrinal statement, so long as they signed it and did not raise any public debate on the disputed areas. When ministers agree to uphold the creeds and confessions of their denomination or church body while privately denying principal articles, they are bearing false witness. I have always been amazed at how nonchalant some people can be in their ordination exams and ceremonies, agreeing to uphold the teachings of their church, when very few people, especially in the mainline churches, expect the candidate to be telling the truth. Surely it is the wrong profession in which one should begin by telling a lie.

That is why Ursinus says there is an opposite direction in which some people may run from suspiciousness: foolish credulity and flattery. In other words, it is equally as dangerous to believe everything you hear or read. It is to assent to something "without just and probable reasons; or, to believe something merely on the basis of the declaration of another, when there are evident and sufficient reasons to the contrary." The Reformers were particularly wary of the idea of implicit faith, that is, the medieval notion that one ought to believe whatever the church says, simply because the church says it. Here again we can take a lesson. As given to believing the worst about our neighbor's moral life as we are, we are just as given these days to an undiscerning mentality that regards those who "ask too many questions" and offer any criticisms as enemies of unity and brotherhood.

Foolish credulity is evidenced in the ease with which many professing Christians accept the "revelations" of self-appointed prophets. We would do well to refresh our memory with God's stern words through Jeremiah: "I [God] have heard what the prophets say who prophesy lies in my name. They say, 'I had a dream! I had a dream!' How long will this continue in the hearts of these lying prophets, who prophesy the delusions of their own minds?" (Jeremiah 23:25–26)

Whereas God intended the prophets to tell the people they would suffer His judgment, they instead "dressed the wound of my people as though it were not serious. 'Peace, Peace,' they say, when there is no peace" (6:14; 8:11). How many of such false witnesses abound in our day? And yet, God promised to Jeremiah, "Therefore, this is what the LORD says about the prophets who are prophesying in my name: I did not send them, yet they are saying, 'No sword or famine will touch this land.' The same prophets will perish by sword and famine" (14:15). This, of course, anticipated the final judgment against the false witnesses and false prophets of all time, when all of a sudden one will come, mounted upon his war-horse, with sword flashing, hunting down His enemies to the last man.

Candor requires truth-telling: putting the best construction on our neighbor's deeds and doctrine, but without slipping into a naive, sentimental optimism that makes us slaves again to new popes and prophets. We must always be aware of the fact that even our religious leaders are not beyond deceit and, therefore, are not beyond the checks and balances placed upon them by Scripture and the people of God.

CONSTANCY

Another word that has passed out of modern usage is the marvelous term *constancy*. Ursinus insists that constancy is included as part of what it means to uphold truthfulness. Constancy is the virtue by which one clings to and defends the truth once he or she has become convinced of it. One of the hallmarks of modern life, and certainly modern education, is open-mindedness, the one virtue secular education seeks to inculcate, according to Allen Bloom. We are not relativists because we think too much, but because we think too little; not because we value the mind and freedom of thought more than previous generations, but because we simply do not want to have to engage in proving and disproving arguments. Similarly, in the church we refuse to come down on one side or another of a particular doctrinal debate because "it causes disunity" or "partakes of a lack of charity." Or, at least, that's what we say. What we mean is that we do not want to risk losing our apathetic acquiescence to the status quo. We do not wish to commit our energies to thinking, arguing, and evaluating. Relativism undermines truth and the life of the mind even while it masquerades as enlightenment and tolerance.

Yet, our seventeenth-century tutor does not want us to go to the other extreme, either, into obstinacy, "which clings to false opinions, and persists in doing what is unjust and unprofitable, although convinced to the contrary. It is a vice which arises from the confidence which any one has in his own wisdom, or from pride and ostentation, and shows itself in an unwillingness to yield its own judgment or opinion, which is seen to be false from many solid arguments." If it is the tendency of relativists to refuse to come to cognitive rest after careful investigation, it is the tendency of funda-mentalists to refuse to give up their opinions even if new evidence makes it clearly impossible to maintain such views.

After centuries, the Bible has withstood the harshest criticisms imaginable and is better for it. Setting out to strip it of its historical accuracy, modern science, especially ar-chaeology, has merely served as a witness for its defense. Though certainly no fundamentalist, postmodernist scho-lar Diogenes Allen announces, as if the cold war between science and Christianity might be cooling down, "There is therefore no need for Christians to continue to be defen-sive. Just as Socrates did in ancient Greece, we have a mis-sion: to challenge the supposition that the status of the universe and our place in it have already been settled by science and philosophy. . . . In the postmodern world Christianity is intellectually relevant."[5] Instead of clinging to interpretations, opinions, and speculations that are not clearly affirmed in the text of Scripture itself, Bible-believ-ing Christians ought to be open to testing their faith. They ought not to fear rational investigation, but invite it. If Christianity is true, do we have anything to lose?

So constancy, that is, a stubborn allegiance to one's convictions, is an essential aspect of bearing witness to the truth; and yet blind dogmatism is as deadly a foe to truth as is relativism.

CONCLUSION

Initially, the prohibition against bearing false witness applied to the courtroom, where it was too often the case that a defendant or a plaintiff could bribe friends into perjury on his or her behalf. Even life hung in the balance, so perjurers were to be themselves put to death. "One witness is not enough to convict a man accused of any crime or offense he may have committed," God commanded Moses. "If the witness proves to be a liar, giving false testimony against his brother, then do to him as he intended to do to his brother. You must purge the evil from among you. The rest of the people will hear of this and be afraid, and never again will such an evil thing be done among you. Show no pity: life for life, eye for eye, tooth for tooth, hand for hand, foot for foot" (Deuteronomy 17:18–21). In our litigious society, where some lawyers specialize in creating false accident claims, this original purpose alone is impressive in its relevance.

Eventually, however, the ninth commandment was carried over, particularly in the New Testament, to include gossip, slander, backbiting, and similar "fruit of the flesh," as Paul sets forth in 2 Corinthians 12:10, Galatians 5:19–20, and elsewhere. We owe our neighbor the truth, whether it is our pledge to pay back a loan or honesty in explaining the Christian message, including its less popular points. We ought to give our neighbor the benefit of the doubt and never judge him or her without proper evidence and even then we must never indulge in suspicious or malicious talk. And yet, truth also demands that we refuse to be naive; we must have convictions, while being willing to correct them if we learn something that causes us to question them. Christians, of all people, must be truth-seeking in every relationship: with God, with parents, children, spouses, co-workers; employers, employees; pastors, parishioners; believer, unbeliever; friend and foe.

For those of us who have violated this commandment (and those who think they haven't, have their own problems telling themselves the truth), there is refuge in the righteousness of the one who is the Truth. In Christ, our deceits, errors, hypocrisy, lies, gossip, and slander are not charged against us because "God made him who had no sin to be sin for us, so that in him we might become the righteousness of God" (2 Corinthians 5:21). With that status before God, in spite of our violations of the ninth commandment, let us "speak the truth to each other, and render true and sound judgment in the courts" (Zechariah 8:16), pressing on toward that day when Zecharaiah's prophecy (v. 3) will be fulfilled in Christ's return and truth will no longer lie slain in the street:

> This is what the LORD says: "I will return to Zion and dwell in Jerusalem. Then Jerusalem will be called the City of Truth, and the mountain of the LORD Almighty will be called the Holy Mountain."

NOTES

1. *Time*, 5 October 1992.
2. Ibid., 32.
3. Ibid., 35.
4. E. Christian Kopff, *Chronicles: A Magazine of American Culture*, December 1992, 21,
5. Diogenes Allen, in *Postmodern Theology* (San Francisco: Harper & Row, 1989), 25.

CHAPTER ELEVEN

WHEN MORE IS LESS

You shall not covet.

Michael Lewis, best-selling author and journalist, began his most recent book, *Money Culture*, by saying,

> At the beginning of the last decade there was a kind of moral fad in parts of the United States that spread almost immediately to the capital cities of industrial Europe. The age-old Anglo-European taboo of handling money was shoved offstage by the sheer force of events in the financial world, clearing the way for a new money culture. . . . In 1985, the average income of the 10 best paid people on Wall Street rose from $29 million to $51 million.

Lewis adds a poignant story to illustrate the lust for money and power characterizing our era:

> One night early that year, Stephen Joseph, a partner of the now bankrupt Drexel Burnham, made what seemed to be a routine business trip to Minnesota and stayed for drinks with a client. "In the course of the evening Joseph happened to mention how much he expected to be paid. The

number made an impression on the client's seven-year-old son, who was eavesdropping on the staircase. Two days later the boy handed his father an essay he had prepared for school. It was called What I Want to Be When I Grow Up and almost perfectly captured the mood of the day.

> I want to be an investment banker. If you had 10,000 sheres [sic] I sell them for you. I make a lot of money. I will make a lot of money. I will be a millionaire. I will have a big house. It will be fun for me.[1]

Contrast this with the example of Louis de Greer, a seventeenth-century Belgian Calvinist who fled the Inquisition, finding solace in Amsterdam at a time of great prosperity for the Dutch business and trade, where he became a famous businessman and banker. Harvard's Simon Schama explains that de Greer strictly followed Calvin's program of low rates of interest for the poor. Schama writes,

> Louis de Greer, who was both an ardent Calvinist and energetic entrepreneur, managed to accommodate a dignified lifestyle with pious expenditure in just these ways. Even though he stocked his home with fine nut wood furniture imported from France and Italy, his self-tithing for the poor was widely known, as was his sincere help for Calvinist refugees from central European theaters of the Thirty Years' War. When in 1646 he drew up his will for his children and heirs, he admonished them to "fear God and keep his commandments and think on the poor and oppressed; then you shall enjoy God's blessings." And he reminded them that when he had come to the Republic, in hard-pressed times, he had made an oath before God to give 200 guilders a year to the poor for every child of his own. God had heard his prayer and had prospered him, and he, in his turn, had kept his oath. He commended his children to do so in their turn.[2]

Notice the contrast in these two families. Both prosperous, both successful. Neither thought money was evil or that prosperity was to be avoided. And yet, one saw prosperity chiefly as a means of acquiring and consuming, whereas the other saw it chiefly as a means of saving and giving. And who said theology wasn't practical?

WHAT DOES THIS COMMANDMENT REQUIRE?

Once again, we are led back to the rich wisdom and insight of our evangelical forebears, as they pull together the wide range of passages from Scripture concerning this final commandment.

All of the evangelical catechisms, Lutheran and Reformed, see the tenth commandment as a summary of the preceding five: the second table of the law, laying out our duty to neighbor. In fact, Luther, in his Large Catechism, comments:

> This last commandment, then, is addressed not to those whom the world considers wicked rogues, but precisely to the most upright—to people who wish to be commended as honest and virtuous because they have not offended against the preceding commandments. . . . Such is nature that we all begrudge another's having as much as we have. Everyone acquires all he can and lets others look out for themselves. Yet we all pretend to be upright. We know how to put up a fine front to conceal our rascality. We think up artful dodges and sly tricks (better and better ones are being devised daily) under the guise of justice. We brazenly dare to boast of it, and insist that it should be called not rascality but shrewdness and business acumen. In this we are assisted by jurists and lawyers who twist and stretch the law to suit their purpose, straining words and using them for pretexts, without regard for equity or for our neighbor's plight.

The Reformers faced a litigious society, not unlike our own, where it was fashionable to even use and abuse the legal system and business opportunities in order to advance one's piece on the board. Notice also Luther's remark that the tenth commandment is meant to deal the final blow to those who think they are left standing after the preceding nine commandments. This commandment, he says, is not addressed to those we usually put behind bars and consider the real criminals, but to the rest who think they have actually conformed to the law. Similarly, the Heidelberg Catechism adds of the tenth commandment's definition, "That there should never enter our heart even the least inclination or thought contrary to any commandment of God, but that we should always hate sin with our whole heart and find satisfaction and joy in all righteousness." In other words, this commandment is treated as a restatement of the rest.

We have seen how the majority of Christians today, like the Pharisees of our Lord's day and the medieval church at the time of the Reformation, think remarkably well of themselves. According to George Barna, most evangelical Christians today do not think they tolerate other gods (76 percent) or fail in their obligation to obey their parents (77 percent); they are guiltless of murder (93 percent), adultery (82 percent), and theft (86 percent). Nearly half do not even think they have fallen short of God's glory by lying (48 percent).[3] So God issues this final commandment, "Thou shalt not covet" (KJV), in order to drive home the point that if any of these commandments have been violated in any of the ways we have considered in the preceding chapters, even by desiring such sinful behavior, we are guilty of offending the whole law. As James warns, "For whoever keeps the whole law and yet stumbles at just one point is guilty of breaking all of it" (James 2:10). This last decree, therefore, is aimed at those who have said, "I'm not really guilty of murder, adultery, or these other sins."

As Jesus, in His Sermon on the Mount, drove the people to realize that the very desire is a violation of the commandment, so even in Moses we find this principle. Even to desire or covet what our neighbor owns makes us lawbreakers as though we had stolen his life, his wife, his property, and his honor. At least we would expect most Christians to come clean on this one, and yet a full majority (53 percent) of evangelicals insist they completely follow this commandment. We ought to be more concerned about the theology behind this mirage than with the obvious and widespread violation of this commandment.

The Westminster Shorter Catechism reinforces this comprehensive view of the tenth commandment: "The Tenth Commandment requireth full contentment with our own condition, with a right and charitable frame of spirit toward our neighbor and all that is his," and "forbiddeth all discontentment with our own estate, envying or grieving at the good of our neighbor, and all inordinate motions and affections to anything that is his." Who among us can say that he or she has never envied the prosperity of a neighbor? Are we never disappointed when we hear that a fellow worker received a raise, even though we have been employed there longer? Is there never a twinge of spite when we see friends we grew up with or with whom we went to school achieve success and prosperity while we have not been able to get our career going? Can we really say that we never even secretly desire our neighbor's new Porsche; that we never scan catalogs or shops wishing we could own the latest fashions, even if we cannot really afford them? Furthermore, who among us can say there has never been a moment when we have failed to revel in our neighbor's success, without the slightest interest in our own material condition? Is there no pastor who craves the success of the church down the street and will even adapt his message to try to compete? We could profit from a visit with the eleventh-century theologian Anselm, who warned those who thought they were keeping their noses clean, "You have not yet considered how great sin is."

Like the boy who stacks his cans, one by one, growing in his pride as he builds the pyramid higher and higher, we stack our character, charity, virtue, spirituality, and obedience as though God saw the same value in our "righteousness" as we do. After graciously tolerating our ignorance and arrogance, God finally descends and, with one blow, strikes the pyramid and scatters all of our well-placed efforts just as surely as He laid siege to the Tower of Babel. The tenth commandment is just such a blow, pointing out in bold relief the prophet's declaration that "all our righteous acts are like filthy rags" (Isaiah 64:6), to say nothing of our wickedness.

THE BASIS OF THIS COMMANDMENT

Just as the other commandments presuppose a particular value—authority, life, marriage and the family, private property and stewardship, truth and honor—so, too, this commandment is based on the value of contentment. We are to live in such a manner that we can say with the apostle Paul, "I have learned to be content whatever the circumstances. I know what it is to be in need, and I know what it is to have plenty. I have learned the secret of being content in any and every situation, whether well fed or hungry, whether living in plenty or in want. I can do everything through him who gives me strength" (Phil. 4:11–12). At the bottom, this final commandment calls us to the conviction that God is good and that even our suffering or lack serves an ultimately benevolent purpose.

Paul gave further instructions to those believers who struggled with this principle:

> But godliness with contentment is great gain. For we brought nothing into the world, and we can take nothing out of it. But if we have food and clothing, we will be content with that. People who want to get rich fall into temptation and a trap and into many foolish and harmful desires that plunge men into ruin and destruction. For the love of money is a root of all kinds of evil. Some people, eager for money, have wandered from the faith and pierced themselves with many griefs. . . .
>
> Command those who are rich in this present world not to be arrogant nor to put their hope in wealth, which is so uncertain, but to put their hope in God, who richly provides us with everything for our enjoyment. Command them to do good, to be rich in good deeds, and to be generous and willing to share. In this way they will lay up treasure for themselves as a firm foundation for the coming age, so that they may take hold of the life that is truly life. (1 Timothy 6:6–10; 17–19)

Notice that this notion of contentment is not sentimental. There is nothing romantic about poverty or repeated business failures. Paul does not tell Timothy to command the people to be content just for the sake of contentment. Rather, he gives them a theological rationale for the command, what theologians call the doctrine of providence. The poor might put their hope in wealth, and some do; but it is far more tempting for those with wealth, success, power, and prosperity to rely on their temporal condition. The poor are just as sinful as the rich, but rarely does a poor person see his poverty as a sign of God's blessing, especially these days. The rich can often ignore the larger spiritual realities of life by either being so consumed with their material success that they are simply out of touch with their own spiritual poverty or by confusing material and spiritual blessing.

As Jesus taught, God "causes his sun to rise on the evil and the good, and sends rain on the righteous and the unrighteous" (Matthew 5:45). The general material condition of men and women is committed to the realm of providence, not redemption. God does not give special privileges to the believers when it comes to material blessing, as even the author of Psalm 73 lamented. Surely his experience jibes with our own:

> But as for me, my feet had almost slipped;
>   I had nearly lost my foothold.
> For I envied the arrogant
>   when I saw the prosperity of the wicked. . . .
>
> When I tried to understand all this,
>   it was oppressive to me,
> till I entered the sanctuary of God;
>   then I understood their final destiny.
>
> Surely you place them on slippery ground;
>   you cast them down to ruin. . . .
>
> Whom have I in heaven but you?
>   And earth has nothing I desire besides you.
> My flesh and my heart may fail,
>   but God is the strength of my heart
>   and my portion forever.
>   (Psalm 73:2–3, 16–18, 25–26)

Like Paul, the psalmist was able to look beyond the shortsightedness of material prosperity to see the final (or theological) meaning of life. Immature religious concepts, such as are common to pagan folk religions, make the easy correspondence between ritual and riches, obedience and material abundance. But God enrolled Job in the school of suffering, for Job's sanctification and God's glory. The apostle Paul prepares us for the same: "We also rejoice in our sufferings, because we know that suffering produces perseverance; perseverance, character; and character, hope" (Romans 5:3–4). If "the fear of the LORD is the beginning of wisdom" (Psalm 111:10), and "suffering produces perseverance; perseverance, character; and character, hope," there is little wonder that modern Christians seem addicted to folly, prone to give up, shallow in character, and looking to secular solutions for hope.

We are in desperate need at the end of this century of a theology of suffering. Liberation theologians have something when they speak of the poor and suffering as those who see the kingdom of God more clearly, although orthodox Christians find difficulties with the "this-world-only" orientation liberation theology seems to share with the materialistic Christianity it seeks to challenge. Nevertheless, there is a deeper, richer theology in the old Negro spirituals than in most of the contemporary "happy-clappy" jingles of congregations often characterized as "yuppy." In those Negro spirituals, the God-centeredness, the longing for heaven, the emphasis on the great events and truths of redemptive history wed personal struggle with hope in the Lord alone.

Those whose personal and corporate stories read like Israel's captivity, Exodus, and wilderness experience see something in the biblical text that the rest of us sometimes miss. That does not mean that we should pray for suffering, but that we ought to see it, when it does come, as an opportunity to deepen in our understanding, roots, and character, to the greater glory of God and the good of our neighbor. As we scan the biblical revelation, we see again and again how suffering brought into a person's life a deeper understanding of the eternal issues and a greater awareness of God's nearness to those who have no shoulder to cry on but their Maker's. Spiritual and material brokenness, though not always companions, are often found together, and God delights in "a broken and contrite heart" (Psalm 51:17). Rare are those whose enjoyment of spiritual blessings comes without any loss in temporal terms.

The story has been told that a reporter asked Nelson Rockefeller, "How much money does it take to be happy?" to which the tycoon replied with refreshing honesty, "Just a little bit more." At the same time, contentment is not a matter of poverty or wealth. Let us be clear about this: coveting is as much the vice of the poor as the rich. Paul did not merely say he was content when he was poor, but that he was also content when he enjoyed wealth. He does not command the rich to empty their savings accounts but urges them to put their hope in God, "who richly provides us with everything for our enjoyment" (1 Timothy 6:17), thereby sanctioning not only wealth but the enjoyment of wealth as God's gracious gift.

But a gift is never to be misused, and if God has given us wealth, we ought to be content; if lack, the same. It is not poverty or wealth that leads us to contentment and trust in the Lord, but the confidence that if God provided so richly for our salvation by choosing, redeeming, calling, adopting, and justifying us, and by sending His Spirit to cause us to grow up into Christ's likeness, then surely we can count on Him for the less essential matters of daily existence. The writer to the Hebrews warned, "Keep your lives free from the love of money and be content with what you have, because God has said, 'Never will I leave you; never will I forsake you.' So we say with confidence, 'The Lord is my helper; I will not be afraid. What can man do to me?'" (Hebrews 13:5–6).

At the bottom of it, coveting is a theological problem. As the psalmist is confused by the prosperity of the wicked in this life until he contemplates their destiny in the next, and Paul anchors our contentment in the God who "blesses us in the heavenly realms with every spiritual blessing in

Christ" (Ephesians 1:3), so the writer to the Hebrews bases his call to contentment, not on some airy, sentimental, blind command, but on the promise God has made to never leave us nor forsake us. God's perseverance with us in spite of our sin and rebellion is enough to justify our perseverance with Him, trusting Him as a careful and loving provider even though He seems to be providing better for the wicked, in material terms.

Israel provides a historical example of this challenge to see God as a provider even in the absence of what we regard as essential provisions. Even though God performed miracles for His people, beginning with the Exodus from Egypt, "they continued to sin against him, rebelling in the desert against the Most High" (Psalm 78:17). They coveted the peace and relative prosperity of Egypt and "willfully put God to the test by demanding the food they craved. They spoke against God, saying, 'Can God spread a table in the desert?'" (vv. 18–19). The root of coveting is the cynicism of the remark "Can God spread a table in the desert?" Of course, that is what is called a rhetorical question. When we rebel against our authorities God has placed over us, it is as though we are calling into question God's own ability or willingness to govern a bad situation and turn evil into good.

When a troubled woman has an abortion, she is questioning God's ability to provide for her and her family if she has another child. When a man steals from the company till, he is challenging God's providence: "Can God spread a table in the desert?" In other words, "I've just been fired, and I don't have any other source of income: I should expect God to drop a treasure chest from the sky?" Not a treasure chest, perhaps; but "our daily bread" is itself more than any one of us deserves at the hand of God.

The lack of contentment, then, is first and foremost a theological issue. That does not mean that those who get their theology straightened out on this and learn more about the sovereignty of God and His providence will suddenly find themselves taking selfless delight in the neighbor's new automotive purchase. But it does mean that we can find an anchor for contentment that isn't carried every way by the waves of either fortune or failure; an anchor, not in our own personal experience, but in the eternal promise of God. In Christ, we are already seated with Him in heavenly realms (Ephesians 2:6). The enemies of the cross cannot know this comfort: a future hope that has the power to liberate here and now. "Their destiny is destruction, their god is their stomach, and their glory is in their shame. Their mind is on earthly things. But our citizenship is in heaven. And we eagerly await a Savior from there, the Lord Jesus Christ, who, by the power that enables him to bring everything under his control, will transform our lowly bodies so that they will be like his glorious body" (Philippians 3:19–21). Those who cannot wait, who demand a realized eschatology, heaven on earth, with perfect health, wealth, and happiness, will not only be disillusioned when they fail to see their earthly dreams materialize; they will fail in the end to enjoy the true life of God that we have in Christ, if in these days they are not content to ride out the storm.

HOW DO WE VIOLATE THIS COMMANDMENT?

We have already seen how this commandment is violated: failing to take pleasure in the success of our neighbor, desiring his or her possessions, prosperity, or position.

I will never forget the ten days I spent a few years ago on an evangelistic mission in Nicaragua. Passing cardboard shacks, with women carrying tremendous loads of firewood and water, we finally arrived for dinner one night at the home of a Pentecostal pastor. He was a fisherman— that is how he made his living, and lobsters were plentiful in the Central American waters. We entered his home, not through a door, for he had none, but through the open-air patio that served as the dining room. The meal was cooked over a window screen that had been set on top of a tire, with kindling providing the coals, while the children chased the pig through the mud beneath us.

Earlier that day, this pastor had traveled, I was later told, forty-five miles to pick up a table and chairs for the occasion. With all candor, this was the first time I had been to this part of the world, and I wasn't certain what we were having for dinner. With some reservation, I asked the host what sort of fish he caught in those waters. "Langosta," he replied—"lobsters," relieving my countenance considerably.

The night was full of ironies. First, here I was, expecting the worst for dinner, and what I could not afford to eat in my own country was plentiful in the waters just yards away from where we were sitting. But then we went on to talk about the influence of the prosperity gospel in North America, particularly among Pentecostals. Even though this pastor was a Pentecostal, the "name it and claim it" heresy was as far-fetched to him as it is to the biblical writers. In the course of the evening, I heard better, sounder theology from my host than from a great many books I've read, even by evangelicals who would not hesitate to condemn the prosperity gospel. This pastor had suffered and had perseverance, character, and hope to show for it. He was not a sappy optimist with rose-colored glasses, passing off his difficult conditions with glib platitudes, but a biblical realist who knew that those who suffer with Christ in this life reign with Him in the next. Whereas he did not shrink from feverish activity in trying to alleviate the misery of his neighbors in very tangible ways, he knew his Bible too well to buy into Marxist or capitalist salvation. The prosperity gospel to him sounded as foreign as the entire scene appeared to me.

Here was a brother showing hospitality beyond that I had ever remembered experiencing at home. I have never heard of a host traveling forty-five winding miles through the mountains simply to pick up a table and chairs for the meal. It was a meal fit for a king, in a situation in which I was simply expecting to "get through" the evening politely. My host's hospitality shamed me.

That is not to say that suffering people do not covet. But we, especially in the United States, have become desensitized to this sin by incessant bombardment by the media, advertisers, and even politicians who tell each group what it wants to hear: "You're the special group; support me and I'll help you get your piece of the pie." "Sure this shampoo costs more, but you're worth it." "You deserve a break today."

We end up filling our lives with things we do not need in the slightest because we have let slogans and images talk us into it. Like Eve, who bit into the fruit "when she saw that the fruit of the tree was good for food and pleasing to the eye, and also desirable for gaining wisdom," we are suckers for the latest products promising the latest cure for what the world has decided to be our latest problem. But this is not unique to our own time and place. James castigated the early church for beginning as a humble congregation of people who suffered and knew they were dependent on God's care and providence and changing to a new generation of more upscale folks. They even began giving subtle, and not-so-subtle, preference to the successful people in society:

> What causes fights and quarrels among you? Don't they come from your desires that battle within you? You want something but don't get it. You kill and covet, but you cannot have what you want. You quarrel and fight. You do not have, because you do not ask God. When you ask, you do not receive, because you ask with wrong motives, that you may spend what you get on your pleasures.
>
> You adulterous people, don't you know that friendship with the world is hatred toward God? . . .
>
> Now listen, you rich people, weep and wail because of the misery that is coming upon you. Your wealth has rotted, and moths have eaten your clothes. Your gold and silver are corroded. Their corrosion will testify against you and eat your flesh like fire. You have hoarded wealth in the last days. Look! The wages you failed to pay the workmen who mowed your fields are crying out against you. The cries of the harvesters have reached the ears of the Lord Almighty. You have lived on earth in luxury and self-indulgence. You have fattened yourselves for the day of slaughter. (James 4:1–5; 5:1–5)

It cannot be denied that this is where evangelicalism, by and large, has staked its claim. The church growth movement even encourages the targeting of yuppies, as Volvo might. The apostle Paul warned Timothy, "In the last days . . . people will be lovers of themselves, lovers of money, boastful, proud, abusive, . . . lovers of pleasure rather than lovers of God" (2 Timothy 3:1–4). And yet, instead of heeding the warning, we have taken the plunge ourselves, meeting the "felt need" for selfishness, greed, and human-centeredness. When, in the fifties, the mental health movement drew the mainline churches into its wake, the Bible was suddenly thought to be all about positive thinking and self-esteem. Then, in the seventies, evangelicals got in on the act and added nationalism to the biblical gospel—another reason to be lovers of ourselves.

Finally, the "decade of money fever," as Wolfe dubbed the eighties, launched the prosperity gospel over the airwaves. Clearly, we are living beyond our means; and this is evident to the world not only in our national debt, placing us in danger of losing the trust of our trading partners, but in our own personal consumerism. Our economy is largely service-based rather than production-based today. Meanwhile, as we pamper ourselves, jobs are traveling overseas. This is not merely a partisan political issue, for we are all caught up in this consumerism, materialism, and greed. And living beyond our means—or even desiring to do so—is a good definition of coveting. We can see how eventually a shift in personal values transforms our businesses and our entire national character in a very short period of time, as historical shifts go.

As we went into the 1980s, the United States Bankruptcy Code was transformed to make it easier for troubled businesses to declare bankruptcy. "The 1980s, in fact, produced the largest growth in bankruptcy cases since the Great Depression of the 1930s," according to Pulitzer Prize-winning journalists Donald Barlett and James Steele.[4] In fact, they write, "Braniff, Inc., the airline, first sought protection in bankruptcy court in May 1982. It emerged two years later, in March 1984, but made a return appearance in September 1989. It emerged again in July 1991, and returned for a third time the following month. . . . All this has been a bonanza for the burgeoning bankruptcy industry—the lawyers, accountants and other specialists who charge up to $500 an hour for their time."[5]

President Reagan told us, "I don't look for a business that's going to render a service to mankind. . . . Greed is involved with everything we do. I find no fault with that."[6] But we have learned after that experiment that greed is not only a moral evil but bad business. With Michael Douglas's character in the movie *Wall Street*, Gordon Gekko, leading Christian celebrities have demonstrated, if not outright declared, "Greed is good!" And how do we reach those who are "lovers of pleasure rather than lovers of God"? By telling them how Jesus can help them "be all they can be," of course. Born-again baseball players tell the teens how Jesus improved their RBI statistics, and beauty queens are testimonies to the worldly success that follows those who put Jesus first.

Instead of challenging the culture and calling men and women to repentance, we have been marketing a false gospel, responding to false needs, reinforcing false gods. We covet praise, money, and pleasure; many of our pastors and church leaders covet success; and the church becomes a cheap instrument of secular aims. If we are to judge by the lifestyles and attitudes of contemporary Christians, we not only covet the vices of the world, we lend them our patronage and blessing. And when God doesn't give them what they covet, smart shoppers move on.

It is not enough, though, to simply issue commands and edicts about coveting. We have to realize that when we covet, we create idols. Once more, every ethical problem is, first, a spiritual and theological problem. What is the character of the god we worship? Who is he/she/it? Beyond merely "not coveting," we need to fill our minds, hearts, and lives with the satisfaction, pleasure, and enjoyment of God and our spiritual blessings in heavenly places, which Paul lists as our election, redemption, inheritance, justification, calling, sealing, and keeping in Christ (Ephesians 1:4–11). Moreover, we need to get beyond self-interest—even interest in our own salvation—and take pleasure in finding new avenues of glorifying God and serving our neighbor.

CONCLUSION

We have seen what a generation's worth of apathy toward theology and doctrinal thinking can produce. Even though Christians pour more energy into moral crusades than almost any other pursuit, Christians themselves do not appear to live any differently, or, for that matter, think differently. Barna observes,

> Survey data supply ample evidence of the bankruptcy of the commonly held world views of Christians. It is undeniable that as a body, American Christians have fallen prey to materialism, hedonism, secular humanism and even to a jaded form of Christianity that rejects much of the commitment required of faithful servants.
>
> A recent national survey discovered that no fewer than seven out of ten Christians are prone to hedonistic attitudes about life.[7]

Further, about two in five evangelical Christians "deny the possibility that pain or suffering could be a means of becoming a better, more mature individual. . . . As a final example, three out of ten Christians agreed that 'nothing in life is more important than having fun and being happy' [and] more than half of the Christian public believes that they 'never have enough money to buy what they need.'"[8] By contrast, secular historians are baffled by the enormous influence the Protestant Reformers had in changing the whole character of the Western world when that was not even their primary aim. How could a movement produce so much fruit in moral, social, and even political terms when, as Luther insisted, "Others attack the life; I attack the doctrine" of the medieval church?

The first objective was to preach the Word, especially the gospel, and administer the sacraments of baptism and Holy Communion. The Reformed added a third mark of the church, church discipline. In other words, the Reformers thought the root problem of individual and societal collapse was spiritual and theological, not moral and political. Consequently, that great movement of God created a distinctive character that, even when it did not succeed, aimed at "glorifying God and enjoying Him forever," seeing duty to neighbor as a tangible means of doing just that. They were saved by grace and by grace alone, so selfish motivations, such as fear of punishment and hope of rewards, were not theologically justified, even when sometimes ignorantly employed. In his *Freedom of the Christian,* Martin Luther drew from the doctrine of justification by grace alone an ethic without self-interest (fear of punishment and hope of rewards) as its motivation. John Calvin offered similar sentiments:

> It is not very sound theology to confine a man's thoughts so much to himself, and not to set before him, as the prime motive of his existence, zeal to illustrate the glory of God. For we are born first of all for God, and not for ourselves. . . . It is certainly the part of the Christian to ascend higher than merely to seek and secure the salvation of his own soul. I am persuaded, therefore, that there is no man imbued with true piety who will not consider as insipid that long and labored exhortation to zeal for heavenly life, a zeal which keeps a man entirely devoted to himself, and does not, even by one expression, arouse him to sanctify the name of God.[9]

Cultural critics may bemoan the loss of the Protestant work ethic and the collapse of ethics in general, but for the evangelical, it is theology that shapes ethics, not the other way around. One is tempted to enjoy the fruit without acknowledging the tree, but Christians no more than secularists can ignore the theology of the Reformation if they wish to recover its grand ethic.

By contrast, however, our ethics are often self-concerned and have little to do with relating to anybody but ourselves, unless being a "testimony" counts, by praying in a public restaurant and making sure no one who knows you sees you at an R-rated movie. We separate our life into "spiritual" and "secular" compartments too often, instead of seeing all of life as the theater of God's glory. Of the English Puritans, the political theorist Michael Waltzer writes that "the saints were responsible for their world—as medieval men were not—and responsible above all for its continual reformation. Their enthusiastic and purposive activity were part of their religious life, not something distinct and separate."[10]

Tom Wolfe told *Time*, "It's the decade of money fever. It's not a decade likely to produce heroic figures." Let's prove Wolfe wrong.

NOTES

1. Michael Lewis, *Money Culture* (New York: Penguin, 1992), 2.
2. Simon Schama, *The Embarrassment of Riches* (Berkeley: Univ. of California Press, 1988), 334–35.
3. George Barna, *The Barna Report: 1991–92* (Ventura, Calif.: Regal, 1992).
4. Donald Barlett and James Steele, *America: What Went Wrong?* (Kansas City: Andrews, McMeel, 1992), 68.
5. Ibid., 69.
6. Ronald Reagan, quoted in the *Los Angeles Times*, 1 February 1984.
7. George Barna and William Paul McKay, *Vital Signs: Emerging Social Trends and the Future of American Christianity* (Westchester, Ill.: Crossway, 1984), 140–41. Data from American Resource Bureau, Wheaton, Ill.
8. Ibid., 141.
9. John Calvin, in *A Reformation Debate*, ed. John Calvin and Jacopo Sadoleto (Grand Rapids: Baker, 1976), 58.
10. Michael Waltzer, *A Revolution of the Saints* (Cambridge: Harvard Univ. Press, 1965), 12.

CHAPTER TWELVE

GOOD NEWS FOR LAW-BREAKERS

For the man who trusts
in the God who justifies the wicked,
his faith is credited as righteousness.

"I am not ashamed of the gospel, for it is the power of God for the salvation of everyone who believes: first for the Jew, then for the Gentile" (Romans 1:16). With this declaration of his own personal confidence in the Christian message, the apostle Paul begins his trek, leading us to the Alpine summits of biblical revelation through what is arguably the most important book of the entire Bible. It was this letter to the Romans that brought reformation and revival throughout church history, unsettling the powers and authorities that were opposed to the clear preaching of the cross. It has been this book that brought comfort to the consciences of the brokenhearted and consternation to those who would tyrannize the consciences of the Christian faithful with threats of wrath even after the furious thunderings of the law had been silenced by that dark Friday afternoon outside of center-city Jerusalem, when God substituted His own innocent Son for all believers.

257

This is precisely why Paul is not ashamed of the gospel, because in it "a righteousness from God is revealed, a righteousness that is by faith from first to last, just as it is written: 'The righteous will live by faith'" (v. 17). In the law, the righteousness *of* God is revealed, a righteousness that condemns all of our pretenses of righteousness as "filthy rags." But in the gospel, a righteousness *from* God, that is, a gift of righteousness, is revealed. Not only does God show us how righteous we must be in order to be saved (in the law), but He actually grants us that very status of perfect righteousness and holiness, and this is known only in the gospel.

FIRST, THE BAD NEWS . . .

According to Deuteronomy 27:26, everyone who does not obey everything we have been discussing in this study of the Ten Commandments is under a curse. Consequently, Paul begins the epistle to the Romans by explaining how the Jews are condemned by the law written on tablets of stone, and the Gentiles by the law written on the conscience through creation. Everyone knows that there is a supreme Judge who makes people give an account of their sins.

The Gentiles suppress the truth about themselves and God's wrath by trying to wipe away God's fingerprints from the divine image stamped upon them. They worship the creature rather than the Creator, exchange the truth for a lie, and turn God's created order upside down (homosexuality is specifically cited) in an attempt to remake the world after their own wickedness so that they can regard their own wickedness as "normal." In this way, they talk themselves into actually believing that there is nothing to worry about—that whatever god that might exist approves of them and does not hold them guilty.

Nevertheless, Paul next turns the guns of the law from the Gentiles to the Jews: "You, therefore, have no excuse, you who pass judgment on someone else, for at whatever point you judge the other, you are condemning yourself, because you who pass judgment do the same things" (2:1).

In other words, by passing judgment on others for their violations of God's revealed commandments, the Jews were admitting that they knew the law in an even clearer way and, therefore, were even more inexcusable. What judging the pagans accomplished was not establishing the righteousness of God's people in contrast to the lawlessness of the Gentiles but merely making the Jews all the more accountable, since they practiced the same sins even though they claimed to be holy. Paul assures them that they will no more escape God's judgment than the heathen (v. 3).

So all the world stands condemned, since "Jews and Gentiles alike are all under sin. . . . 'There is no one righteous, not even one; there is no one who understands, no one who seeks God. All have turned away, they have together become worthless; there is no one who does good, not even one'" (3:9–12). God, therefore, issues the threats of the law, "so that every mouth may be silenced and the whole world held accountable to God. Therefore no one will be declared righteous in his sight by observing the law; rather, through the law we become conscious of sin" (vv. 19–20). In other words, the purpose of the law is to remind us how wicked we are.

It is easy for us, like the Jews of old, to assume that because we have the Bible, the church, Judeo-Christian values, and the like, we are righteous, holy, and good. The wicked are those who promote secular values. But here the apostle Paul levels us just as he did his own countrymen. After all, we practice the same sins. The only difference is that our (often self-righteous) claims to adhering to traditional values accuses rather than excuses us. Instead of showing that God is on our side, it merely shows us that God has even more reason for condemning us, because we claim to know better and pretend that we do better, while in fact we engage in the same sins as our unbelieving neighbor.

So, the law comes to tell all of us that "there is no one who does good, not even one" before the pure eyes of Him who can see filthiness in things we consider pure and holy. The one who trusts in his own righteousness knows who the wicked are: the homosexuals, the feminists, the pornographers, the secular humanists, the abortionists, and so on. But if our Lord was right in His Sermon on the Mount, we are all adulterers, fornicators, murderers, false witnesses, thieves, covetous, false worshipers, blasphemers, and self-seekers. In this tradition, Paul assures us that the law locks us all up in the same jail cell together with common criminals, regardless of how much we may protest in defense of our own godliness. As we have seen from the Barna surveys, even most evangelical Christians believe they are conforming to the Ten Commandments. It is no small wonder, then, that most cannot name more than five of them. If ever our generation is going to know the power of the gospel, it will first have to know its own powerlessness against the threats of God's demand for perfect, inward holiness of heart and life. God does not demand *our* best, but *His* best, which is to say, simply, the original righteousness in which we were created.

JUSTIFICATION: BEING *DECLARED* RIGHTEOUS

Once we come to the place where we realize that we cannot recreate that original righteousness—even with God's help—we are ready for the good news and the Savior's words of absolution: "Your guilt is taken away and your sins are forgiven." This is precisely where Paul picks up:

> But now a righteousness from God, apart from law, has been made known, to which the Law and the Prophets testify. This righteousness from God comes through faith in Jesus Christ to all who believe. There is no difference, for all have sinned and fall short of the glory of God, and are justified freely by his grace through the redemption that came by Christ Jesus. (3:21–24).

Only in this way could God be both "just and the one who justifies those who have faith in Jesus" (v. 26). Therefore, there is no place for boasting, "for we maintain that a man is justified by faith apart from observing the law" (v. 28). Abraham is called to the witness stand to testify to justification by grace alone through faith alone. We receive the gift of righteousness, not as a reward, as though we could do anything that would obligate God to respond in kind, but by giving up on our own performance. "However, to the man who does not work but trusts God who justifies the wicked, his faith is credited as righteousness" (4:5). And that is the important phrase: "God who justifies *the wicked.*" How can God declare righteous those who are unrighteous and, in fact, wicked? How can He say something about us that is untrue?

Here is where the Pharisees of Jesus' day failed to grasp the gospel (Luke 18:9–14), as did the Judaizers (Galatians 3:10–14), the medieval church, and all today—Catholic and Protestant—who see their relationship with God primarily in terms of moral transformation. Such people have always insisted that God cannot declare us righteous until we actually become righteous. As Wesley pleaded, "O warn them [the Calvinists] that if they remain unrighteous, the righteousness of Christ will profit them nothing!"[1]

Luther's phrase captures the Pauline thought: *simul iustus et peccator,* "simultaneously justified and sinful." In other words, the Christian is to believe, on the authority of God's promise in the Word, that he or she is righteous because of someone else's obedience to the law and satisfaction of his or her violations of it. If we are in Christ, God regards us as though we had never sinned and, in fact, as though we had obeyed the law perfectly already. This is a fact, a once-and-for-all declaration that is not in any way dependent on our own performance. But moralists of all ages have found this impossible to believe. One contemporary evangelical scholar writes, "But can it really be true— saint and sinner simultaneously? I wish it were so. . . . *Simul iustus et peccator?* I hope it's true! I simply fear it's not."[2]

We are convinced that our righteousness has to fit in there somewhere. God cannot provide all of the righteousness, for that would be unjust. This is how we reason, but the gospel, unlike the law, is not something we can learn from reason or from nature. It comes only from divine revelation, in no other place than God's written Word. In fact, whereas the law makes sense, the gospel is "foolishness to those who are perishing" (1 Corinthians 1:18). Who ever heard of someone being declared "not guilty" even when he continued committing crimes? How can the law-keeping of someone else be credited to a law-breaker? To the degree that we try to make God's method of saving sinners more acceptable to the sinful mind, to that degree it will be something other than the gospel of Jesus Christ.

Thus, from Genesis 15:6, where "Abraham believed the LORD, and it was credited to him as righteousness," to Jesus, where the sinner who cried out, "God, have mercy on me, a sinner," "went home justified" rather than the Pharisee who thanked God that he was not like the others (Luke 18:13–14), to Paul and the other apostles, the main idea is that God justifies sinners, not by *making* them holy, but by *declaring* them holy even though they will never live up to that declaration this side of heaven. The Christian, therefore, lives by promise, not by sight. He or she knows that what God says is true, even if it does not match his or her own experience. One day we will be glorified as we see God for the first time "as he is," face to face.

So Paul argues in Romans 5 that Adam was the federal head or representative spokesperson for the whole human race. Just as Thomas Jefferson spoke for all future Americans in his Declaration of Independence, so Adam spoke for all of his descendants. We are born sinners, with both the imputation of Adam's guilt (since we were in some sense with him, united with him in his sin) and the corruption of Adam's nature. But in Christ, we are taken from the covenant of works, by which we are judged law-breakers and sentenced to judgment—even from birth—to the covenant of grace. Adam, our covenant head, ruined us by his disobedience, but Christ, the Second Adam, rescued us by His obedience. As Adam's guilt is imputed to us even apart from our own personal actions, so Christ's righteousness is imputed to us even apart from our own personal actions. This is justification. But also, as Adam's corruption was passed on to us, so too in Christ we are given new life, resulting in actual righteousness, personal acts of obedience flowing out of a renewed heart. This is sanctification.

SANCTIFICATION: BEING *MADE* RIGHTEOUS

By the end of Paul's major section on justification, the apostle anticipates the most likely reaction: "What shall we say then? Shall we go on sinning that grace may increase?" (Romans 6:1). After all, he had just said, "Where sin increased, grace increased all the more" (5:20). Surely this is a recipe for license. If people do not sense that they can still be condemned for their sins—especially great ones—what will keep them from saying, "I have my fire insurance, and now I'll live any kind of life I wish"? Martyn Lloyd-Jones observed that if, upon hearing our presentation of the gospel of God's free grace, we do not hear the same criticism raised, we have not really preached the gospel.

One of Luther's students asked the professor, "If what you're saying is true, then we may live as we want!" to which Luther replied, "Yes. Now what do you want?" As Jesus argued that it was the tree that made the fruit, so Paul here will argue that it is God's unconditional acceptance that produces real change, not the other way around. So Paul turns from the discussion of what God does in Christ *for* us and *outside of* us (justification) to what he does in Christ *within* us. God has yet to justify someone He leaves unconverted. The same God who grants someone who is "dead in trespasses and sins" (Ephesians 2:1) the life to believe and trust in Christ for his or her justification also grants that person the faith to grow in Christ and trust in him for his or her sanctification and perseverance in faith (Philippians 1:6).

God not only justifies; He sanctifies. These must be clearly distinguished so that we do not end up slipping back into confusing God's declaring us righteous by legal decree with the process of making us righteous. Nevertheless, we must not separate these divine actions, either. One is a pronouncement, based on Christ's finished work; the other is a process, based on Christ's finished work; but both belong to every believer by grace alone, through the same simple faith God gives us to trust in Christ. Through this faith, we are assured that we are righteous in Christ, even though we do not perceive it in ourselves, and through this same faith we are assured that Christ's life flows through us, sanctifying us just as surely as the life of the vine forms the shape, color, health, and vitality of the branches.

That is why Paul answers the question, "Shall we go on sinning so that grace may increase?" (Romans 6:1) in such strong terms:

> By no means! We died to sin; how can we live in it any longer? Or don't you know that all of us who were baptized in into Christ Jesus were baptized into his death? We were therefore buried with him through baptism into death in order that, just as Christ was raised from the dead through the glory of the Father, we too may live a new life.
>
> If we have been united with him like this in his death, we will certainly also be united with him in his resurrection. For we know that our old self was crucified with him so that the body of sin might be done away with, that we should no longer be slaves to sin—because anyone who has died has been freed from sin. (vv. 2–7)

What the apostle is saying is this: Two things are true of you, through faith in Christ. First, you *are* justified. That is, God has declared you righteous apart from your works. Second, you are *being* sanctified because you have not only been freed from the guilt of your sin, but from its all-consuming power and tyranny as well. It can no longer master you, because Christ has seen to its dethronement.

Many of us are familiar with the booklets that depict the two options for the believer. In the first circle, self is on the throne; in the second, Christ. "In which circle are you?" the booklet asks the believer. Many have argued in a similar vein what has come to be called the "carnal Christian" teaching; that is, the idea that the Christian may be saved from the guilt of sin and, therefore, be assured of salvation even though the same person is not free from the rule of sin. One can know Christ as Savior but not accept Him as Lord. Thus, the goal of the preacher in this kind of system is to get the person to make a second decision, this time "allowing" Jesus to gain victory over sin's dominion.

But according to Paul's declaration in Romans 6, *every* believer is in the same circle, with Christ on the throne! Notice that Paul does not urge the Romans to enter into a higher life, to gain victory over sin, or to live "the victorious Christian life." He says that all of this has already been accomplished for the believer in Christ and is given all at once to the believer through faith. The moment God grants the sinner faith, the guilt *and* the control of sin are both conquered immediately and completely. Never again does the believer have to worry either about being judged for his sins or about being controlled by his sins. We do not achieve the victory; Christ already has! So, Paul says, we *have* died to sin; our sinful nature *was* crucified with Christ; we *have been* raised with Christ. "Anyone who *has* died *has been* freed from sin" (v. 7, italics added). He does not call us to die to sin and live to Christ, but rather to "*count* [regard, recognize, acknowledge] yourselves dead to sin but alive to God in Christ Jesus" (v. 11).

Here we return to a point we made in the opening chapter: the distinction between the *indicative* and the *imperative*. According to the indicative, we are already holy in Christ; sin has already been dethroned; we are already dead to sin, buried, and raised in new life, seated with Christ in the heavenlies. Because this is *already* true about us, according to God's promise, and not dependent on our own decisions or efforts, we are to obey the imperatives laid out for us in Scripture. For instance, Paul says in Colossians 3:12, "Therefore, *as* God's chosen people, holy and dearly loved, *clothe* yourselves with compassion, kindness, humility, gentleness and patience" (italics added). He does not say, "Therefore, as you attempt to become God's people and seek to enter into the holiness and love of God," do thus and so. We do not *become* by doing or entering, surrendering or gaining victory. Because of *Christ's* victory, we are already victorious; we are called not to enter into victory, but to live in the light of it.

Think of all the ways in which Paul could have answered the criticism that this doctrine would lead to license. He could have answered, "By no means! Don't you know that those who do not put Jesus on the throne of their lives will never experience the real joy and fulfillment that comes from doing the will of God?" Or, in another appeal to man's happiness rather than to what God has done for his own glory in Christ, "By no means! Don't you know that if you do not subdue sin in your life and let Jesus take control, you will fall under God's judgment again?" Or, in the same vein, "By no means! How shall those who have not yet died to sin enjoy rewards in the next life?"

But against all of these, Paul declares that we *have* died to sin and already enjoy all of the spiritual blessings in Christ as we long for the day when we shall fully experience the freedom not only from sin's tyranny, but from its very presence in our lives.

And still, this victory is not the only thing that is true about us. Just as the reader might wrongly conclude, after Paul's discussion of justification, that one may live in sin without fear, so too the reader might wrongly conclude, after Paul's declaration "Anyone who has died has been freed from sin" (Romans 6:7), that the believer is perfected in sanctification the moment he or she believes. In other words, one may infer, "If I am really united with Christ, I will no longer continue to sin." But once more, Paul is ready with a response to such a conclusion, and as a caring pastor, he uses his own failures as an illustration:

> . . . So then, the law is holy and the commandment is holy, righteous and good.
> Did that which is good, then, become death to me? By no means! . . .
> We know that the law is spiritual; but I am unspiritual, sold as a slave to sin. I do not understand what I do. For what I want to do I do not do, but what I hate I do. And if I do what I do not want to do, I agree that the law is good. . . . I know that nothing good lives in me, that is, in my sinful nature. For I have the desire to do what is good, but I cannot carry it out. For what I do is not the good I want to do; no, the evil I do not want to do—this I keep on doing. . . .
> So I find this law at work: When I want to do good, evil is right there with me. For in my inner being I delight

in God's law; but I see another law at work in the members
of my body, waging war against the law of my mind and
making me a prisoner of the law of sin at work within my
members. What a wretched man I am! Who will rescue me
from this body of death? Thanks be to God—through Jesus
Christ our Lord!

So then, in my mind I am a slave to God's law, but in
the sinful nature a slave to the law of sin. (7:12–25)

Many have argued that Paul must be speaking of his
preconversion experience, since it seems inappropriate for
an apostle to refer to himself as "unspiritual, sold as a slave
to sin," and finding himself falling into the same sins again
and again. But however incongruous as this passage may
seem next to the optimism of Romans 6, Paul does say that
even when he does engage in sins, it is contrary to his
deeper commitment to the law of God. He states, in fact,
that he loves God's law and delights in it. And yet, he states
in just the next chapter that "the sinful mind is hostile to
God. It does not submit to God's law, nor can it do so"
(8:7). Further, in 1 Corinthians 2:14, "The man without
the Spirit does not accept the things of the Spirit of God,
for they are foolishness to him, and he cannot understand
them, because they are spiritually discerned." So the experience of Paul is clearly the experience of someone who
does have the Spirit of God, and it is the very fact that he
does possess the Spirit that makes Paul is so frustrated with
his condition. The unbeliever is not disturbed about his
law-breaking, but Paul here is outraged at his own failures
precisely because he does love the law and does delight in
it. Furthermore, Paul writes here in the present tense, and
has used other tenses regularly in the surrounding passages;
therefore, there would be no reason to use the present
tense here if it were not describing an ongoing experience.

Why is all of this important? Anyone who struggles as
a believer with ongoing sinful habits, behaviors, and desires knows why it is so important. Far from advancing
some sort of perfectionism, Paul uses this testimony to his
own failures as an example of the realism we ought to have

in the Christian life. One cannot truly grow in Christ unless one is prepared for failure. When it comes, as it inevitably will, the Christian must know why it comes and not be disillusioned with the gospel simply because of overly optimistic schemes of victorious living. Instead, one must simply acknowledge God's forgiveness and move on in the strength of the Holy Spirit.

So, while we are new people, baptized into a new identity, wild branches grafted onto a new vine, we are still the same people we were before. We still bring with us the sinful affections we had before we were converted. The difference is that we have a new heart and can never love our sins as we love the law of God, and that is what creates the tension. Only believers struggle in their conscience over obedience to God's law and giving in to temptation, for they have been made new and the law of God is no longer merely written on tablets or on their conscience, but on the very heart; in other words, it is the new frame of their affections. This is why the Heidelberg Catechism says that even though "the holiest of them [Christians] make only a small beginning in obedience in this life," they nevertheless "begin with serious purpose to conform not only to some, but to all of the commandments of God" (Q. 114). Here Romans 6 and 7 come together: On the one hand, our whole soul, not just part of it, has been converted, so that there is not a single part of our soul that is not turned back to God; and yet we know by our own experience that this newness that pervades our soul is at war with the ejected tenant. That within us which used to reign wants its throne back and, although Christ's victory insures that this will never happen, the war will not end until we are brought into that place where we will be glorified and the presence of sin banished.

That is why Paul then returns, in chapter 8, to his former optimism. He assures us that he was not optimistic because of anything he saw in his own Christian experience necessarily (for war is often discouraging), but because of the promise that Christ *has* achieved victory once and for all. "Therefore, there is *now*"—not in some future moment, when we "surrender all"—"no condemnation for those who are in Christ Jesus, because through Christ Jesus the law of the Spirit of life *set me free*"—past tense again —"from the law of sin and death. For what the law was powerless to do in that it was weakened by the sinful nature, God did by sending his own Son in the likeness of sinful man to be a sin offering" (8:1–3). The law cannot change us; it cannot save us; it cannot even assist grace in saving us. The law can only condemn—not because of a weakness in it, but because of our own sinfulness. Therefore, even in the Christian life, we are always brought back to the cross.

Sometimes we think that the law only condemns all of our righteousness done before our conversion. Now that we are believers, we often reason, our works now must keep us from punishment and gain for us rewards. And then tragedy comes. When we thought we were the strongest against temptation, we suddenly find ourselves wrapped up in a sin in which we were entangled before we were converted. What of all of those "before and after" testimonies of people who were suddenly converted from a life of debauchery to an instant life of service? *Surely I must not really be converted,* we reason.

But when our conscience agrees with the law that we are unholy and unrighteous, we must seek the verdict of God in Christ: "God made him who had no sin to be sin for us, so that in him we might become the righteousness of God" (2 Corinthians 5:21). The good news is for believers, too! Not only can unbelievers be saved from their guilt and shame; even believers who return to their sins can be forgiven. Our God is not a stingy God with His grace; He is not grudging in His forgiveness but is more anxious to clothe us in Christ's righteousness than we are to be clothed in it.

The Heidelberg Catechism asks an important question at this point. After making it plain from Scripture that even the best Christians in this life make only a short beginning in holiness, it asks, "Why then does God have the Ten Commandments preached so strictly since no one can keep them in this life?" In response, it says, "First, that all our life long we may become increasingly aware of our sinfulness, and therefore more eagerly seek forgiveness of sins and righteousness in Christ. Second, that we may constantly and diligently pray to God for the grace of the Holy Spirit, so that more and more we may be renewed in the image of God, until we attain the goal of full perfection after this life."

First, we need to constantly hear the law of God, in spite of our failure to conform to it, so that we will forever be running to Christ. Imagine, if the believer could conform to the demands of the law in this life, he or she would be inclined to rest more and more on his or her own righteousness. Since it is only the perfect righteousness of Christ, and not our approximations, that God accepts, our holiness in that scenario would be damning. Even the believer must be reminded that his best works are spotted with sin, and never does one advance to the position where he can begin to be graded on his own work before God. Not only our justification, but even our sanctification, depends on Christ's righteousness and never on our ability to keep the law—either God's or man's; either the Ten Commandments or the Ten Steps to Victory.

Second, the law must be preached in all of its perfection, never lowered to our standards, so that we will be drawn to pray for God's Spirit to conform us more to the image of Christ and to live every day in longing anticipation for that great day when we will be able to love God and our neighbor as the law commands.

"Even so, Lord Jesus, come quickly!"

NOTES

1. John Wesley, *Works,* ed. Albert C. Outler (Oxford: Oxford Univ. Press, 1964), 1:127.
2. Russel Spittler, in *Christian Spirituality,* ed. Donald Alexander (Downers Grove, Ill.: InterVarsity, 1988), 84.

APPENDIX

INTRODUCTION

Many modern believers are put off by the term *catechism*. Nevertheless, the word simply means "instruction guide." Christians, ever since the earliest days of the church, have found it necessary to draw out from Scripture the main points and arrange them in a systematic way, in the form of questions and answers, so they could pass down through the generations at least a basic knowledge of the faith. During the Sunday morning service, the question and answer for the week would be read; then, in the evening service, the sermon would be a study of that teaching throughout Scripture. Throughout the week, usually at the dinner table, parents would lead their children in a discussion of that topic and make sure that they were memorizing the question, answer, and supporting verses.

If we get beyond the term *catechism*, we can see that the idea makes a good deal of sense. The Jews used just such a pattern for learning the Scriptures, and Christians followed suit, including evangelicals, until gradually the pressures of modern life and the downplaying of doctrine in general led them to abandon these teaching manuals. Below you will find a sample from the Heidelberg Catechism, one of the Reformation catechisms that sought to bring unity between German evangelicals. This is followed by a selection from the Westminster Shorter Catechism. The reader is encouraged to also see Luther's small and larger catechisms.

It is my prayer that regular catechetical teaching *in the home* will be revived as a remedy for biblical illiteracy, the degeneration of the family's spiritual significance, and for raising covenant children in the fear and admonition of the Lord.

The texts used in these appendixes are the following:

For the Heidelberg Catechism, the translation that appears in *Ecumenical Creeds and Reformed Confessions*, edited by The Christian Reformed Church (Grand Rapids: CRC Publication, 1987); Copyright © 1987 by CRC Publications.

For the Westminster Shorter Catechism, the text published by the Office of the General Assembly, The United Presbyterian Church (New York, 1970).

SELECTION FROM THE HEIDELBERG CATECHISM

LORD'S DAY 32

86 Q. We have been delivered
from our misery
by God's grace alone through Christ
and not because we have earned it:
why then must we still do good?

A. To be sure, Christ has redeemed us by his blood.
But we do good because
Christ by his Spirit is also renewing us to be like
himself,
so that in all our living
we may show that we are thankful to God
for all he has done for us,[1]
and so that he may be praised through us.[2]

And we do good
so that we may be assured of our faith by its fruits,[3]
and so that by our godly living
our neighbors may be won over to Christ.[4]

1. Rom. 6:13; 12:1–2; 1 Pet. 2:5–10.
2. Matt. 5:16; 1 Cor. 6:19–20.
3. Matt. 7:17–18; Gal. 5:22–24; 2 Pet. 1:10–11.
4. Matt. 5:14–16; Rom. 14:17–19; 1 Pet. 2:12; 3:1–2.

87 Q. **Can those be saved**
who do not turn to God
from their ungrateful
and impenitent ways?

 A. By no means.
Scripture tells us that
no unchaste person,
no idolater, adulterer, thief,
no covetous person,
no drunkard, slanderer, robber,
or the like
is going to inherit the kingdom of God.[1]

1. 1 Cor. 6:9–10; Gal. 5:19–21; Eph. 5:1–20; 1 John 3:14.

LORD'S DAY 33

88 Q. **What is involved**
in genuine repentance or conversion?

 A. Two things:
the dying-away of the old self,
and the coming-to-life of the new.[1]

1. Rom. 6:1–11; 2 Cor. 5:17; Eph. 4:22–24; Col. 3:5–10.

89 Q. **What is the dying-away of the old self?**

 A. It is to be genuinely sorry for sin,
to hate it more and more,
and to run away from it.[1]

1. Ps. 51:3–4,17; Joel 2:12–13; Rom. 8:12–13; 2 Cor. 7:10.

90 Q. **What is the coming-to-life of the new self?**

 A. It is wholehearted joy in God through Christ[1]
and a delight to do every kind of good
as God wants us to.[2]

1. Ps. 51:8, 12; Isa. 57:15; Rom. 5:1; 14:17.
2. Rom. 6:10–11; Gal. 2:20.

91 Q. **What do we do that is good?**

A. Only that which
    arises out of true faith,[1]
    conforms to God's law,[2]
    and is done for his glory;[3]
and not that which is based
    on what we think is right
    or on established human tradition.[4]

1. John 15:5; Heb. 11:6.
2. Lev. 18:4; 1 Sam. 15:22; Eph. 2:10.
3. 1 Cor. 10:31.
4. Deut. 12:32; Isa. 29:13; Ezek. 20:18–19; Matt. 15:7–9.

LORD'S DAY 34

92 Q. What does the Lord say in his law?

A. God spoke all these words:

The First Commandment
I am the LORD your God,
    who brought you out of Egypt,
    out of the land of slavery.
You shall have no other gods before me.

The Second Commandment
You shall not make for yourself an idol
    in the form of anything in heaven above
    or on the earth beneath
    or in the waters below.
You shall not bow down to them or worship them;
    for I, the LORD your God, am a jealous God,
    punishing the children for the sin of the fathers
      to the third and fourth generation
      of those who hate me,
    but showing love to a thousand generations of those
      who love me and keep my commandments.

The Third Commandment
You shall not misuse the name of the LORD your God,
    for the LORD will not hold anyone guiltless
    who misuses his name.

The Fourth Commandment
Remember the Sabbath day by keeping it holy.
Six days you shall labor and do all your work,
but the seventh day is a Sabbath to the LORD your God.
On it you shall not do any work,
    neither you, nor your son or daughter,
    nor your manservant or maidservant,
    nor your animals,
    nor the alien within your gates.

For in six days the LORD made the heavens and
the earth,
the sea, and all that is in them,
but he rested on the seventh day.
Therefore the LORD blessed the Sabbath day
and made it holy.

The Fifth Commandment
Honor your father and your mother,
so that you may live long
in the land the LORD your God is giving you.

The Sixth Commandment
You shall not murder.

The Seventh Commandment
You shall not commit adultery.

The Eighth Commandment
You shall not steal.

The Ninth Commandment
You shall not give false testimony against your
neighbor.

The Tenth Commandment
You shall not covet your neighbor's house.
You shall not covet your neighbor's wife,
or his manservant or maidservant,
his ox or donkey,
or anything that belongs to your neighbor.[1]

1. Ex. 20:1–17; Deut. 5:6–21.

93 Q. **How are these commandments divided?**

A. Into two tables.
The first has four commandments,
teaching us what our relation to God should be.
The second has six commandments,
teaching us what we owe our neighbor.[1]

1. Matt. 22:37–39.

94 Q. **What does the Lord require
in the first commandment?**

A. That I, not wanting to endanger my very salvation,
avoid and shun
all idolatry,[1] magic, superstitious rites,[2]
and prayer to saints or to other creatures.[3]

That I sincerely acknowledge the only true God,[4]
trust him alone,[5]
look to him for every good thing[6]
humbly[7] and patiently,[8]
love him,[9] fear him,[10] and honor him[11]
with all my heart.

In short,
That I give up anything
rather than go against his will in any way.[12]

1. 1 Cor. 6:9–10; 10:5–14; 1 John 5:21.
2. Lev. 19:31; Deut. 18:9–12.
3. Matt. 4:10; Rev. 19;10; 22:8–9.
4. John 17:3.
5. Jer. 17:5, 7.
6. Ps. 104:27–28; James 1:17.
7. 1 Pet. 5:5–6.
8. Col. 1:11; Heb. 10:36.
9. Matt. 22:37 (Deut. 6:5).
10. Prov. 9:10; 1 Pet. 1:17.
11. Matt. 4:10 (Deut. 6:13).
12. Matt. 5:29–30; 10:37–39.

95 Q. What is idolatry?

A. Idolatry is
having or inventing something in which one trusts
in place of or alongside of the only true God,
who has revealed himself in his Word.[1]

1. 1 Chron. 16:26; Gal. 4:8–9; Eph. 5:5; Phil. 3:19.

LORD'S DAY 35

**96 Q. What is God's will for us
in the second commandment?**

A. That we in no way make any image of God[1]
nor worship him in any other way
than he has commanded in his Word.[2]

1. Deut. 4:15–19; Isa. 40:18–25; Acts 17:29; Rom. 1:23.
2. Lev. 10:1–7; 1 Sam. 15:22–23; John 4:23–24.

97 Q. May we then not make any image at all?

A. God can not and may not
be visibly portrayed in any way.

Although creatures may be portrayed,
yet God forbids making or having such images
if one's intention is to worship them
or to serve God through them.[1]

1. Ex. 34:13–14, 17; 2 Kings 18:4–5.

98 Q. But may not images be permitted in the churches
as teaching aids for the unlearned?

A. No, we shouldn't try to be wiser than God.
He wants his people instructed
by the living preaching of his Word—[1]
not by idols that cannot even talk.[2]

1. Rom. 10:14–15, 17; 2 Tim. 3:16–17; 2 Pet. 1:19.
2. Jer. 10:8; Hab. 2:18–20.

LORD'S DAY 36

99 Q. What is God's will for us
in the third commandment?

A. That we neither blaspheme nor misuse the name
of God
by cursing,[1] perjury,[2] or unnecessary oaths,[3]
nor share in such horrible sins
by being silent bystanders.[4]

In a word, it requires
that we use the holy name of God
only with reverence and awe,[5]
so that we may properly
confess him,[6]
pray to him,[7]
and praise him in everything we do and say.[8]

1. Lev. 24:10–17.
2. Lev. 19:12.
3. Matt. 5:37; James 5:12.
4. Lev. 5:1; Prov. 29:24.
5. Ps. 99:1–5; Jer. 4:2.
6. Matt. 10:32–33; Rom. 10:9–10.
7. Ps. 50:14–15; 1 Tim. 2:8.
8. Col. 3:17.

100 Q. Is blasphemy of God's name by swearing and
cursing
really such serious sin
that God is angry also with those
who do not do all they can
to help prevent it and forbid it?

A. Yes, indeed.[1]
No sin is greater,
no sin makes God more angry
than blaspheming his name.
That is why he commanded the death penalty for
it.[2]

1. Lev. 5:1.
2. Lev. 24:10–17.

LORD'S DAY 37

101 Q. But may we swear an oath in God's name
if we do it reverently?

A. Yes, when the government demands it,
or when necessity requires it,
in order to maintain and promote truth and
trustworthiness
for God's glory and our neighbor's good.

Such oaths are approved in God's Word[1]
and were rightly used by Old and New Testament
believers.[2]

1. Deut. 6:13; 10:20; Jer. 4:1–2; Heb. 6:16.
2. Gen. 21:24; Josh. 9:15; 1 Kings 1:29–30; Rom. 1:9; 2 Cor. 1:23.

102 Q. May we swear by saints or other creatures?

A. No.
A legitimate oath means calling upon God
as the one who knows my heart
to witness to my truthfulness
and to punish me if I swear falsely.[1]
No creature is worthy of such honor.[2]

1. Rom. 9:11; 2 Cor. 1:23.
2. Matt. 5:34–37; 23:16–22; James 5:12.

LORD'S DAY 38

103 Q. What is God's will for us
in the fourth commandment?

A. First,
that the gospel ministry and education for it be
maintained,[1]
and that, especially on the festive day of rest,
I regularly attend the assembly of God's people[2]
to learn what God's Word teaches,[3]
to participate in the sacraments,[4]
to pray to God publicly,[5]
and to bring Christian offerings for the poor.[6]

Second,
that every day of my life
I rest from my evil ways,
let the Lord work in me through his Spirit,
and so begin in this life
the eternal Sabbath.[7]

1. Deut. 6:4–9, 20–25; 1 Cor. 9:13–14; 2 Tim. 2:2; 3:13–17; Tit. 1:5.
2. Deut. 12:5–12; Ps. 40:9–10; 68:26; Acts 2:42–47; Heb. 10:23–25.
3. Rom. 10:14–17; 1 Cor. 14:31–32; 1 Tim. 4:13.

4. 1 Cor. 11:23–24.
5. Col. 3:16; 1 Tim. 2:1.
6. Ps. 50:14; 1 Cor. 16:2; 2 Cor. 8–9.
7. Isa. 66:23; Heb. 4:9–11.

LORD'S DAY 39

**104 Q. What is God's will for us
in the fifth commandment?**

    A. That I honor, love, and be loyal to
        my father and mother
        and all those in authority over me;
    that I obey and submit to them, as is proper,
        when they correct and punish me;[1]
    and also that I be patient with their failings—[2]
    for through them God chooses to rule us.[3]

1. Ex. 21:17; Prov. 1:8; 4:1; Rom. 13:1–2; Eph. 5:21–22; 6:1–9; Col 3:18–4:1.
2. Prov. 20:20; 23:22; 1 Pet. 2:18.
3. Matt. 22:21; Rom. 13:1–8; Eph. 6:1–9; Col. 3:18–21.

LORD'S DAY 40

**105 Q. What is God's will for us
in the sixth commandment?**

    A. I am not to belittle, insult, hate, or kill my
        neighbor—
    not by my thoughts, my words, my look or
        gesture,
    and certainly not by actual deeds—
    and I am not to be party to this in others;[1]
    rather, I am to put away all desire for revenge.[2]

    I am not to harm or recklessly endanger myself
    either.[3]

    Prevention of murder is also why
    government is armed with the sword.[4]

1. Gen. 9:6; Lev. 19:17–18; Matt. 5:21–22; 26:52.
2. Prov. 25:21–22; Matt. 18:35; Rom. 12:19; Eph. 4:26.
3. Matt. 4:7; 26:52; Rom. 13:11–14.
4. Gen. 9:6; Ex. 21:14; Rom. 13:4.

106 Q. Does this commandment refer only to killing?

    A. By forbidding murder God teaches us
        that he hates the root of murder:
        envy, hatred, anger, vindictiveness.[1]

    In God's sight all such are murder.[2]

1. Prov. 14:30; Rom. 1:29; 12:19; Gal. 5:19–21; 1 John 2:9–11
2. 1 John 3:15.

107 Q. Is it enough then
that we do not kill our neighbor
in any such way?

A. No.
By condemning envy, hatred, and anger
God tells us
to love our neighbor as ourselves,[1]
to be patient, peace-loving, gentle,
merciful, and friendly to him,[2]
to protect him from harm as much as we can,
and to do good even to our enemies.[3]

1. Matt. 7:12; 22:39; Rom. 12:10.
2. Matt. 5:3–12; Luke 6:36; Rom. 12:10, 18; Gal. 6:1–2; Eph. 4:2; Col. 3:12; 1 Pet. 3:8.
3. Ex. 23:4–5; Matt. 44–45; Rom. 12:20–21 (Prov. 25:21–22).

LORD'S DAY 41

108 Q. What is God's will for us
in the seventh commandment?

A. God condemns all unchastity.[1]
We should therefore thoroughly detest it[2]
and, married or single,
live decent and chaste lives.[3]

1. Lev. 18:30; Eph. 5:3–5.
2. Jude 22–23.
3. 1 Cor. 7:1–9; 1 Thess. 4:3–8; Heb. 13:4.

109 Q. Does God, in this commandment,
forbid only such scandalous sins as adultery?

A. We are temples of the Holy Spirit, body and soul,
and God wants both to be kept clean and holy.
That is why he forbids
everything which incites unchastity,[1]
whether it be actions, looks, talk, thoughts, or
desires.[2]

1. 1 Cor. 15:33; Eph. 5:18.
2. Matt. 5:27–29; 1 Cor. 6:18–20; Eph. 5:3–4.

LORD'S DAY 42

110 Q. What does God forbid
in the eighth commandment?

A. He forbids not only outright theft and robbery,
punishable by law.[1]

But in God's sight theft also includes
cheating and swindling our neighbor
by schemes made to appear legitimate,[2]
such as:
inaccurate measurements of weight, size, or
volume;
fraudulent merchandising;
counterfeit money;
excessive interest;
or any other means forbidden by God.[3]

In addition he forbids all greed[4]
and pointless squandering of his gifts.[5]

1. Ex. 22:1; 1 Cor. 5:9–10; 6:9–10.
2. Mic. 6:9–11; Luke 3:14; James 5:1–6.
3. Deut. 25:13–16; Ps. 15:5; Prov. 11:1; 12:22; Ezek. 45:9–12; Luke 6:35.
4. Luke 12:15; Eph. 5:5.
5. Prov. 21:20; 23:20–21; Luke 16:10–13.

**111 Q. What does God require of you
in this commandment?**

  A. That I do whatever I can
for my neighbor's good,
that I treat him
as I would like others to treat me,
and that I work faithfully
so that I may share with those in need.[1]

1. Isa. 58:5–10; Matt. 7:12; Gal. 6:9–10; Eph. 4:28.

LORD'S DAY 43

**112 Q. What is God's will for us
in the ninth commandment?**

  A. God's will is that I
never give false testimony against anyone,
twist no one's words,
not gossip or slander,
nor join in condemning anyone
without a hearing or without a just cause.[1]

Rather, in court and everywhere else,
I should avoid lying and deceit of every kind;
these are devices the devil himself uses,
and they would call down on me God's intense
anger.[2]
I should love the truth,
speak it candidly,
and openly acknowledge it.[3]

And I should do what I can
   to guard and advance my neighbor's good
     name.[4]

1. Ps. 15; Prov. 19:5; Matt. 7:1; Luke 6:37; Rom. 1:28–32.
2. Lev. 19:11–12; Prov. 12:22; 13:5; John 8:44; Rev. 21:8.
3. 1 Cor. 13:6; Eph. 4:25.
4. 1 Pet. 3:8–9; 4:8.

LORD'S DAY 44

**113 Q. What is God's will for us
in the tenth commandment?**

   A. That not even the slightest thought or desire
      contrary to any one of God's commandments
      should ever arise in my heart.

     Rather, with all my heart
      I should always hate sin
      and take pleasure in whatever is right.[1]

1. Ps. 19:7–14; 139:23–24; Rom. 7:7–8.

**114 Q. But can those converted to God
obey these commandments perfectly?**

   A. No.
     In this life even the holiest
     have only a small beginning of this obedience.[1]

     Nevertheless, with all seriousness of purpose,
     they do begin to live
     according to all, not only some,
     of God's commandments.[2]

1. Eccles. 7:20; Rom. 7:14–15; 1 Cor. 13:9; 1 John 1:8–10.
2. Ps. 1:1–2; Rom. 7:22–25; Phil. 3:12–16.

**115 Q. No one in this life
can obey the ten commandments perfectly:
why then does God want them
preached so pointedly?**

   A. First, so that the longer we live
      the more we may come to know our sinfulness
      and the more eagerly look to Christ
        for forgiveness of sins and righteousness.[1]

     Second, so that,
      while praying to God for the grace of the
        Holy Spirit,
      we may never stop striving

to be renewed more and more after God's
image,
until after this life we reach our goal:
perfection.[2]

1. Ps. 32:5; Rom. 3:19–26; 7:7, 24–25; 1 John 1:9.
2. 1 Cor. 9:24; Phil. 3:12–14; 1 John 3:1–3.

SELECTION FROM THE
WESTMINSTER SHORTER CATECHISM

Q. 39. What is the duty which God requireth of man?
A. The duty which God requireth of man is obedience to his revealed will.

Q. 40. What did God at first reveal to man for the rule of his obedience?
A. The rule which God at first revealed to man for his obedience was the moral law.

Q. 41. Where is the moral law summarily comprehended?
A. The moral law is summarily comprehended in the Ten Commandments.

Q. 42. What is the sum of the Ten Commandments?
A. The sum of the Ten Commandments is: to love the Lord our God with all our heart, with all our soul, with all our strength, and with all our mind; and our neighbor as ourselves.

Q. 43. What is the preface to the Ten Commandments?
A. The preface to the Ten Commandments is in these words: "I am the Lord thy God, which have brought thee out of the land of Egypt, out of the house of bondage."

Q. 44. What doth the preface to the Ten Commandments teach us?
A. The preface to the Ten Commandments teacheth us that because God is the Lord, and our God and Redeemer, therefore we are bound to keep all his commandments.

Q. 45. Which is the First Commandment?
A. The First Commandment is, "Thou shalt have no other gods before me."

Q. 46. What is required in the First Commandment?
A. The First Commandment requireth us to know and acknowledge God to be the only true God, and our God; and to
worship and glorify him accordingly.

Q. 47. What is forbidden in the First Commandment?
A. The First Commandment forbiddeth the denying, or not
worshiping and glorifying, the true God as God, and our God;
and the giving of that worship and glory to any other which is
due to him alone.

**Q. 48. What are we specially taught by these words, "before
me," in the First Commandment?**
A. These words, "before me," in the First Commandment
teach us that God, who seeth all things, taketh notice of, and is
much displeased with, the sin of having any other god.

Q. 49. Which is the Second Commandment?
A. The Second Commandment is, "Thou shalt not make unto
thee any graven image, or any likeness of any thing that is in
heaven above, or that is in the earth beneath, or that is in the water under the earth: thou shalt not bow down thyself to them,
nor serve them: for I the Lord thy God am a jealous God, visiting
the iniquity of the fathers upon the children unto the third and
fourth generation of them that hate me; and showing mercy
unto thousands of them that love me, and keep my commandments."

Q. 50. What is required in the Second Commandment?
A. The Second Commandment requireth the receiving, observing, and keeping pure and entire all such religious worship
and ordinances as God hath appointed in his Word.

Q. 51. What is forbidden in the Second Commandment?
A. The Second Commandment forbiddeth the worshiping of
God by images, or any other way not appointed in his Word.

**Q. 52. What are the reasons annexed to the Second Com-
mandment?**
A. The reasons annexed to the Second Commandment are:
God's sovereignty over us, his propriety in us, and the zeal he
hath to his own worship.

Q. 53. Which is the Third Commandment?
A. The Third Commandment is, "Thou shalt not take the
name of the Lord thy God in vain: for the Lord will not hold him
guiltless that taketh his name in vain."

Q. 54. What is required in the Third Commandment?
A. The Third Commandment requireth the holy and reverent use of God's names, titles, attributes, ordinances, Word, and works.

Q. 55. What is forbidden in the Third Commandment?
A. The Third Commandment forbiddeth all profaning or abusing of anything whereby God maketh himself known.

Q. 56. What is the reason annexed to the Third Commandment?
A. The reason annexed to the Third Commandment is that, however the breakers of this commandment may escape punishment from men, yet the Lord our God will not suffer them to escape his righteous judgment.

Q. 57. Which is the Fourth Commandment?
A. The Fourth Commandment is, "Remember the Sabbath day, to keep it holy. Six days shalt though labor, and do all thy work: but the seventh day is the Sabbath of the Lord thy God: in it thou shalt not do any work, thou, nor thy son, nor thy daughter, thy manservant, nor thy maidservant, nor thy cattle, nor thy stranger that is within thy gates: for in six days the Lord made heaven and earth, the sea, and all that in them is, and rested the seventh day: wherefore the Lord blessed the Sabbath day, and hallowed it."

Q. 58. What is required in the Fourth Commandment?
A. The Fourth Commandment requireth the keeping holy to God such set times as he hath appointed in his Word; expressly one whole day in seven, to be a holy Sabbath to himself.

Q. 59. Which day of the seven that God appointed to be the weekly Sabbath?
A. From the beginning of the world to the resurrection of Christ, God appointed the seventh day of the week to be bc the weekly Sabbath; and the first day of the week ever since, to continue to the end of the world, which is the Christian Sabbath.

Q. 60. How is the Sabbath to be sanctified?
A. The Sabbath is to be sanctified by a holy resting all that day, even from such worldly employments and recreations as are lawful on other days; and spending the whole time in the public and private exercises of God's worship, except so much as is to be taken up in the works of necessity and mercy.

Q. 61. What is forbidden in the Fourth Commandment?
A. The Fourth Commandment forbiddeth the omission, or careless performance, of the duties required, and the profaning the day by idleness, or doing that which is in itself sinful, or by unnecessary thoughts, words, or works, about our worldly employments or recreations.

Q. 62. What are the reasons annexed to the Fourth Commandment?
A. The reasons annexed to the Fourth Commandment are: God's allowing us six days of the week for our own employments, his challenging a special propriety in the seventh, his own example, and his blessing the Sabbath Day.

Q. 63. Which is the Fifth Commandment?
A. The Fifth Commandment is, "Honor thy father and thy mother: that thy days may be long upon the land which the Lord thy God giveth thee."

Q. 64. What is required in the Fifth Commandment?
A. The Fifth Commandment requireth the preserving the honor, and performing the duties, belonging to everyone in their several places and relations, as superiors, inferiors, or equals.

Q. 65. What is forbidden in the Fifth Commandment?
A. The Fifth Commandment forbiddeth the neglecting of, or doing anything against, the honor and duty which belongeth to everyone in their several places and relations.

Q. 66. What is the reason annexed to the Fifth Commandment?
A. The reason annexed to the Fifth Commandment is a promise of long life and prosperity (as far as it shall serve for God's glory, and their own good) to all such as keep this commandment.

Q. 67. Which is the Sixth Commandment?
A. The Sixth Commandment is, "Thou shalt not kill."

Q. 68. What is required in the Sixth Commandment?
A. The Sixth Commandment requireth all lawful endeavors to preserve our own life, and the life of others.

Q. 69. What is forbidden in the Sixth Commandment?
A. The Sixth Commandment forbiddeth the taking away of our own life, or the life of our neighbor unjustly, or whatsoever tendeth thereunto.

Q. 70. Which is the Seventh Commandment?
A. The Seventh Commandment is, "Thou shalt not commit adultery."

Q. 71. What is required in the Seventh Commandment?
A. The Seventh Commandment requireth the preservation of our own and our neighbor's chastity, in heart, speech, and behavior.

Q. 72. What is forbidden in the Seventh Commandment?
A. The Seventh Commandment forbiddeth all unchaste thoughts, words, and actions.

Q. 73. Which is the Eighth Commandment?
A. The Eighth Commandment is, "Thou shalt not steal."

Q. 74. What is required in the Eighth Commandment?
A. The Eighth Commandment requireth the lawful procuring and furthering the wealth and outward estate of ourselves and others.

Q. 75. What is forbidden in the Eighth Commandment?
A. The Eighth Commandment forbiddeth whatsoever doth, or may, unjustly hinder our own, or our neighbor's, wealth or outward estate.

Q. 76. Which is the Ninth Commandment?
A. The Ninth Commandment is, "Thou shalt not bear false witness against thy neighbor."

Q. 77. What is required in the Ninth Commandment?
A. The Ninth Commandment requireth the maintaining and promoting of truth between man and man, and of our own and our neighbor's good name, especially in witness-bearing.

Q. 78. What is forbidden in the Ninth Commandment?
A. The Ninth Commandment forbiddeth whatsoever is prejudicial to truth, or injurious to our own or our neighbor's good name.

Q. 79. Which is the Tenth Commandment?
A. The Tenth Commandment is, "Thou shalt not covet thy neighbor's house, thou shalt not covet thy neighbor's wife, nor his manservant, nor his maidservant, nor his ox, nor his ass, nor any thing that is thy neighbor's."

Q. 80. What is required in the Tenth Commandment?

A. The Tenth Commandment requireth full contentment with our own condition, with a right and charitable frame of spirit toward our neighbor and all that is his.

Q. 81. What is forbidden in the Tenth Commandment?

A. The Tenth Commandment forbiddeth all discontentment with our own estate, envying or grieving at the good of our neighbor, and all inordinate motions and affections to anything that is his.

Q. 82. Is any man able perfectly to keep the commandments of God?

A. No mere man, since the Fall, is able, in this life, perfectly to keep the commandments of God, but doth daily break them, in thought, word, and deed.

Moody Press, a ministry of the Moody Bible Institute,
is designed for education, evangelization, and edification.
If we may assist you in knowing more about Christ
and the Christian life, please write us without obligation:
Moody Press, c/o MLM, Chicago, Illinois 60610.